D1034955

Lavery Library

St. John Fisher College
Rochester, New York

Gloria Naylor

Gloria Naylor

Strategy and Technique, Magic and Myth

Edited by
Shirley A. Stave

DELAWARE

Newark: University of Delaware Press
London: Associated University Presses

© 2001 by Associated University Presses, Inc.

All rights reserved. Authorization to photocopy items for internal or personal use, or the internal or personal use of specific clients, is granted by the copyright owner, provided that a base fee of $10.00, plus eight cents per page, per copy is paid directly to the Copyright Clearance Center, 222 Rosewood Drive, Danvers, Massachusetts 01923. [0–87413–705–5/01 $10.00+ 8¢ pp, pc.]
Other than as indicated in the foregoing, this book may not be reproduced, in whole or in part, in any form (except as permitted by Sections 107 and 108 of the U.S. Copyright Law, and except for brief quotes appearing in reviews in the public press).

Associated University Presses
440 Forsgate Drive
Cranbury, NJ 08512

Associated University Presses
16 Barter Street
London WC1A 2AH, England

Associated University Presses
P.O. Box 338, Port Credit
Mississauga, Ontario
Canada L5G 4L8

The paper used in this publication meets the requirements of the American National Standard for Permanence of Paper for Printed Library Materials Z39.48–1984.

Library of Congress Cataloging-in-Publication Data

Gloria Naylor : strategy and technique, magic and myth / edited by Shirley A. Stave.
   p. cm.
  Includes bibliographical references and index.
  ISBN 0-87413-705-5 (alk. paper)
  1. Naylor, Gloria—Criticism and interpretation.   2. Women and literature—United States—History—20th century.   3. Afro-American women in literature.
4. Afro-Americans in literature.   5. Naylor, Gloria—Technique. 6. Magic in literature.   7. Myth in literature.   I. Stave, Shirley A., 1952–
PS3564.A895 Z682 2001
813'.54—dc21

00-037384

PRINTED IN THE UNITED STATES OF AMERICA

Contents

Acknowledgments

During the time this work has taken to come to fruition, I have incurred debts of gratitude to many wonderful people. First of all, I wish to acknowledge my friend and former colleague Jean Tobin for all her practical advise and encouragement. I can honestly say that without her input, the volume would never have seen the light of day. Second, I wish to acknowledge my former student Thomas Pinckney, who agreed to volunteer his time to serve as my research assistant on this project, even though his theater projects were very demanding. His contribution was enormous—and predictably, it was the sort of work that was not intellectually stimulating or rewarding. I also wish to thank my friends and former colleagues Peg Rozga and Elizabeth Zanich-kowsky for sharing my excitement as various stages of the project were accomplished. Their enthusiasm allowed me to deal with the various frustrations that accompany a work of this sort. My brother in spirit, Chad Rackowitz, deserves thanks for both practical assistance and emotional support. Finally, I wish to thank my contributors, who dealt with my frantic e-mails and deadlines with grace and kindness.

My contributors also wish to acknowledge the following:

- Carol Bender and Roseanne Hoefel would like to acknowledge each other for consistent professional, collegial and personal support; their students for the challenges, rewards, and continued growth they embody and elicit; and the late Paulo Freire and Agusto Boal, for the pedagogy of peace and justice and methodology of transformation their spirits release.
- Mark Hall would like to extend his thanks to his friend Katharine Purcell for the title of his essay. Lead on with light.
- Johnny Lorenz says Obrigado, Mãe. Thank you, Harvey. Thank you, Lisa Sánchez González. Thank you, Thu, for so much.
- Kerry Regan would like to thank Andrea K. Newlyn for her compelling insights, encouragement and continued support of all her work.
- Mark Simpson-Vos wishes to thank Linda Wagner-Martin for her profound influence on and encouragement of his interest in Gloria Naylor.
- Julie Tharp acknowledges the articles and books by African American

7

feminists such as Patricia Hill Collins and Barbara Christian which have led to the development of her article. She also expresses her gratitude to Shirley Stave for her careful editing and thoughtful revision suggestions.
• Anissa Wardi would like to thank Keith Gilyard for his guidance and encouragement during this project.

For permission to use sources, I acknowledge

—Faber and Faber, Ltd., for the right to cite *The God of the Witches* by Margaret A. Murray.
—Excerpts from *Linden Hills* by Gloria Naylor. Copyright © 1985 by Gloria Naylor. Used by permission of Viking Penguin, a division of Penguin Putnam Inc.
—Excerpts from *Mama Day.* Copyright © 1988 by Gloria Naylor. Reprinted by permission of Houghton Mifflin Company. All rights reserved.
—Excerpts from *Cane* by Jean Toomer. Copyright 1923 by Boni & Liveright, renewed 1951 by Jean Toomer. Reprinted by permission of Liveright Publishing Corporation.
—Excerpts from *The Spiral Dance* by Starhawk. Copyright © 1979 by Miriam Simos. Used by permission of HarperCollins Publishers Inc.

Introduction

For many scholars and readers of contemporary women's writing, Toni Morrison, Alice Walker, and Gloria Naylor have come to represent a kind of "holy trinity" of African-American women's literature. In an area of tremendous literary achievement, these three authors stand out as standards of excellence, as the writers who, in their different ways, define the contemporary African-American novel in the way that Dickens and Eliot have been seen as defining English Victorianism and Joyce and Faulker high modernism. However, while Morrison and Walker's works are widely known, likely because of the tremendous literary and filmic success of *The Color Purple* in Walker's case and the Nobel Prize for Literature in Morrison's case, Naylor remains more generally unknown outside of academe. And even there, her works typically appear in African-American literature classes or contemporary women's literature classes, while they remain in some cases unknown even to scholars of twentieth century literature. This situation will, of course, change and my hope in bringing out this collection of essays is obviously to contribute to a greater cultural recognition of a writer whose contribution to contemporary literature is significant. My impetus is my own tremendous respect for Naylor's work, my delight in teaching it, my joy in reading it, a respect, delight, and joy I hope other readers may come to share.

The essays in this volume specifically explore Naylor's third and fourth novels, *Mama Day* and *Bailey's Cafe*. These two works, woven together through the character of George, are profoundly spiritual and narratively powerful. They are outrageously and wickedly funny in places, hauntingly grim and despairing in others. However, they also differ from each other in significant ways. *Mama Day,* set on an island off the coast of Georgia and South Carolina, focuses on a rich, unified rural community, celebratory of its origins and way of life, even as it must face changes wrought by the passing of time and the attempted encroachment of the outside world. *Bailey's Cafe,* on the other hand, takes place in an unnamed city on a mystical street accessible only to those who are at the very bottom edge of despair. Its characters are wounded, lost, in many cases lacking identity. What unifies the two novels is Naylor's brilliant play with narrative—with the complexity and the

9

differences of the voices who speak: Mama Day, an old conjure woman; Cocoa, her educated and citified niece; George, Cocoa's gentle-spoken, hard-working, successful husband; the unnamed cook/proprietor of Bailey's Cafe, who defers to the women in his life; Eve, an ancient, brittle businesswoman; Peaches, a beautiful woman damaged by a culture that categorizes women into bi-polar opposites; Jesse Bell, a lusty, fierce, working class woman who is undone by her wealthy husband's haughty uncle; and the others. The works also share in their concern with geography. Repeatedly, Naylor's novels prioritize setting, each highlighting a locale that shapes and itself is created by the characters who inhabit it. In Naylor, while characters are psycho-logically believable and their situations reflect the contemporary world, the novels in which these characters appear do not fall within the parameters of the "realistic" novel but rather, as is the case with much contemporary women's writing, are more akin to works of magical realism in that the scientific laws of time, space, and probability are unraveled.

The questions posed by the novels, which I believe are addressed by this volume, are various. Obviously, as with any writer who is studied seriously, Naylor must be considered in light of her influences, her placement within a tradition of literature. Equally obviously, Naylor's use of language must be explored. Additionally, within the novels themselves, questions of crit-ical interpretation come into play. The collection of essays in this volume address themselves to one or more of these issues.

Mark Simpson-Vos's essay, "Hope from the Ashes: Naylor, Faulkner, and the Signifyin(g) Tradition," argues that Gloria Naylor's novels explore the issue of empowerment for her characters of both genders, a view which challenges those readers who perceive Naylor's work as univocally gyno-centric. While these characters arrive at an understanding of their indi-vidual identities, they do so in the context of community, which requires interaction and negotiation. Simpson-Vos parallels Naylor's meticulous construction of a world of interwoven individuals and geographies with Faulkner's creation of Yoknapatawpha County, and more specifically, reads Naylor's second novel, Linden Hills, as a play upon Faulkner's Absalom, Absalom! Exploring the African-American literary tradition of "signify-ing" articulated by Henry Louis Gates in The Signifying Monkey, a work cited frequently throughout this volume, Simpson-Vos perceives Naylor's impetus in writing Linden Hills as an undermining and revision of Faulk-ner's narrative exploration of repression. In the paralleling of Thomas Sut-pen with Luther Nedeed, both outsiders who create dynasties which are subsequently destroyed, partly as a result of the color of their heirs, Simpson-Vos contends that Naylor "reworks and provides an antidote to the negative, destructive conclusion of Nedeed's legacy." Her agent of difference is Willa Nedeed, whose narrative "reconstructs and reclaims a distinctly female history" lacking in the Faulkerian text. Naylor's subsequent *Mama Day,* Simpson-Vos argues, appears after "the legacy of Luther Nedeed [is] destroyed and completes the narrative project begun in the earlier novel." Tracing Cocoa's journey illustrates a repetition and revision of Naylor's own narratives in order to propose a path toward individual and communal strength.

The issue of signifying appears again in Anissa J. Wardi's essay, "Divergent Paths to the South: Echoes of *Cane* in *Mama Day.*" Wardi sees an African-American text, Jean Toomer's *Cane,* as one of the major influences on Naylor's third novel. Wardi argues that the Naylor novel signifies on Toomer's work both in terms of structure and theme, showing how Naylor has not simply repeated central tropes from *Cane,* but also how she has continued Toomer's exploration of geography, specifically in terms of the role it assumes in the development of the individual and community. Specifically, Wardi cites section three of *Cane,* the "Kabnis" section, as Naylor's basis for textual play. Both texts, Wardi contends, engage the concept of the pastoral, re-articulating it in ways that allow for the inclusion of the African-American experience. Toomer's character Kabnis, like Naylor's George, is a Northerner who returns to the South to recover his identity as an African-American man. However, Wardi argues, Naylor "expands and elaborates on Toomer's treatment of the Southern journey," so that George is "able to embrace his ethnic heritage and reconcile his identity," whereas Kabnis's pastoral journey fails because Kabnis "will not or cannot reclaim the history and lineage that would redeem him."

Naylor's signifying on familiar texts is the theme of a third essay in the collection, in this case my essay, "Re-writing Sacred Texts: Gloria Naylor's Revisionary Theology," which argues that Naylor's source for both *Mama Day* and *Bailey's Cafe* is the Bible, a text she reworks for her feminist purposes. In the *Mama Day* section of the paper, I contend that Naylor essentially rewrites the Genesis account of creation and the fall into sin to provide an "alternative mythology of redemption." Reading Mama Day as representative of the Great Goddess, the primal mother, I argue that George's choice of saving Cocoa without Mama Day's assistance, a decision that results in his own death, identifies him as a Christ figure who chooses to be sacrificed for love; the plan proposed by Mama Day and rejected by George would have enabled a theology of love rather than justice, a theology free from sacrifice. In *Bailey's Cafe,* I assert that Naylor gives voice to Biblical characters who are rendered mute, whose stories are shaped and focalized by a patriarchal narrative voice. Whether these characters are "virtuous" women like Esther, Sarah, or the Virgin Mary, or "fallen" women like Eve, Jezebel, or the Magdalene, in Naylor's narrative the stories they tell challenge canonical interpretation of these characters and allow for a feminist reading of their lives and texts.

Naylor's use of religion and spirituality also figures in R. Mark Hall's essay, "Serving the Second Sun: The Men in Gloria Naylor's *Mama Day*." However, Hall's focus shifts from Judeo-Christian theology to an older form of spirituality, one more specific to Africa, that form of Paganism we call Witchcraft. In addressing the charges of "male-bashing" that have been hurled against Naylor, Hall argues that Naylor is not simply trafficking in rogue stereotypes, but rather that the assortment of males who populate Willow Springs—and George, as well—constitute various manifestations of the multi-faceted God of the Witches, often referred to as the Horned God. Using both African and Western concepts of Witchcraft as his theoretical base, Hall contends that George's sacrificial death aligns him with the Horned God, who is sacrificed yearly (in August, the time of George's death). Hall reads the Horned God as he is represented both historically as well as through the character of George as offering a challenge to contemporary definitions of masculinity. The essay goes on to argue that through her balanced presentation of both the "male" and the "female" principles of Witchcraft, Naylor transcends an oversimplified "negative/positive" dichotomy and "resist evoking a monolithic homogeneous representation of black masculinity."

Hall's focus on masculinity in Naylor's work is balanced by Julie Tharp's essay, "The Maternal Aesthetic of *Mama Day*," which interrogates the role of mothering in the novel. Tharp agrees with many other critics that the character of Mama Day must be read through the African/American tradition of conjure; however, Tharp complicates the conjure-figure, insisting on pushing beyond the parameters of the spiritual to consider the political and economic implications of conjure. Reading both the character of Mama Day and the text as a whole from this expanded perspective, Tharp argues that the novel presents "a road map for an alternative civilization, one based on a rendering of mainstream philosophy as holistic, spiritual, and natural, rather than dichotomous, rational and technocratic." In the alternative civilization, depicted by the community of Willow Springs, women have had the privilege of raising their own children, an option not available to many African/American women in the past or even now for economic or political reasons. While the various mothers on Willow Springs are not idealized— Tharp insists that they are "demanding, powerful, and at times dangerous"— the concept of black mothering as Naylor writes it becomes linked "to a gender and ethnic identity which undermines, if not inverts, the destructive fragmentation of capitalism, racism, and patriarchy."

One of the great pleasures of reading Naylor is her brilliant play with voice, her use of multiple and fused narrators, her ability to write in specific, localized dialect. However, Naylor's "speakerly" narratives are deceptive in their seeming simplicity. For that reason, several of the essays in the collection focus specifically on Naylor's use of language. In "Talking in Metaphors: Problems of Language and Knowledge in Gloria Naylor's *Mama Day*," Carol Howard addresses the characters' use of "semantic indirection," which she identifies with the language of signifying. Howard explores the novel's scenes of characters signifying on each other, showing how such speech acts "[reinforce] the community's social ties and the unofficial hierarchy of its citizens." However, in a detailed exploration of the signifying that occurs in the novel's opening chapter, when the communal narrator recounts the antics of a benighted anthropology student who attempt to understand the discourse of Willow Springs without knowing how to listen to the stories he is told, Howard suggests that the narrated incident exists to model an appropriate reading of the book's most vexing scene—the death of George. Howard contends that the "problem that defeats the possibility of connection between George and Mama Day is both epistemic and rhetorical." Insisting that George must not be read as "an unflagging agent of Western culture," Howard argues that "George's resistance to Mama Day's alternative ways of knowing is clearly circumstantial," driven by his frenzy at his wife's severe illness and rapid decline. However, Howard also sees much of the miscommunication that occurs in Willow Springs as tied to the cosmogony of the island itself. Reading Sapphira Wade as a "wandering signifier," Howard argues that she is "the Logos, the Living Word, rather than the dead letter of the text."

Johnny Lorenz's "*This Mumbo-Jumbo:* Vocabularies and Communities in Gloria Naylor's *Mama Day*" also explores the binary oppositions in Naylor's text. In direct contrast to both my and R. Mark Hall's readings of the magic in *Mama Day,* Lorenz argues that the presence of conjure in the text should not point at its extradiegetic existence but rather functions as a means by which characters in the novel act out their desires and, in the process of doing so, forge communities. By constructing overt and subtle binaries involving Willow Springs and anywhere "beyond the bridge," the novel, Lorenz contends, creates situations wherein characters—most notably George—must reconstruct their realities to account for, if not accommodate, the unfamiliar, the "other." George's "authorial pretentiousness," Lorenz argues, "limits his ability to shape the outside forces that actively shape the narrative of his life." When he is confronted with an experience "that threatens to refigure the character of the 'real,'" George refuses to "reconstruct his vocabulary" and therefore is destroyed by his experience. Mama Day, on the other hand, finds spiritual strength through her acknowledgment of history and through her conscious decision to engage that history. She does not approach the present "simply as an opportunity to impose her individual will or to define the moment with a discrete action, but rather as a chance to shape reality by negotiating between history and possibility."

Kerry Regan's essay, "Return to Sender: Correspondence(s) in Gloria Naylor's *Mama Day*," explores the novel's repeated reliance on the second person "you" in all the various narrators' segments of communication, each of which, Regan argues, can be read as an epistle sent to an other. Regan links this novel to the "readerly" text in the African-American tradition, a tradition she understands as providing "instances of dialogic relation between margin and center, between what dominant culture refuses to say and the already-said, the authorized." Regan's essay explores the positioning of the reader by the text and argues that the "reader has a purpose in the narrative, but the role requires a disavowal of particular identity." Citing the text's self-contradictory discussion of the legendary Sapphira Wade, Regan shows how "the legend itself responds to its changing readers." Ultimately, according to Regan, the novel "interrogates the way in which exchanges of dialogue, moments of correspondence, come together to create a changing, progressive narrative truth."

Carol Bender and Roseanne Hoefel turn their collective gaze to *Bailey's Cafe*, which they read as a challenge to the master narratives of our culture, narratives that in themselves foster oppression. Seeing the proprietor of the cafe as the reader's "model for empathy," they argue that he "reduces reader resistance through his own respectful demeanor and intermittent consciousness-raising." His own horrifying experiences during World War II allow him to understand "the devastation incurred by an abuse of power" and thereby to listen to the stories of the other characters, all of whom have suffered violation themselves; his narrative essentially "teaches" the novel's readers how to listen as well and his humane responses to the devastating stories he hears model the appropriate response in readers. Furthermore, they argue, the moments of humor he interjects serve as conduits that enable readers to disperse the pain they encounter in the reading of the novel. Ultimately, the authors argue, "communal catharsis," such as exists in the theatre of the oppressed, occurs at the novel's end in the birth of Miriam's child. The group assembled in the cafe, most of whom are not Jewish, "model the benefits of inhabiting another's culture when they assume a collective Jewish identity and participate in the naming ceremony and circumcision."

Gloria Naylor

Hope from the Ashes: Naylor, Faulkner, and the Signifyin(g) Tradition

MARK SIMPSON-VOS

I

Throughout the history of black women's writing, novelists from Ann Petry and Frances Harper to Toni Morrison and Alice Walker have challenged social conventions and called for racial justice while creating significant space for their female protagonists to construct and explore personal histories, relationships, and other forms of discovery, facilitated by a protagonist's ties to communities of strong women. Within these communities, protagonists recognize opportunities for collective empowerment in what Barbara Christian calls "a community of sisters" which can alter stereotypes for both women and men.[1] While contemporary novelists vary in their optimism that such empowerment may actually occur, many present possible avenues toward it. Gloria Naylor is one such author; issues of self-exploration, empowerment, and community are central to each of her novels. A variety of pressures within the fabric of a given text may limit the extent to which Naylor's characters construct a positive sense of self, but Naylor is clearly committed to exploring paths toward empowerment, for both her female and male characters.

While these characters work toward a re-valuing of the self, they constantly interact and negotiate with the communities around them. In much the same way as Faulkner creates his Yoknapatawpha County, Naylor in her novels meticulously constructs a world of interwoven geographies and individuals—one great community. Within this larger intertextual framework, each of Naylor's narratives also focuses on a small community, its fabric as dependent on its inhabitants as on its location and structures. Thus, as Yoknapatawpha is made of places, colorful characters, and troubled histories, Naylor's fictional world similarly holds Willow Springs, Bailey's Café, and the Putney Wayne neighborhood, linked by the shared experiences of such people as Mama Day, Lester Tilson, and Kiswana Browne. Each

individual community has a profound effect on its inhabitants' journeys toward self-discovery; one may prevent the journey altogether, while another
may be vital to its completion. Whether or not Naylor's characters find empowerment through themselves and each other, however, each of Naylor's
novels presents a path toward realizing this goal. While her narratives may
not provide happy endings, they almost inevitably leave room for hope.

While Naylor's oeuvre is perhaps best considered as an interwoven whole,
her two middle novels, *Linden Hills* (1985) and *Mama Day* (1988), clearly
demonstrate her interest in possibilities for self-discovery and reconciliation
between diverse groups and individuals within the larger black community.
Given their different narrative styles, geographical settings, and apparent
narrative purpose, *Linden Hills* and *Mama Day* may seem an unlikely pair
to be coupled critically. *Linden Hills,* an urban-suburban novel in which
Naylor attacks racially and economically divisive notions of success, is her
most overtly political book, ending in violence and flames. *Mama Day,* on
the other hand, seems less political and more mystical and reflective, pre-
senting a strong community, primarily rural and presided over by women,
which enables the novel's protagonists to complete difficult journeys toward
spiritual and emotional communion.

Despite these surface differences, I would argue that *Linden Hills* and
Mama Day function as companion texts: we cannot fully appreciate the path
toward self-discovery and empowerment suggested in *Mama Day* without
first considering the ways in which Naylor sets the groundwork in *Linden
Hills.* As the bleak story of Willa Prescott Nedeed unfolds in the first text,
we see a woman whose exploration of self-consciousness is cut short by
an oppressive husband and a community which forgets its history, denies
its mothers, and spurns genuine love for appearances. Ultimately, these re-
pressive social constructs lead to the collapse of both the community and
its inhabitants. Naylor not only describes this collapse, however, but also
employs the strategy of "signifyin(g)" to revise and reverse its causes and
effects. Using Faulkner's *Absalom, Absalom!* as an intertext in *Linden Hills*
and Luther Nedeed's story, Naylor repeats Faulkner's narrative about repression and collapse only to undermine and revise this repression through
the narrative of Nedeed's wife, Willa. Creating textual space for black self-
discovery by challenging tradition, Naylor allows her readers to hope that
although Willa's journey ends too soon, another character may complete
the path.

As we examine the family tree with which Naylor begins *Mama Day,*
readers see that this hope is to be fulfilled by Willa's cousin, Ophelia (Cocoa) Day, and by her aunt, Miranda (Mama) Day herself. Cocoa's story is

in many ways the completion of Willa's, drawing *Linden Hills* and *Mama Day* into one linked narrative. While the characters in the earlier novel suffer alienation from the power of history, the nurturing of motherhood, and the companionship of racial brothers and sisters, *Mama Day's* community of Willow Springs provides all these means of support. Cocoa, like her cousin Willa, has left this community behind, but unlike Willa, Cocoa is able to maintain contact with the people and places of Willow Springs, a literal and figurative "motherland." This sustained contact, along with the companionship of her husband, George, enables Cocoa to overcome a range of forces which threaten her self-discovery, and ultimately to rejoin a strong community of sisters and brothers. Tracing Cocoa's journey, we may see how Naylor repeats and revises her own narratives in order to propose a path toward individual and community strength. As we see and understand *Mama Day's* completion of the narrative project begun in *Linden Hills,* we may begin to appreciate Gloria Naylor's contribution to the emerging tradition of black women's fiction.

II

If we reduce *Linden Hills* to an essential narrative, it tells the story of the rise and fall of one family's effort to construct and maintain an empire. Luther Nedeed, the fifth in a line of fathers and sons to possess the same name, inhabits the same house as his fathers and shares their work as the community's undertaker. He inherits Linden Hills, a series of showcase homes rented to the most affluent, successful blacks in America and beyond. As we learn from Naylor's narrative history of Linden Hills, Nedeed's empire was carved from absolute nothingness by the first Nedeed, a freed slave who moved to the North from Mississippi, purchasing with his only money a tract of infertile land along the front face of a hill. Over nearly a century, through hard work, meticulous planning, and rigidly willful control, the Nedeeds transformed the land first into a row of shacks and eventually into a series of mansions; the worthless land owned by a worthless black man becomes an "ebony jewel" admired across the world. This empire depends on perpetuation through a single, black male heir, produced with a wife chosen solely for her ability to perform the birthing duty with proper subservience. When the fifth Nedeed is unable to produce the proper heir with his wife, however, the dynasty crumbles. The line is broken, and in the novel's final pages, Nedeed, his home, and the legacy he inherits are consumed by fire.

From this simplified version of the plot, we can see that *Linden Hills* bears a provocative similarity to the Thomas Sutpen story of *Absalom, Absalom!* Sutpen, like the first Nedeed, is an outsider—a man with no history, no evident financial means, and no place within the community structure. Through sheer force of will, and despite the opposition of those around them, Sutpen and Nedeed both create empires, metaphorically represented by the construction of an edifice. Sutpen's is his "Hundred," the plantation of epic dimensions; Nedeed's is Linden Hills, equally epic in size and notoriety. The future of both the Sutpen and Nedeed dynasties relies on the founders' bearing a male heir of the proper race, and both pursue the production of that heir with all-consuming intensity. Finally, Nedeed's effort to create this heir and project his empire into history, like Sutpen's, collapses upon itself, resulting in the death of the founder and the ultimate decay of the project.

If one were to focus entirely on Nedeed's story, one could easier conclude that Naylor is retelling the Sutpen story of *Absalom, Absalom!,* perhaps in an effort to critique a growing division of upper- and lower-class blacks.[2] But to focus on the rise and fall of Luther Nedeed is to focus on, at best, one side of the narrative. Naylor novel shows us that as Nedeed's world is collapsing around him, along with the lives of many Linden Hills residents, another character is regaining strength and ascending through the decay. This distinctly different side of the story is inscribed from within the darkest part of Nedeed's empire by the last Nedeed wife, Willa Prescott Nedeed. Naylor intently focuses her readers' attentions on the story of Willa's reconstruction of her personal history and discovery of the female lineage to which she belongs. Luther Nedeed's narrative, accompanied by stories of pain and decay from within the walls of Linden Hills, repeats much of the Sutpen story. But as the other side of the narrative simultaneously develops in Willa's story, we see much of the Sutpen/Nedeed story rejected, even reversed. *Linden Hills,* then, reworks and provides an antidote to the negative, destructive conclusion of *Absalom, Absalom!,* even as it repeats this destruction. In this way, Naylor constructs the type of subversive, "double-voiced" narrative Henry Louis Gates, Jr. describes in his seminal work on African and African-American vernacular theory, *The Signifyin(g) Monkey.*[3] The result is a story in which Naylor not only critiques the male-dominated, oppressive, and ultimately misguided project of Luther Nedeed, but provides the reader with a (re)vision empowering the female, and denying that black success necessitates imitating white social and economic (not to mention literary) structures. By first considering in more depth how Nedeed's story repeats Sutpen's, and then by evaluating the multiple ways in which the Sutpen/Nedeed story is reversed, we can see Naylor's sig-nifyin(g) process at work.

The parallels between Sutpen's story and Luther Nedeed's history be-come apparent early in the narrative of *Linden Hills*. As Naylor describes the dark genesis of Nedeed's plans, she demonstrates that his motivations, like Thomas Sutpen's, are based in an insult. Faulkner's young Sutpen determines to establish himself among the weathly, land-owning elite after he is spurned by a house-slave. This slave insists that Sutpen—poor, but white—go to the back door (the slave door) to deliver a message to the owner of the plantation where Sutpen's family lives. Motivated by rejec-tion, Sutpen decides his only recourse is to avenge this insult by imitating the plantation owner in as ruthless and cold a fashion as Sutpen felt he him-self had been treated.[4] Nedeed's project grows out of a similar, yet ironi-cally reversed insult—enslavement and humiliation at the hands of white culture. Though the insults differ in degree, and to an extent, in kind, as they are internalized they create similar effects on Sutpen and Nedeed. Both men are branded outsiders by their communities and denied a role in soci-ety. Just as Sutpen seeks some vengeance for his insult, Nedeed determines that he must overcome his shame. Consequently, Nedeed and his descendants dream of success defined by wealth and status that puts the white world to shame:

> Sure, they thought him a fool—look at the fools that he had to claim [from his own race]. When they laughed at them, they laughed at him. Well, he would show them. This wedge of earth was his—he couldn't rule but he sure as hell could ruin. He could be a fly in that ointment, a sport on that bleached sheet, and Linden Hills would prove it. He had given his people some of the most expensive property. They had the land for a millennium. Now just let them sit on it. . . . Nedeed's last vision when he closed his puffy eyelids . . . was of Wayne County forced to drive past Linden Hills and being waved at by the maids, mammies, and mules who were bringing the price of that sweat back to his land and his hands. [It would become a] wad of spit right in the white eye of Amer-ica (Naylor; *Linden Hills,* 8–9).

To overcome these insults, both Sutpen and Nedeed deny their histories entirely so that nothing can blemish their present achievements. In *Absa-lom, Absalom!,* Faulkner describes Sutpen as the man "who came out of nowhere and without warning."[5] Because he has no history, Sutpen's neigh-bors in Jefferson ostracize him from the first moments of his arrival to the community. As Faulkner's novel unfolds, we learn that Sutpen has actively rejected the past in order to avoid his shameful ties to poor parents with no genealogical legacy and the insults of the planter's slave. Sutpen wants no one to pierce this anti-historical shroud, fearing that his past will destroy the status he eventually gains through his plantation's size and worth. Sutpen plans to be judged solely on the basis of his actions, not on their source. Luther Nedeed, like Sutpen, is a character without a history. Nedeed renounces his history, as Sutpen has, because his past has no cultural value. As a slave, Nedeed was a possession; as property, he had no individual worth, historical or otherwise. Nedeed leaves his past behind in his move to the North, where although he is still black and marginalized, he is left alone, allowed to create some degree of self. In his reidentification process, Nedeed not only discards his enslaved past, but tries to reject the very fact of his race. As Luke Bouvier writes, Nedeed's idea of "blackness" is, in fact, "forgetting blackness" through an ignorance of the past and a concentration on replicating the success of white society.[6]

As later generations of Nedeeds are born, we see that they, like Sutpen, forget their genealogy. Each generation's son bears the same name, and even the same appearance, as his father, leading to the illusion of no past but rather a present in which one Luther Nedeed exists for now and always. This denial of genealogy extends to a forgetting of mothers. As we are shown in the marginalia of Luwana Packerville's Bible, the wives and mothers of the various Luther Nedeeds are denied all ties to their sons, and slowly become invisible, nonexistent once they have fulfilled their procreative duty. Nedeed's denial of the past is shown most clearly in his caveat to those who inhabit Linden Hills. "Just stay right here," he says, "you step outside Linden Hills and you've stepped into history—someone else's history about what you couldn't ever do" (16). This history, as we see from Luther Nedeed's every word and deed, must be avoided at all costs.

Ironically, although both Sutpen and Nedeed attempt to forget their own genealogies, the continuation of their dynasties relies on the creation of a family line. Much of *Absalom, Absalom!* is centered around Sutpen's obsession with producing an heir, and with the grim consequences of these efforts. For the line of Nedeeds, the continuation of a male line takes on a similar importance. The reproductive act—and sex is simply that for Nedeed— takes on the tenor of a religious (satanic?) ritual. As we read about the fifth Nedeed's effort to produce a son, we are introduced to

the journals and charts that were locked in the ancient rolltop desk in his den. Weeks were spent tracing the date and times of penetrations, conceptions, and births for every Luther Nedeed in Linden Hills. . . . and it all verified what had been passed down to him about the facts of life: 'There must be five days of penetration at the appearance of Aries, and the son is born when the sun has died. (19).

Just as Sutpen must have a male heir, so Nedeed needs a son to maintain the integrity of his patriarchal empire. For both men, however, their dynasties begin to crumble when their actions produce the "wrong son." In an even stronger parallel, this wrong son is problematic for both Nedeed and Sutpen because of the son's race. Sutpen's part black child, Charles Bon, sparks the downward spiral which ultimately destroys Sutpen's empire; Sutpen's forgotten son of the past returns to haunt his present. Nedeed's downfall, too, begins with the birth of a son—a white son. As Naylor explains, Nedeed's son had

[the] same squat bow legs, the same protruding eyes and puffed lips, but a ghostly presence that mocked everything his fathers had built. How could Luther die and leave this with the future of Linden Hills? He looked at this whiteness and saw the destruction of five generations (18).

Nedeed, like Sutpen, is struck down by his ignorance of the past. Forgetting his mother and the line of women called only "Mrs. Nedeed," he cannot realize that the birth of this white son is only logical, given that the pattern of his fathers was to marry only pale-skinned women. It was only a matter of time before genetics caught up. But Nedeed only knows what he has been taught by his fathers—that the women "were chosen for the color of their spirits, not their faces" (18). Therefore, the birth of this pale-skinned son is a complete shock. He cannot accept that the explanation lies in his own actions and those of his fathers. Nedeed concludes, instead, that his wife has been unfaithful and the son is not his own. Locking his wife and son in his basement morgue, Nedeed insists "it would be a cold day in hell before he saw some woman tear . . . down" the work of five generations (20).

For Nedeed, however, like Sutpen, this day comes all too soon. Sutpen's desperate efforts to produce a white male heir are futile, and they end at last in his murder. Sutpen's legacy, as represented by the house at Sutpen's Hundred, is left to decay, along with the withered figure of his heir, Henry Sutpen. In a final conflagration, the house, along with all it represents, burns and is destroyed. Nedeed's pale-skinned son, too, dies in the basement in which he and his mother are imprisoned. When Willa recovers from her bereavement long enough to escape her basement prison, she starts a fire which kills her, Nedeed, and the legacy her husband wanted so desperately to preserve. Ultimately for Sutpen and Nedeed, the return of a forgotten past and the inability to produce a male heir bring about the catastrophic collapse of the patrilinear dynasties.

When Nedeed first banishes Willa and his son to the basement morgue for her supposed infidelity, it appears that Willa will soon share the decay and death seen in the conclusion of the Sutpen and Nedeed narratives. Nedeed takes brutal measures to assert his dominance over Willa, controlling her access to food, water, and light with the ruthlessness of a concentration camp overseer. We see Nedeed muse over Willa's punishment as he reflects on the sour turn his legacy is taking:

> His father was right: breaking in a wife is like breaking in a good pair of slippers. Once you'd gotten used to them, you'd wear them until they fell apart, rather than go to the trouble of buying a new pair. Well, in a few weeks she would have learned her lesson (67).

Initially, Nedeed's plan to "break" his family works all too well. His son dies, unable to withstand the inhumane conditions, and Willa is left hopelessly unable to mourn her child; "any possibility of salvation lay withered in her arms" (71).She floats along the edge of sanity, convinced that she, too, will die. Left only to pass the counting seconds, Willa thinks:

> Just let the mind swing out—she could never leave this basement alive now. Because Luther knows he's a dead man. Swing out—he knows that she would rest, eat, grow strong. And wait. Yes, she was doomed here. So put your mind on the clock. Right there. On the clock. And let it swing you to death (66).

As she slips closer to madness, she also slips further into the grip of Nedeed's destructive, anti-historical narrative. When Nedeed calls to Willa over an intercom to warn her that she is about to receive her allotment of water, she is unable to comprehend his words. "There was no meaning to those patterns of empty noises," Naylor writes. "The words didn't connect inside her to any history or emotion" (71). Willa is reduced to a starved, mucus-caked skeleton, laughing and screaming with uncontrollable anguish and near a final collapse.

The narrator hints, however, that this is not to be Willa's fate. Even as she falls from sanity, her brain insists, "Iwantyoutolive . . . Iwantyoutolive . . . I wantyouto. . . ." (70) Quickly, we begin to see that Willa will not fall prey to Nedeed's scheme, but will instead work to subvert it. As her narrative develops alongside, or rather, underneath Nedeed's, Willa signifies on the Nedeed/Sutpen story, reversing its decay. The first clue pointing toward the subversive nature of Willa's narrative is that it is presented in a type-face bolder than the rest of the text. The difference draws extra attention to Willa's story—a method also used by Faulkner to present Rosa Coldfield's narrative in *Absalom, Absalom!* But while the technique may be borrowed, the result is distinctly revised. Rosa's narrative can only repeat her version of Sutpen's story as her story is pushed to the margins by the more author-itative narratives of Faulkner's male characters; Willa's narrative is power-fully different from Nedeed's.

The difference between Naylor's two narratives lies in their relationship to history. While Nedeed's story repeats the patrilinear, anti-historical as-pects of his fathers and the textual/literary history of Sutpen's narrative, Willa's reconstructs and reclaims a distinctly female history. This history places Willa in a tradition which undercuts and reverses the authority of the male Nedeed line. Willa's process of recovery—both of this history and her self—begins as she allows herself to remember, reuniting herself with the recent past of her experiences. Immediately after her son's death, Willa re-fuses to remember his life or to mourn, fearing the grief will kill her. Soon, however, the memories come flooding back despite her efforts to block them:

> She paced by the cot [where her son's body lay], pressing her temples so tightly the skull bone threatened to give way. But the memory had al-ready splintered into blinding needles of white light that burned so badly she knew if it didn't stop, she would have to bash her head against the concrete floor (92).

Willa decides that if she cannot mourn, she will at least dress her son for burial. As she prepares to wrap his body using something from a nearby trunk of old clothes, "remembering silk dresses and brocades in her search for extra blankets weeks ago," Willa makes a discovery that decisively changes the direction of her narrative from mere repetition to signifying. Among the scraps of fabric, wound in a roll of lace, Willa finds

> a leather- and gold-bound Bible. LUWANA PACKERVILLE 1837 was etched in fading gold on the bottom border. . . .
> She threw the Bible on the cot and began to wrap the lace veiling around the child's body. How strange; what must that woman have seen or lived . . . ? Tupelo, Mississippi. She was probably this child's great-grandmother or one of the many mothers that Luther never talked about (92–93).

Willa's assumption is correct. The Bible is the first in a series of inscriptions Willa finds which enable her to reconstruct the lost history of the Mrs. Nedeeds. This initial discovery encourages Willa to dig deeper, and her search reveals possessions from three generations of women, buried within boxes, hidden symbolically in the morgue constructed by the first Luther Nedeed. As a narrative develops around these artifacts, Willa discovers elements of her own history in the stories of those before her. By reassembling the fragmented women's histories Nedeed's fathers had fractured and suppressed, Willa reweaves history into autobiography, reversing her husband's anti-historical world.[7]

As Willa recovers and retells the history of the Mrs. Nedeeds, we learn that each played a subversive role similar to Willa's own. As Willa pages through Luwana Packerville's Bible, she finds that Luwana has used the "master text" as a place to record her own story. We learn that Luwana writes literally and metaphorically out of the margins. Willa struggles "to decipher the fine, webbed scrawl that was crammed onto the gold-edged tissue paper that separated one book . . . from another" (117). In these cramped spaces, Luwana tells how she is pushed away from her son's life as he grows closer to his father. We learn that over time, Luwana becomes so isolated that she can only talk to herself for companionship. In a final letter to herself recorded in the Bible, Luwana explains that she has not spoken except for "332 times to answer [her husband's] good mornings and 333 times to do the same in the evening," (124) only one answer away from 666 words, a full descent into the literal and figurative hell toward which Luther has driven her. Luwana is able to keep track of these instances because she cuts herself with a hat pin each time she speaks, subverting Luther's control by writing on her own body—the only thing which she can still claim as her own.

Willa recovers the names and histories of two other Mrs. Nedeeds as she discovers additional fragments from their lives. In the cookbooks of Evelyn Creton, Willa learns about a woman who signifies on her marginal role as wife and cook by altering and creating her own traditional "recipes." Evelyn's cookbooks include not only recipes multiplied to create enormous amounts of food, but formulas for concoctions used as purgatives. Cookbooks and recipe cards, normally records of life-providing food and family history, are inscribed with Evelyn's slow death by bulimia. Priscilla McGuire, the third woman Willa rediscovers, signifies on a series of photograph albums. Though the albums ostensibly capture the growth of her son—the rise of the patrilinear—Priscilla simultaneously creates a different history by scraping and burning her images from the photos. Willa realizes that "the only thing growing in these pictures was [Priscilla's] absence" (209). Evelyn and Priscilla, like Luwana, subvert traditional family artifacts to inscribe their histories—histories of disappearance.

In her recovery of these histories, Willa finds a place for herself in the tradition of women who were forced to endure the Nedeed's oppression: "Using these ancient records as signposts, [Willa] had found at least one place that could offer an anchor of validity to the inner flow of her life" (118). Thanks to her predecessors, Willa recalls her own genealogy, linked to her great-aunt Miranda Day and the strong female community of sisters Naylor presents in her third novel, *Mama Day*. Through these matriarchal lineages which reverse Nedeed's anti-historical patriarchy, Willa is reborn into her own strong womanhood, even though the discoveries of her "mothers" and "sisters" ironically occur as she is ostensibly preparing her son for burial. From death, through sisterhood, life is recreated, as Willa reclaims the simple act of breathing that had been linked to her near-insanity only a few pages earlier:

> She breathed in to touch the very elements that at the beginning of time sparked to produce the miracle some called divine creation and others the force of life. An unconscious journey in toward the power of will that had crept alone in primordial muck. . . . Then she breathed out. Out, past cells that divided to form ovaries, wombs, glands. . . . She breathed in and out, her body a mere shelter for the mating of unfathomable will to unfathomable possibility. And in that union, the amber germ of truth she went to sleep with conceived and reconceived itself. . . . Like other emerging life, her brain, heart, hands, and feet were being programmed to a purpose (288–89).

As Willa restores a voice to the history of the women who went before her, she regains her own metaphorical voice—her will to live, and her will to reorder the world in which she had been forced to dwell.

The reborn Willa sets to "keeping house," first straightening the basement, and then heading back upstairs toward the kitchen. As with her predecessors, Willa's participation in traditional household duties is symbolically charged. Though her house cleaning begins with folding sheets and repacking boxes, in Willa's final moment she acts decisively to clean Linden Hills of Nedeed's influence once and for all. As she reaches the top step and escapes her basement prison, the typeface in which Willa's narrative is written changes to match the rest of the novel. But Willa is not simply rejoining Nedeed's narrative world; she is assuming control. With determination repeatedly compared to that of a queen ant, Willa symbolically cleans everything in sight, and then, carrying the body of her dead son, she confronts her husband:

> ... [S]he kept walking when he called her, walking when he touched her. ... That brought them face to face. He had never encountered the eyes of a lone army ant, marching in defiance ... ; so the dilated eyes in front of him registered insanity. Her fists lashed out and caught him across the Adam's apple, making him bend and choke. ... Then he reached for the child. The moment his fingers touched the wrapped body ... her arms loosened for one to shoot around his neck, the other his waist, and the three were welded together (300).

Luther Nedeed's final inability to perceive correctly is his final damnation. Willa completes her reversal of Nedeed's narrative as she brushes against a candle, quickly enveloping the home and the legacy in fire. Reclaiming the matriarchal history Nedeed had tried so hard to suppress, Willa's final act completes her signifying on Nedeed's story and its repetition of Thomas Sutpen's by bringing about Nedeed's literal and textual end.

III

Following the publication of *Linden Hills,* a number of scholars criticized Naylor's conclusion, deeply dissatisfied that a woman author would bring her female protagonist to the threshold of freedom, only to have her die before the journey can be completed. Indeed, our first instinct may be to question why Naylor invests so much narrative energy in Willa's reclamation of history, only to snuff it out so bluntly. Many readers undoubtedly feel that in the ashes of Luther Nedeed's home, something is clearly left incomplete. Certainly, several factors limit Willa's journey to self-discovery. First, Naylor sets *Linden Hills* in a dystopia, a place where neither plans nor individuals can grow naturally. Ultimately, there is not community to nurture Naylor's protagonist. Second, while Willa works to uncover and revalue a portion of female history, this reclamation remains incomplete. Willa recovers dead mothers of the Nedeeds, but is never reunited in body or spirit with her own *living* mothers—she is unable to rejoin fully a vital community of sisters. With an incompletely reclaimed history and a dystopia as its backdrop, it may be tempting to view *Linden Hills* solely as a novel of shortcomings and betrayed hope.

Ultimately, we must recognize however, that the ashes at the conclusion of *Linden Hills* are not Naylor's last comment on the search for history, community, or empowerment. In the text, Naylor challenges a wide range of conventions, both literary and social, seeking to clear narrative space so that she may later explore and create a more hopeful fictive world; moreover, Willa Prescott Nedeed makes great strides toward the recovery of personal and communal history. Finally it seems, though, that Naylor's primary concern in the text is less with building up her characters and more with tearing down the social constructs which constrain both protagonists and audience. If we view the text in this light, we see that burned ruins of Nedeed's home are a fitting emblem for what Naylor accomplishes in *Linden Hills;* self-discovery and growth may suffer setbacks, but the novel works hard to make such projects easier in the future.

It becomes easier still to understand Naylor's project in *Linden Hills* as we begin to consider her next novel, *Mama Day.* With the legacy of Luther Nedeed destroyed, and having established a foothold for her text by signifying on previous literary traditions, Naylor is left with fertile ground on which to continue a reversal of Nedeed's hell and to create the fictive paradise of Willow Springs. In *Mama Day,* then, Naylor completes the process begun in her earlier work. Building on the open narrative spaces created by previous challenges of convention, Naylor fashions a text where a female protagonist reconstructs her history and strives toward a self-discovery that can be completed. Where Willa Prescott Nedeed's journey ends, Ophelia Day's begins, and ultimately concludes in empowerment and reunion with the community of strong women that gave her life.

Mama Day's narrative structure provides the first clues that the novel mirrors *Linden Hills* in many ways, but goes a step further, providing a positive backdrop for Ophelia Day's journey. Like *Linden Hills, Mama Day* is a story told from multiple narrative perspectives, and in several different voices. The many voices of *Linden Hills,* however, create a dissonant set of stories which struggle against one another throughout the text. Luther Nedeed's story and legacy battle to restrain the narratives woven by Willa and Naylor's two other protagonists, Willie Mason and Lester Tilson; finally the competition of voices works to cancel out both sides. In contrast, the multivocal nature of *Mama Day* enhances the fabric of the narrative. An omniscient narrator joins the voices of Ophelia Day, George Andrews, and Mama Day within the novel, with each voice lending a unique perspective on Willow Springs and those who inhabit it. These multiple narratives blend to reinforce rather than contradict each other. The cooperation of many voices to form one text creates a strong atmosphere of community from the first pages of *Mama Day.*

This community atmosphere is reinforced constantly by the place where

Naylor grounds her narrative—Willow Springs. Before we meet Cocoa,
George, or even Mama Day, the novel is anchored by an introduction to this
distinctive community. In fact, Willow Springs seems to exist as a character itself, constantly interacting with and influencing those who come in
contact with it. Through the voice of Naylor's third-person "community
narrator," we become acquainted with the island's geography and history.
In combination with the other narratives, the community narrator helps the
reader to understand how Willow Springs revises Linden Hills and provides
a perfect textual location for self-discovery. While Linden Hills is imaged
as a barren ridge of land, Willow Springs seems geographically perfect to
encourage and sustain life. Surrounded by water and covered with trees, the
island reverses the arid terrain claimed by Luther Nedeed. While the community narrator is quick to point out that mosquito-breeding marshes, sandy
soil, and hurricanes make Willow Springs a less than perfect place, it is difficult to deny George's perceptions when he first crosses "The Sound" and
reaches the island: "I had to be there and see—no, feel—that I was entering
another world," he explains; "Where even the word *paradise* failed once I
crossed over"[8] (Naylor, *Mama Day,* 175). Clearly, there is an edenic quality
about Willow Springs, emphasized by its location as a "place nowhere," a
liminal world, between former slave states, that cannot be marked by the
political control of governments or the spatial definitions of maps. Balanced
perfectly between places, Willow Springs seems a harmonious middle ground
for community to be established.

Since no one but its inhabitants can lay claim to the island, Willow Springs
is able to maintain geographical and figurative distance from those on the
mainland. While a bridge forms an important link to places beyond, and
while visitors are welcomed (provided their intentions are good),[9] the island stays removed from much of what the community narrator sees as the
foolishness of the outside world. This foolishness is exposed as the community narrator tells the story of Reema's boy and his attempt to explain
the traditions of Willow Springs in anthropological terms:

> Look at what happened when Reema's boy—the one with the pear-shaped
> head—came hauling himself back from one of those fancy colleges main-
> side, dragging his notebooks and tape recorder and a funny way of curl-
> ing up his lip and clicking his teeth, all excited and determined to put
> Willow Springs on the map (7).

Naylor's community voice concludes that for all his scholarly language and
ornate equipment, the boy makes a completely incorrect set of conclusions

from his research. Reema's son forgets his heritage and ends up looking like a buffoon to his former neighbors, having conformed to outside definitions of success and knowledge—definitions like those embraced in Luther Nedeed's world. As a community removed from such pretensions, Willow Springs remains true to its historical and cultural identity, helping prevent the betrayals of self witnessed in *Linden Hills*.

Just as Willow Springs's geography aids the community's nurturing of its inhabitants, its historical traditions act as an empowering body of folklore—proud, though sometimes painful stories which bind together past, present, and future. While Luther Nedeed insists, with terrible consequences, that history is to be feared and avoided at all costs, the history of Willow Springs is an inseparable part of its people's lives. As the community narrator explains, history is a force which everybody in Willow Springs knows, but nobody speaks; it exists in a realm apart from the conscious mind. Yet while historical traditions remain somehow intangible, they are not difficult to access: by knowing how to listen, the community narrator states, the stories of Willow Springs can be "heard . . . without a single living soul really saying a word" (10). Beginning the novel with a sketch of the sometimes mysterious history of the community, then, Naylor creates a framework which values history and prepares the reader for a text in which Cocoa, George, and Mama Day weave their own historical reflections into a cohesive narrative.

The specifics of the island's legends are clouded by the passage of time, but everyone understands that the history of Willow Springs is tied permanently to the legend of Sapphira Wade, conjure woman, great mother of the community, a slave woman who somehow wrested control of the island from a man who may have been her owner, lover, or both, and in so doing, sparked the legend of "18 & 23," the year in which these events supposedly began. Already embodying the land's origins, Sapphira's claim as first mother is strengthened by the family tree which Naylor includes before her first page of the text. From Sapphira Wade seven sons are born, and from the seventh son, another seven sons; these children are Mama Day's ancestors, and together shape the island through their lives. Invoked repeatedly, Mama Day's family tree bears an almost scriptural quality, and constantly reminds us that Willow Springs is a productive, life-giving place—what Helen Fiddyment Levy has called a "vital female pastoral."[10] Through a line of great mothers, fathers, and legends, then, the island is drawn together as a single family which nurtures and empowers its members.

While the island's geography and historical traditions form a strong backbone for the community, ultimately the people of Willow Springs are responsible for creating its atmosphere of growth. Certainly the legend of Sapphira Wade is omnipresent in each resident's consciousness, but as the community narrator explains, the true meaning of "18 & 23" is in knowing your neighbors, in being able to hear and understand their stories. These stories, missed by outsiders and those who forget their roots, demonstrate self-sacrifice for the common good, and illustrate the personal character of Willow Springs' residents, willing to disregard personal pain and danger for the good of the whole. For instance, the narrator tells us about Winky, whose name comes from the injury hot tar caused to his eye when he worked to rebuild the community's bridge after a hurricane (8). Clearly, such strong men and women have much to teach their children, and stand in stark contrast to the residents of Linden Hills, where the only important virtue is material success.

As we continue to meet the inhabitants of Willow Springs, we see the community is marked not only by strong character, but by considerable diversity. Joining Mama Day and her sister, Abigail, on the island are colorful individuals such as Buzzard, a moonshiner and "hoodoo man;" Junior Lee, usually drunk and cheating on his wife; and Ruby, bitterly jealous and a practitioner of black magic. Despite this presence of less-than-savory folk, however, a sort of harmony is found between discordant personalities as each blends with the others to balance and form the whole of the community. A similar balance exists between Willow Springs and those beyond the bridge; this balance is represented in the relationship between Mama Day and Dr. Smithfield, a "real" doctor from the mainland, with each knowing "their limitations and where to draw the line" (84). These lines are sometimes crossed, and conflicts of varying seriousness result, but such conflict only seems natural in a community where people try to work cooperatively. Indeed, we cannot help but welcome some conflict alongside genuine neighborliness when we consider the disastrous sterility of Linden Hills, where community is little more than lipservice.

Nowhere is Willow Springs's revision of Linden Hills clearer, however, than in the island's unique tradition of Candle Walk. In this annual rite, geography, history, and people are drawn together by an exchange of gifts as members of the community walk through Willow Springs with lighted candles and the greeting, "Lead on with light" (110). As neighbors give of themselves according to their means, they renew their community by helping those in need, thanking those who have been helpful, and sharing the memories which unite them. The tradition goes back as far as the legends of Sapphira Wade, but each year brings changes and concerns that Candle Walk will die with the older generation. Yet, as the community narrator reassures, "Miranda, who is known to be far more wise than wicked, says there's nothing to worry about" (111). In her wisdom, Mama Day holds a deep sense that history is not only the past, but a progression of present and future as well, and that in this progression, Candle Walk will remain constant.

It can be no coincidence that Candle Walk, an annual December celebration of gifts and light, bears resemblance to, yet clearly is not Christmas. Naylor's purpose in signifying on the Christian holiday becomes evident when we compare Christmas in *Linden Hills* with Candle Walk in *Mama Day*. Christmas in the former text is a night of destruction and death, a night when a candle knocked over by Willa and Luther's desperate struggle results in a fire which consumes them both. Candle Walk, on the other hand, is a validation of life, encompassing every trait of Willow Springs that makes it an ideal home where "being new and old [is] all rolled into one," and where geography, history, and community blend to enable Cocoa's journey toward self-discovery and love. Naylor thus returns to a strategy of repetition and revision, signifying on a textual tradition—her own—and creating a place where her narrative can evolve.

While Willow Springs seems a community ideal for nurturing personal growth, as Ophelia Day[11] begins to tell her story, we see that she has joined the stream of young Willow Springs residents who have left for cities and opportunities beyond the bridge. This decision seems particularly foreboding considering the fate of Willa Prescott Nedeed, the last Day to leave Willow Springs. Ophelia risks being swept up in the same falseness and repression which consumed her cousin, and we cannot be surprised that the less-than-comforting atmosphere of New York leaves Ophelia feeling lost and uncertain. Though she remains scornful of city institutions designed for "assembly-line nutrition" and job interviews like "cattle calls," the pace of city life allows her only a moment to be critical, and no apparent alternatives.

To cope with being faceless in such a mass of people, and to soften the pain of loneliness, Ophelia tries to develop a mental edge over her "competition," believing she can distinguish those who have jobs from those who don't by their haircuts, the hang of their briefcases, and how their newspapers are folded—a skill she credits to the "second sight" passed on as an inheritance from Mama Day (14). Sadly, while Ophelia has not lost sight of her roots and inheritance as a Day, her "second sight" remains largely superficial. An even more disturbing defense mechanism, however, is her habit of viewing people as food; a white receptionist is "Cherry Vanilla," a gay Asian man a "kumquat," and a dark black woman "licorice" (20). This apparent bigotry demonstrates how far Ophelia has come from her diverse, yet largely accepting Willow Springs home.

Ophelia grants readers these insights into her state of mind as she recalls first seeing the man who is to become her husband, George. She finds him attractive, yet difficult years of dating in New York have left her too jaded to believe any connection between them can occur. As she continues to reflect on the difficulties of being single in the city, Cocoa reveals exactly how much pain she has experienced at the hands of those she has admitted into her life by creating a list of relationship disasters. Failed attempts to find companionship leave Cocoa convinced that it is not worth the emotional risk to pursue George.

As we learn about George, he appears to be exactly what Cocoa needs to remedy her loneliness. He co-owns a successful business, is honest, and seems extremely practical; as George states, "To believe in fate or predestination means you have to believe there's a future, and I grew up without one" (22). George's attitudes stem largely from his upbringing in a boys' shelter, where he was taught respect, but little tenderness or love. Still, George recognizes his second chance as an orphan and is remarkably accepting of its pains; like Ophelia, he never loses sight of his roots, demonstrating an ongoing connection to personal history.

Although George's practicality enables him to see through the illusions of city life and overcome his difficult beginnings, he still lacks one crucial thing: a mother. While unlike Luther Nedeed, who chooses to forget his mothers and their histories, George still lacks the love and nurture a mother would have provided. The closest person to a mother for George is Mrs. Jackson, the orphanage's rigid supervisor. But instead of providing George with a connection to family and history, Mrs. Jackson works to make her charge forget the past with her constant refrain, "Only the present has potential, sir" (23). It would seem that such a childhood would leave George at risk for slipping into the artificiality and drive for money that consumes Linden Hills in its pursuit of upward mobility, yet he remains simple in his goals and earnest in care for those around him. As he says, "I understood exactly what they were protecting themselves against, and I was willing . . . to be the shoulder they could cry on when it got too heavy" (32).

When Ophelia applies for a position at George's firm, despite a disastrous interview, both feel that some higher purpose has drawn them together. While they cannot fill each other's respective needs for a secretary and employment, they seem strangely able to fill each other's personal and emotional needs. Ophelia longs for someone to provide her with a sense of belonging, and is amazed then, at George's genuine empathy as she explains how she must visit home following the death of her cousin, rather than start work at George's firm. George's dream of a woman who is genuine and connected to home is fulfilled by Cocoa, who allows him "to imagine . . . jasmine-scented nights, warm biscuits and honey. . . ." (33). While both conclude initially that a relationship with the other would be as disastrous as the job interview, their first encounter foreshadows the companionship which will soon follow—companionship integral to each one's growth.

Cocoa's subsequent visit to Willow Springs reveals that George will not be her only companion along her journey of self-discovery. During this visit, we begin to understand how important Grandma Abigail and Aunt Mama Day are to Cocoa's growth. In particular, Mama Day is to be a mother-figure for Cocoa, completely reinscribing the motherless narratives of Luther Nedeed and *Linden Hills*. While Nedeed is an undertaker, for instance, Mama Day is in every way a keeper of life, the island's midwife and healer. Nedeed is an aloof suburban landlord, while Mama Day is the touchstone of her rural community. Where Nedeed spurns his history to pursue material wealth, Mama Day binds her community together as a keeper of the past. Through Mama Day, then, Cocoa maintains contact with a nurturing mother—a benefit Willa, her cousin, lives and dies without.

As the community narrator takes us into the lives of Abigail and Mama day, we see that Miranda acts not only as a mother to her community, but also as a sister. Mama always greets Abby with the same words, "You there, Sister?", words originating in the pain they feel following the death of their sister, Peace. Emotionally torn by the tragedy of their sister's death and mother's subsequent madness, Miranda and Abigail seek solace in one another:

> So climbing up on the bed, she shakes the younger child awake. "You there, Sister"?" The answer is coated with phlegm, on the edge of tears. "Uh, huh." Miranda's small fingers place themselves around the rhythm of Abigail's breathing. Nestled under the quilt, they are four arms and legs, two heads, and one heartbeat (36).

Willow Springs history, then, is not only a tradition of mothers, but also of sisters, drawing together to form a supporting and strong community throughout the passing years.

While home offers Cocoa so much support and guidance, time away from Willow Springs and her mother-figures has caused her to lose sight of community. Instead of viewing those around her with accepting eyes and a cooperative mind, Ophelia sees only a mass of isolated individuals. Having lost her ability to reason in community-based terms, Ophelia is not ready to accept the nurturing Mama Day might provide. While Ophelia's love for her grandmother and aunt are evident, her visits back to Willow Springs are marked with tension, particularly when Mama Day seeks to offer advice; Ophelia does not want to receive it. As her relationship with George grows, however, his companionship helps restore her community vision, opening her heart for the love and historical knowledge that awaits. Meanwhile, recognizing that Cocoa is not yet ready to accept her family's past and to return to Willow Springs as part of the community, Mama Day waits behind the scenes, knowing that her grandniece has found companionship which, like the brotherhood of Willie and Lester in *Linden Hills,* will enable her to sift through the illusions of the city and rediscover the history and community which awaits her.

Developing love between Ophelia and George both helps clear Ophelia's vision and enables George to discover ways to remedy the pain he feels from lacking a mother and a past. The process begins with George's challenging Ophelia's tendency to turn people into "[stuff] you chew up in your mouth until it's slimy and then leave behind as shit the next day" (62). Though this challenge comes from anger, and is met with anger in return, George's accusations are incisive, and Ophelia begins to confront the fears of change and difference that have changed her. Next, George further restores Ophelia's sense of community as he guides her on a journey to see the "real" New York City. As Ophelia sees the diversity of her surroundings, she admits how narrow her life had become. Standing on the George Washington Bridge, Ophelia recalls the bridge to Willow Springs, and seeing the balance of island and a larger community, her new vista enables refreshed insight into her own balance and connection to the worlds around her:

> Standing there under and over all that incredible space, I saw how small and cramped my life had been. I actually lived on this island—somewhere down there on Ninety-sixth Street, among all the clutter of those buildings looking as if any minute they would push themselves into the river. And I had told Mama Day I knew New York—God, what a fool I had been (98).

George can see the change occurring in Cocoa. As he accompanies her, he delights that she has "stopped calling people food" and is "learning the difference between a Chinese, a Korean, . . . and a Filipino, that Dominicans and Mexicans weren't all Puerto Ricans" (100). Having persevered through initial doubts that a relationship was possible, George's companionship helps restore Cocoa to the community-based mindset of her mothers, brothers, and sisters in Willow Springs. But George also realizes that Cocoa is helping him grow as much as he helps her. First, Ophelia helps George realize his long-time relationship with a woman named Shawn has become stagnant, and that he truly loves Ophelia instead. Then, within the context of this now mutually-recognized love, and through its strength, Cocoa enables George to come to grips with the painful reality of his past as an orphan. Explaining his affinity for *King Lear,* George reveals that his physical heart, damaged by rheumatic fever, is an apt reminder of his emotionally injured heart, damaged by "the rage of a bastard son, my own father having disappeared long before I was born" (106).

At first, Cocoa cannot understand this rage, but following a bitter fight in which she calls George an "uptight son-of-a-bitch," George delves into the depths of his history, uncovering the root of his hatred for that term. Cocoa recalls George literally dragging her to a Harlem brownstone, where he explains in a burst of emotion:

> My mother was a whore. And that's why I don't like being called the son of a bitch. . . .
> I found out that's where I was born. She was fifteen years old. And she worked out of that house. My father was one of her customers. . . .
> The man who owned the place found me one morning, lying on a stack of newspaper. He called the shelter and picked me up. I was three months old. . . .
> Later, her body washed up down there. I don't have all the pieces. But there are enough of them to lead me to believe that she was not a bitch (130–31).

Though this catharsis comes as the immediate result of an argument, Cocoa's love makes it possible; her companionship and support give George the strength he needs to confront his pain and recover the memory of his mother. Having opened themselves both to love and their personal histories, then, George and Cocoa take their relationship to a new plateau—marriage. Validating their love and companionship in their vows, they demonstrate readiness to move on in their journey toward the more powerful history and community of Willow Springs.

As George and Ophelia build their lives together, preparing for new paths toward self-discovery, Mama Day makes preparations in Willow Springs for Cocoa's return as a full member of the community. As she and Abigail prepare their niece and granddaughter's wedding gift, a quilt sewn as much from family history as from cloth, Mama Day uncovers stories which, though painful, Ophelia must share. When Ophelia returns home for the first time following her wedding, then, Mama Day takes the younger woman to the "Other Place," the symbolic heart of all her family's knowledge. As Cocoa and Mama Day walk through the woods, the "talk is of avoiding the poison sumac, marveling at lightning-struck edges of tree limbs . . . , but they're walking through time" into a mythic history—"the beginning of the Days" (150).

In the Other Place, Ophelia begins to witness all that Mama Day has seen, claiming her inheritance as a child of Sapphira Wade's line: "An old house with a big garden. And it's seen its share of pain" (152). Ophelia learns that she shares the name of Mama Day's mother, a woman who broke her husband's heart by drowning herself after the death of Peace, her youngest child. Ophelia hears the voice of her mother testify:

> I gave the first and only baby my grandmother's name. Ophelia. I did it out of vengeance. Let this be another one, I told God, who could break a man's heart. Didn't women suffer enough? Eight months heavy with this child and he went off to chase horizons. I hoped he'd find them in hell. If I had known then what I was knowing all along, I woulda named her something else. Sapphira. My grandmother only softly broke a heart. My great-great grandmother tore one wide open (151).

Though much of what Ophelia learns remains shrouded in mystery, she finds herself in a line of men and women who suffer broken relationships. Yet, she sees, this line has given birth to Mama Day, a woman of extraordinary power who can "even turn a patch of zinnias into butterflies with a wave of her walking stick." As the discovery of her history nears completion, Ophelia takes great hope that her love will be different, like Mama Day—that she, with George's love, will be a healer rather than a breaker of hearts. As the two women return from the Other Place, then, Ophelia returns a reunited member of Willow Springs, fully aware of its traditions and her place in them, yet uncertain how they will play out.

Having merged her life with George's, however, Ophelia's reunion with Willow Springs can only be complete when he joins her there. George's nurturing companionship shows Cocoa the ability to understand truly the importance of community and leads her back to the land of her mothers, so in leading him over the bridge to the island for the first time, Cocoa is returning this love. Because of his orphaned childhood, George has never truly known the power of a mother's love nor a sense of belonging within

a familial community. Willow Springs provides him with both. Accepted instantly into the Day family circle, George is overwhelmed by the love he feels:

> Their laughter had been waiting for me, and as it circled around us, I could finally tell that they were sisters. The heads thrown back in similar angles to let out a matching pitch of flowing sound. Miss Abigail put her hands up on each side of my face—Well, bless your heart, child— and a lump formed in my throat at their gentle pressure. Up until that moment, no woman had ever called me her child (176).

George feels welcomed more fully than ever before, and on his own, he quickly becomes acquainted with the many personalities of the island, leading Cocoa to remark, "It was amazing how much you had managed to find out about people I thought I had known all my life" (190). Even after Cocoa has become aware of her own history, through George's companionship, her understanding of the community's heritage grows.

Yet while George continues to help Cocoa see those around her in new ways, he himself never fully comprehends the legacy of the Days or their community. When Dr. Buzzard explains how he earns his living making potions and charms, George mistakenly assumes that Buzzard's abilities are of the same nature and caliber as Mama Day's. Though Mama Day takes him to the tombstone of Bascombe Wade, George cannot hear the voices of history which tell him of pain and heartbreak. Understanding a portion of the island's history as he marvels at hundred-year-old trees, he still looks for ways to "improve" Willow Springs with "stations for solar energy [and] marine conservation" (185). While he is smitten with the island's beauty and nurturing atmosphere, ultimately George continues to view the community through the eyes of a New Yorker—an outsider. The women of Willow Springs and the community at large provide George with a sense of peace he never dreamed possible, yet it is precisely this limited ability to believe which hinders him from full understanding, and causes a crisis which threatens to destroy all the self-discovery he and Cocoa have enjoyed.

This crisis arises when Ruby, filled with misguided hate and jealousy, poisons and bewitches Ophelia. When Ophelia first falls ill, George presumes the problem is strictly medical, and is confident Mama Day's healing abilities will cure his wife. Although Mama Day's treatments provide some initial relief, Cocoa quickly worsens. At this, George can only believe that Cocoa needs "real" medical treatment from beyond the bridge; he cannot fathom that something far greater than a physical ailment is plaguing

Ophelia. He also cannot understand that even if he had found a way to the mainland without using the washed out bridge, it would have done Ophelia no good. As Dr. Buzzard first tries to explain what must be done to save Cocoa lies in the realm of magic, George replies:

> What do you do when someone starts telling you something that you just cannot believe? You can walk away. You can stand there and challenge him. Or in my case, you can fight the urge to laugh if it wasn't so pathetic: the grizzled old man with his hat of rooster feathers and his necklace of bones. . . . (286).

As Cocoa's symptoms begin to resemble madness, George grows more desperate. He gives an almost super-human effort to try and repair the bridge so that he can take Cocoa away from what he sees as pure insanity, yet cannot work quickly enough. When Dr. Buzzard tries to convince George to go the Other Place instead and follow Mama Day's directions, George tries to insist on his own way, claiming "[we're] going to be fine because I believe in myself." Buzzard wisely replies, however, "That's where folks start, boy—not where they finish up" (292). George must recognize finally that only when he reaches beyond himself, to Mama Day and a realm of forces he cannot understand, is he able to provide what Cocoa needs to save her life. Following a final, willful battle with his doubts, George sacrifices his disbelief, immersing himself one last time in a history not fully his own. He takes Mama Day's staff and Bascombe Wade's ledger—the full weight of the island's history—upon himself, but as he makes the last steps toward Cocoa's bedside, the burden is too much. Exhausted, George's heart bursts just as he reaches Ophelia, and before he can speak a word, he dies.

Although George's sacrifice in the name of love returns Ophelia to life, it appears that his death is only one more heartbreak in the long legacy of pain owned by the Days. While their loves were strong, those who went before George and Ophelia were unable to bring back Peace—neither the children of two generations, both with the same name and dying too young, nor the tranquillity of soul and mind. After George's death, Ophelia believes her own life is over, and contemplates suicide. But Mama Day preservers with a mother's strength and wisdom: "There ain't no pain—no pain—that you could be having worse than what that boy went through for your life," she tells Cocoa. "And you would throw it back in his face, heifer?" And in time, George's voice returns from beyond the grave to reassure Cocoa that his fate *was* different from all those who went before:

But I want to tell you something about my real death that day. I didn't feel a thing after my heart burst. As my bleeding hand slid gently down your arm, there *was total peace.* [emphasis mine] (302).

Indeed, as we realize that Ophelia's conversation with her husband has all been carried out silently, in a spiritual realm mediating between life and death, we see that their companionship does not end with George's broken heart. Instead, their love survives, both in Ophelia's mind, and in her son who bears George's name. When Ophelia remarries a good man, she makes it clear that "any man would have to come in second" to George (306). Living on with her new family and the continued presence of Mama Day, however, Ophelia completes one journey as she begins a new one, taking her place among the Days and writing a new history for herself. As she looks ahead to the future, we know she will be enabled both by the community of strong women and men that gave her life, and by memories of the companion with whom she shared her journey home.

With the completion of this narrative, then, Naylor decisively rejects the destructive, anti-historical legacy of Linden Hills in favor of a different path—a path marked by empowerment and self-discovery for her protagonists, both male and female. Naylor replaces Willa's voiceless death with Ophelia's life, speaking on beyond the conclusion of the text, just as Naylor replaces the uncertain brotherhood of Willie and Lester with the companionship of George and Ophelia, enduring even beyond death. Most remarkably, however, Naylor replaces the ashes of Luther Nedeed and his dead world with a final image of Mama Day. "Some things stay the same," Naylor writes as she gives us one last glimpse of this woman who so powerfully embodies history and community, "[some] things change. . . . [and] some things are yet to be" (312). From Naylor's vision in *Mama Day*, we must believe that she is optimistic about these things to come; if Naylor's audience accepts that her vision for personal discovery and growth, enabled by love, is possible, then perhaps, we should be optimistic as well.

NOTES

All citations of *Linden Hills* are from New York: Penguin, 1985. All citations of *Mama Day* are from New York: Vintage Books, 1993.

1. Barbara Christian, "Trajectories of Self-Definition: Placing Contemporary Afro-American Women's Fiction." In *Conjuring: Black Women, Fiction, and Literary Tradition,* edited by Marjorie Pryse and Hortense J. Spillers. (Bloomington, IN: Indiana University Press, 1985). Christian constructs a framework history tracing the development of black

women's fiction from past to present, describing how novels of the 1980s (and, presumably, the 1990s) have particularly focused on individual and collective women's empowerment, as opposed to earlier fiction, which focused more on correcting racism's broader social injustices.

2. Luke Bouvier, "Reading Black and White: Space and Race in *Linden Hills*." In *Gloria Naylor: Critical Perspectives Past and Present,* edited by Henry Louis Gates, Jr. and K. A. Appiah. (New York: Amistad Press, 1993). Bouvier focuses on Naylor's critique of a rising black elite's "commodity fetishism" as the driving force behind *Linden Hills*. As I argue above, however, this class-based reading of the novel only considers one part of the story.

3. Henry Louis Gates, Jr. *The Signifying Monkey*. (New York: Oxford University Press, 1988), p. xxv.

4. Carl Rollyson, *Uses of the Past in the Novels of William Faulkner* (Ann Arbor, MI: UMI Research Press, 1984), p. 82.

5. William Faulkner, *Absalom, Absalom!* (New York: Vintage Books, 1986), p. 5.

6. Bouvier, "Reading Black and White," p. 143.

7. Teresa Goddu, "Reconstructing History in Linden Hills." In *Gloria Naylor: Critical Perspectives*, p. 215.

8. Naylor, *Mama Day* (New York: Vintage Books, 1993), p. 175.

9. Naylor, *Mama Day,* pp. 79–81. Here we are reminded of how Sheriff Hart's deputy, intent on finding "northern agitators," crosses the bridge uninvited, only to meet with a frightening and embarrassing encounter with Mama Day.

10. Helen Fiddyment Levy, "Lead On With Light." In *Gloria Naylor: Critical Perspectives*, p. 275. Earlier in the piece, Levy notes, as I have, the stark contrast between Willow Springs and the "male-controlled American dystopia" of Linden Hills.

11. For the purposes of this essay, I will refer to Ophelia interchangeably by her given name and her "pet name," Cocoa, following the pattern set by the novel's other characters.

BIBLIOGRAPHY

Bouvier, Luke. "Reading Black and White: Space and Race in *Linden Hills*." In *Gloria Naylor: Critical Perspectives Past and Present,* edited by Henry Louis Gates, Jr. and K. A. Appiah, 140–51. New York: Amistad Books, 1993.

Christian, Barbara. "Naylor's Geography: Community, Class, and Patriarchy in *The Women of Brewster Place* and *Linden Hills*." In *Gloria Naylor: Critical Perspectives Past and Present*, 106–25.

———. "Trajectories of Self-Definition: Placing Afro-American Women's Fiction." In *Conjuring: Black Women, Fiction, and Literary Tradition*, edited by Marjorie Pryse and Hortense J. Spillers, 233–48. Bloomington, IN: Indiana University Press, 1985.

Faulkner, William. *Absalom, Absalom!* New York: Vintage Books, 1986.

Gates, Henry Louis, Jr. *The Signifying Monkey*. New York: Oxford University Press, 1988.

Gates, Henry Louis, Jr., and Appiah, K.A., eds. *Gloria Naylor: Critical Perspectives Past and Present*. New York: Amistad Books, 1993.

Goddu, Teresa. "Reconstructing History in *Linden Hills*." In *Gloria Naylor: Critical Perspectives Past and Present*, 215–30.

Levy, Helen Fiddyment. "Lead on with Light." In *Gloria Naylor: Critical Perspectives Past and Present,* 270–87.

Naylor, Gloria. *Linden Hills.* New York: Penguin Books, 1985.

———. *Mama Day.* New York: Vintage Books, 1993.

Pryse, Marjorie, and Spillers, Hortense J., eds. *Conjuring: Black Women, Fiction, and Literary Tradition.* Bloomington, IN: Indiana University Press, 1985.

Rollyson, Carl A. *Uses of the Past in the Novels of William Faulkner.* Ann Arbor, MI: UMI Research Press, 1984.

Saunders, James Robert. "The Ornamentation of Old Ideas: Naylor's First Three Novels. In *Gloria Naylor: Critical Perspectives Past and Present,* 195–214.

Divergent Paths to the South:
Echoes of *Cane* in *Mama Day*

Anissa J. Wardi

Gloria Naylor's *Mama Day* and Jean Toomer's *Cane* share many intertextual traits. In a Gatesian sense, Naylor signifies on *Cane* in her work in terms of both structure and theme.[1] Naylor not only repeats tropes and reworks scenes from *Cane,* but, more importantly for this analysis, continues Toomer's exploration of the African American pastoral. The African American pastoral is both part of, and counter to, what is generally characterized as the southern pastoral. Toomer can be seen as heralding a comprehensive pastoral vision in the African American expressive tradition.[2]

Definitions of American southern pastoral literature are many, yet at its most fundamental level, Kermode states, the pastoral is "any work which concerns itself with the contrast between simple and complicated ways of living."[3] Classifying works of American literature as pastorals suggests a connection with European pastorals insofar as these American texts incorporate elements of the tradition, including mood, tone, and narrative strategy. According to Osborne, "The spirit that underlay the older pastoral . . . was retained [in the modern pastoral]—the impulse to go back in time and place to a remembered innocence, the nostalgic backward glance to times when life was uncomplicated or to natural locales that were uncorrupted."[4] He further claims that "[i]n our time, the term 'pastoral' has come to refer to almost any literature which juxtaposes the complexities of urban life with the simplicities of a life removed."[5] While the rural-urban dichotomy is prevalent in pastorals, any tension concerning seemingly antagonistic elements upholds the design of the tradition.

Irony also figures in pastoral designs. The ritual journey to an Arcadian landscape, although redemptive and spiritually nourishing, is undermined by the knowledge that it is brief and that the realities of the harsh world still await. The primacy of irony in pastorals is exemplified in the phrase, "Et in Arcadia Ego" (Even in Arcadia am I), which is spoken by death, itself.[6] According to Bakker, this "epitaph . . . [was] inscribed on a sepulcher in

Arcady and topped by a skull in a seventeenth-century painting by Guer-
cino," signifying the irony of searching for an "idyllic rural existence in the
face of contemporary realities."[7]

Because of the political nature of pastorals—that is, their critique of a
modern world through fond remembrances of an earlier, more "pure" time—
use of this genre became popular during the post-Civil War era. For notable
Reconstruction writers Thomas Nelson Page and Joel Chandler Harris, the
pastoral became an ideal vehicle for criticizing the modern world by eulo-
gizing the Old South as an Arcadian landscape of order, graciousness and
dignity. These writers created a southern landscape where all members of
society lived harmoniously and peacefully together. Indeed, one of their
most popular narrative strategies was to position the African American
slave as a modern-day shepherd, a seemingly simple man, who sang the
praises of the institution of slavery.[8] MacKethan explains that the plantation school of writers, as they are known, believed that the "plantation provided the last and greatest bastion for the promotion of the pastoral ideal."[9]
They espoused that in this simpler world, "mutual affection between the
races was the natural state of affairs."[10] These writers distorted history in
order to promote their own agenda, using the pastoral's inherent desire for
order and unity to this end.

This kind of political propaganda was critiqued and undermined in the
writing of Charles Chesnutt. Chesnutt, an African American male writer of
the same period, exposed the brutality and inhumanity of chattel slavery.
He reversed the myth of the Old South as Arcady with a realistic portrait
of the horror and human devastation inherent in the institution of slavery.
MacKethan elaborates on Chesnutt's anti-pastoral writings: "he might employ the language as well as the settings of an idealized rural South, but always and only as an ironic counterpoint to his own ideals. For Chesnutt the
pastoral mode as a strategy for dealing with the black man's problems in a
world controlled by whites was a form to be mocked or undermined from
within."[11]

Jean Toomer's *Cane,* in contrast to Chesnutt's fiction, reveals a distinctly
African American pastoral vision. The import of Toomer's text lies in the
fact that it renders the complexity of pastoral yearnings in the African
American expressive tradition, while concomitantly critiquing notions of
the Old South as a site of Arcady. The overarching African American pastoral sentiment, as articulated through *Cane* and reified through the fiction
of contemporary authors such as Ernest Gaines, Toni Morrison, and Gloria Naylor, is one which celebrates the kinship that African Americans felt
with the Southern land while reconciling the oppression that their forbears

suffered on that land. These African American pastoral writers temper the
sense of belonging and identity that African Americans achieved through
a close relationship with the land with the historical systems of oppression
(including slavery, racism, and sharecropping) that took place on the Southern land. Thus, the ritual pastoral journey that so many of the characters
undertake is not one motivated by a temporary escape from harsh reality.
In African American pastorals, the South is not conceived as an "ideal" or
innocent world, nor is it positioned as merely a landscape of oppression (as
it was for early African American writers). Contemporary African American writers are recuperating the South as a site of contradiction which, despite the tangible history of violence, oppression and enslavement, fortifies
members of the community by enabling a close relationship with their
forebears and the land.

Indeed the southern land holds such a prominent position in both *Cane*
and *Mama Day* that many characters are narrated as part of the landscape.
This is unlike Euro-American pastoral writers, who wax eloquently about
the Southern land, but who in fact had a relationship to it that was marked
solely by ownership. MacKethan claims that the Southern aristocrats, as
portrayed in Page's fiction, regarded working with the land as "degrading."
She further argues that "while he loved basking in the atmosphere of simplicity that plantation life afforded, the southern gentleman . . . is incapable of participating in that life as its most elemental level. He might
'commune' with nature but it is his slaves who work in it to maintain his
paradise."[12] The level of intimacy with the southern land that is rendered in
African American pastorals is captured poetically by Alice Walker: "In the
cities it cannot be so clear to one that he is a creature of the earth, feeling
the soil between the toes, smelling the dust thrown up by the rain, loving
the earth so much that one longs to taste it and sometimes does."[13] The
spirit of the African American pastoral, then, is characterized by a closeness
and familiarity with the earth.

Naylor's third novel, *Mama Day* is a signifying text to Jean Toomer's
"Kabnis" (the third and final section of *Cane*) specifically through its treatment of the African American pastoral impulse—one which employs mainstream tropes while creating a uniquely cultural pastoral vision. *Cane*'s form
adheres to a traditional pastoral. The setting of the first section of Toomer's
text is rural Georgia and various women of the region dominate the narrative. In section two of *Cane*, Toomer moves his narrative to an urban,
northern landscape which is dominated by images of modernism and in-
dustrialism. In a traditionally pastoral vein, Toomer reveals the spiritual
death of a culture immersed in artifice.

In section three of *Cane*, Toomer again returns to the agrarian landscape of rural Georgia. However, the women who dominate section one of *Cane* are notably absent from this portrait and are replaced primarily by a northern male figure, Ralph Kabnis, and a cast of male characters. "Kabnis" differs from the previous sections of the text in that it is not a collection of short stories and poetry, but rather is a continuous narrative best defined as a drama. The protagonist, Ralph Kabnis, is a teacher from Washington, D.C. (the setting for a great deal of section two) who journeys to Sempter, Georgia ostensibly to teach. However, the reader soon learns that Kabnis, a northern man with southern ancestry, has made this journey in an effort to understand and come to terms with his ethnic and cultural heritage. Feeling displaced and alienated in the North, Kabnis yearns to understand his identity as an African American man. The circularity of *Cane*'s pastoral design, then, is realized in this section as Toomer attempts to synthesize North and South, male and female, and urban and rural. This attempt at reconciliation is a seminal pastoral trope. In the Reconstruction South, for example, the reconciliation theme was often employed by Euro-American writers through narratives of Union Soldiers marrying southern belles and living on plantations. Toomer's structure in *Cane,* then, is in keeping with this pastoral tendency to reconcile seeming oppositions.

The journey theme is a consistent trope in the African American expressive tradition. While Euro-American literature often focuses on the West as a site of progress and advancement, African American literature since the slave narrative has been concerned with the movement from the South to the North. Because the earliest works of African American literature were concerned with exposing the brutality of the South, the North was necessarily positioned as the land of freedom and opportunity. The North has remained a symbolic site of freedom for a number of years in African American letters. However, African American pastoral authors have balanced this vision by recuperating the South as a locale of community, history and identity. Robert Stepto sheds light on the narrative strategy of the southern trek, which he refers to as the "ritual of immersion" or a journey into group consciousness. Stepto defines the immersion journey thusly:

the immersion narrative is fundamentally an expression of a ritualized journey into a symbolic South, in which the protagonist seeks those aspects of tribal literacy that ameliorate, if not obliterate, the conditions imposed by solitude. The conventional immersion narrative ends almost paradoxically, with the questing figure located in or near the narrative's most oppressive social structure but free in the sense that he has gained or regained sufficient tribal literacy to assume the mantle of an articulate kinsman.[14]

Journeying to this ancestral space and gaining tribal literacy through the folk culture, can, according to Stepto, be spiritually freeing. Here, an obvious pastoral motif is sounded. The typical pastoral journey from urban to rural is appropriated but is not configured as an idyllic escape in contemporary African American literature. Toni Morrison's *Song of Solomon* is a notable example of this literary movement. Milkman, the protagonist, is consistent with the portrait of isolated Northern figures who dominate section two of *Cane*. He is steeped in materialism and individualism, and is consequently spiritually malnourished. Having been raised by his father, Macon Dead, a businessman who has abandoned his culture and his family, Milkman is physically and spiritually alienated from his culture. Milkman does not begin his journey to the South thinking that he will be, in fact, reconciling his identity. Yet in his search for material goods (he has traveled looking for gold), he discovers his family's name and history, which enable him symbolically to name himself. In keeping with the African American pastoral tradition, it is only through being on the land of his ancestors that Milkman comes to appreciate and understand the lives of those who have gone before him; thus, he surrenders himself to the pain and glory of the southern African American heritage.

The anti-materialist sentiment of Morrison's novel is also a predominant pastoral theme. Southern writers often portrayed the ante-bellum South as a society uninterested in money, but predicated on family name and honor. Clearly, this theme lacked cogency insofar as the system of slavery was concerned. Nevertheless, the Reconstruction writers tried to convince their readership that plantations were not motivated by profit, but were simply in existence to maintain the owner's aristocratic lifestyle—a lifestyle they held was necessary for establishing order in that social milieu.

This trend to look toward the South for spiritual regeneration, which has gained popularity in contemporary African American literature,[15] can be understood in terms of *Cane*. Although Toomer does not, finally, celebrate the South as a viable space for disinherited northern African Americans, he does explore the possibilities that exist there in "Kabnis." Gloria Naylor's *Mama Day* is read as a revision of "Kabnis" insofar as Naylor expands and elaborates on Toomer's treatment of the southern journey.

Toomer poignantly illustrates the African American pastoral problem in "Kabnis." The title character is consistently drawn towards and repelled by the southern landscape which is a symbol of African American history and culture. This seeming paradox is reflected in his own tormented identity— at once proud and strong, yet confused and pained. While the reader is certain that Kabnis is plagued with this dilemma in the North, it becomes overwhelming to him on the soil of his ancestors. Kabnis' living space in the South is a one room cabin in the quarters; thus, he literally inhabits the space of his enslaved ancestors.[16] Stepto argues that the slave quarters are the "prototypical ritual ground," which he defines as those "specifically Afro-American spatial configurations within the structural topography that are, in varying ways, elaborate responses to social structure."[17] The quarters, emblematic of the African American pastoral, are a sign-system of seeming contradiction—a space of slavery, dehumanization, and enclosure which African Americans redefined as an area of "community, protection, progress, learning and religious life."[18] In postbellum pastoral literature, the plantation house or "great house" is the symbol of order: "The great house, with its simple and stately facade, its ordered arrangement of buildings and gardens and fields, its aura of serenity and grace, was easily equated with the southerner's idea of what Eden must have been."[19] Thus, Toomer reverses this configuration of so-called order by shifting the emphasis to the slave quarters. In so doing, Toomer mines a painful, yet spiritually sustaining, cultural symbol.[20]

Notably, Kabnis' room is described as "whitewashed," which suggests that there has been an attempt to cleanse or erase the stain of slavery from the facade of this structure and from the South itself. Yet, the "blackness" is visible in the cracks of the wall, just as the remnants of slavery are evident despite attempts to obscure historical reality. The whitewashing also refers to Kabnis, himself. As a person of mixed race, he has attempted to erase his African American identity in the North, yet ultimately, like the living quarters of his ancestors, he cannot hide his "blackness."

On the first night of his stay, he is tormented by the night sounds as he imagines the violence and brutality that has taken place in these quarters. In keeping with the pastoral tradition, the land is personified throughout *Cane*—the moon casts spells, cane fields whisper, and the night winds sing. Kabnis, on this first night, is greeted by the song of the night winds in Georgia which, significantly, is heard through these cracks in the wall: "The winds, like soft-voiced poets sing: White-man's land. / Niggers, sing. / Burn, bear black children / Till poor rivers bring / Rest, and sweet glory / In Camp Ground."[21] The land, in fact, introduces Kabnis to the African American Southern experience. The cracks in the wall which are referred to as "lips" that give voice to the night songs also shower Kabnis with the red dust of the slave fields. The song from the night winds culminates with the falling earth that physically baptizes Kabnis, as Nellie McKay suggests, "into the community of his past."[22] Kabnis' displacement in the North is alluded to through the description of the falling earth: "[d]ust of slave fields, dried, scattered."[23] Later in that scene, Kabnis describes himself as an "atom of dust," which suggests that he is beginning to articulate his identity in terms of the land and his forebears. Kabnis' first night in the South is marked by historical visions of terror and violence. A distraught Kabnis, however, is unable to accept and look beyond this history and instead becomes an actor in this theater of violence himself, killing a hen out of frustration and fear. Kabnis wanders into the night searching to make meaning of this senseless brutality:

> Kabnis is about to shake his fists heavenward. He looks up, and the night's beauty strikes him dumb. He falls to his knees . . . The shock sends a shiver over him. He quivers. Tears mist his eyes. He writhes . . . 'Dear Jesus, do not chain me to myself and set these hills and valleys, heaving with folk-songs, so close to me that I cannot reach them. There is a radiant beauty in the night that touches and . . . tortures me.'[24]

In this scene, Toomer's writing epitomizes the African American pastoral. Kabnis is overwhelmed by the conflation of beauty and pain that inhabits the physical and symbolic space of the South. Kabnis' epiphanic moment, however, does not enable him to embrace that which would release him from his suffering. That Toomer describes Kabnis as feeling chained and therefore bound to the southern land is particularly fitting. Although Kabnis continually positions himself as an outsider, his utterances symbolically begin to undermine that chasm. Toomer explicitly connects Kabnis to his enslaved forebears, thus completing a historical circle—the symbol of *Cane*—as Kabnis' pain arches back to its origins.

Greene elaborates on Kabnis' "journey quest," which he, like Stepto, views as a quest in which the individual is "drawn back to the spirituality of his black roots, back to the South."[25] Most obviously in *Cane,* this type of spirituality is embodied in folk songs. Greene asserts that "folk art becomes . . . indicative of the luring powers of southern black life, a life that may brutalize the body but one that nourishes the soul."[26] Kabnis' inability to reach the folk songs which reconcile the complexity of the African American pastoral symbolizes his alienation from the African American folk culture. Returning to the opening night song in "Kabnis," it is clear that Toomer is establishing the theme of racial violence while also revealing the import of voice in establishing identity through community. Indeed, pairing the burning of Black bodies with song recalls, specifically, African American spirituals, which Bernard Bell characterizes as similar to chanted sermons, as they are "inspired by the Bible, informed by the group experience, and characterized by occasional rhyme, improvised graphic phrases, and dramatic lines delivered in a call-and-response manner."[27] Toomer establishes in this opening verse a distinctly African American oral tradition, one which is rooted in suffering, yet bespeaks the creativity and spirit of the community. The significance of these folk songs is the underlying message of hope. DuBois, in *The Souls of Black Folk,* characterizes these "Sorrow Songs" as promising a message of ultimate justice, if not in this world, then in the after life. However, because Kabnis cannot read the complexity of this message, he is enveloped by the real and imagined horror of the Southern landscape.

After a restless night, Kabnis concludes that there is "no use to read," which ostensibly refers to his futile attempt to read himself to sleep in this alien environment. In terms of the journey motif, however, this statement yields a more complex message. Kabnis, being from the North, symbolically has completed what Stepto labels the "ritual of ascension," and consequently has gained literacy. Stepto's ritual of ascension (a journey into self-consciousness) is counter to his ritual of immersion. The ascension ritual, thematized in slave narratives, is a journey to freedom and literacy.[28] Toomer stresses Kabnis' achievement of completing the ritual of ascension through his occupation as a school teacher. However, Kabnis' textual literacy solely cannot emancipate him. To negotiate successfully the ritual of immersion he is engaged in, it is imperative that Kabnis become fluent in his "tribal literacy," which is symbolized in this instance by reading the text of the folk songs. Toomer is positioning a dichotomy, fundamentally, between the written and oral modes of discourse which can be understood as embodying the African American's dual heritage: African and Western.

In this first scene, Toomer introduces Kabnis' desire to become a poet, thus connecting him to this oral tradition: "[i]f I, the dream (not what is weak and afraid in me) could become the face of the South. How my lips could sing for it, my songs being the lips of its soul."[29] Here, Kabnis reveals his dream of singing the songs of his people; yet, by his own admission, he is afraid of confronting the devastation and fear that his forebears endured. Ironically, as McKay rightly asserts, "[o]nly in embracing this history can he ever be free of it."[30] Furthermore, only in balancing this vision of violence with the communal strength of the culture can he become the "face of the South."

In scene two, Toomer establishes the male community which dominates section three of *Cane.* Kabnis is introduced to southern men who daily confront the realities of the African American pastoral. Fred Halsey, a wagon shop owner, and Professor Layman, an educator and preacher, attempt to help Kabnis understand the contradictions of the South. Unfortunately, the men's conversation only serves to exacerbate Kabnis' anxiety. Halsey and Layman animate the very real fears that Kabnis has about lynching and murders in the South. They relate the story of Mame Lamkins, which has both structural and thematic implications for *Cane*. The story involves a pregnant African American woman who, because she refuses to reveal the whereabouts of her husband to an angry mob, is lynched viciously. The mob's terror does not end there. They proceed literally to cut the living fetus from the mother's stomach and hang it from a tree. This horrific scene of racial violence in the southern landscape illuminates a significant division between European and Euro-American pastoral texts. The notion of placing the voice of death (Et in Arcadia Ego) in the idyllic landscape so that the inhabitants will recognize that their pastoral interlude is fleeting and that the "real" world awaits is irrelevant in the African American pastoral. In the African American pastoral, the voice of death is assumed: it is inherent in the very conceptualization of a southern land—a historical site of inhumanity, brutality and violence.

Kabnis is overwhelmed by the horror of this story, positioning himself in the role of Mame Lamkins. In fact, Toomer may be equating Kabnis's art to the aborted fetus. Kabnis later recognizes that his art could be the vehicle for his rebirth, but only if he will resign himself to the realities of the South. If he does not, the text implies, Kabnis' art will suffer a fate similar to Mame Lamkins' unborn child. Later, Kabnis recalls this episode in discussing his aborted attempts at creating poetry. Even though Kabnis claims that he has "[b]een shapin words t fit [his] soul,"[31] his art tortures rather than redeems him. Because he will not allow himself to create art from the material of his life, he continues, in vain, to feed his soul with "[m]isshapen, split-gut, tortured, twisted words," and thus wishes that "some lynchin white man ud stick his knife through it an pin it to a tree."[32] Alan Golding sheds light on Kabnis' approach, arguing that Kabnis "mistakenly wants to feed the soul through limited mental consciousness while denying the 'symbol, flesh, and spirit of the [black] past.'"[33] Golding further states that Kabnis wants to create words for his soul, "but he has no access to the beautiful language of *Cane*'s Part 1,"[34] which implies that he has not reconciled the contradictions inherent in the African American pastoral.

Kabnis is able to understand the horror that is still taking place in the South, yet he is unable to balance this with the positive aspects of the African American community which, in this scene, are expressed in the spiritual regeneration that the church provides. Layman's story of Mame Lamkins is punctuated by the shouts from a nearby church. Kabnis rejects this overt

expression of emotion coming from the church: "Couldnt stand the shout-
ing, and thats a fact. We don't have that sort of thing up North. We do, but,
that is, some one should see to it that they are stopped or put out when they
get so bad the preacher has to stop the sermon for them."[35] Thus, Kabnis
is overcome with the threat of southern racial violence, but refuses to participate in or even accept the indigenous folk tradition. Despite Kabnis'
journey, then, he is steeped in northern traditions, which Toomer characterizes as sterile and emotionally detached. In fact, as one of Toomer's
northern characters, Kabnis is described as an "artificial man." Unlike
Halsey (an artisan), Layman (an orator / preacher) and the church community (a chorus singing songs of freedom and redemption), Kabnis cannot
be the poet who sings his people's songs. He is incapable of creating art
because of his refusal to fully accept the pain and joy of his cultural past.
Therefore, he is "a promise of a soil-soaked beauty," who is "[s]uspended
a few feet above the soil whose touch would resurrect him."[36] His failed
artistry can, again, be understood in terms of the African American pastoral. Rooting himself in the folk culture, Toomer suggests, is Kabnis's only
chance at redemption.

Lewis, who is also a northerner, is part of Kabnis' social milieu in the
South. Lewis is portrayed as both a compliment to and antithesis of Kabnis:
"He is what a stronger Kabnis might have been, and in an odd faint way resembles him."[37] Unlike Kabnis, Lewis successfully has negotiated his immersion journey and, consequently, his insight into Kabnis is telling. Lewis
explains Kabnis' ultimate failure in becoming the voice of the South: "Cant
hold them, can you? Master; slave. Soil; and the overarching heavens.
Dusk; dawn. They fight and bastardize you."[38] This statement at once reaf-
firms Kabnis' position as a cultural orphan who is bastardized by a history
of incongruity. While seeking cultural identity in the South, Kabnis also
rejects the heritage he finds there, which suggests that he accepts this "bastardize[d]" identity.

The action of section three culminates with another symbolic immersion
journey as Kabnis descends into the "hole"—the basement of Fred Halsey's
workshop. "Kabnis" begins with the title character alone in the quarters,
moves toward Kabnis' initiation into the community and ends with Kabnis
literally facing his racial and cultural history. While there is a great deal of
circumlocution around the subject of slavery in "Kabnis," it is not directly
addressed until the last scene of the drama. Beneath Fred Halsey's wagon
shop (where Kabnis now works as a result of being fired from his teaching
position) there sits an old man, Father John, who is the symbolic embodiment of slavery. Father John cannot hear or see and rarely speaks. He is

tended to by Fred Halsey's young sister, Carrie Kate, who is a composite of the women in section one of *Cane*.[39] Carrie Kate, a pious and self sacrificing woman, feeds and cares for Father John, which suggests her connection to her cultural history. Indeed, the characters' reaction to Father John bespeaks their connection to their cultural past. The focus on Father John becomes apparent in the party that Halsey holds in the basement of his shop. The mood here is not joyous; rather, the "air is too tense and deep for that."[40] Literally faced with Father John, the characters must confront their personal pain of racism and their collective history of slavery. Again, Kabnis and Lewis have differing reactions to Father John. Lewis embraces Father John, responding to him as a symbol and text of slavery:

> Lewis . . . merges with his source and lets the pain and beauty of the South meet him there. White faces, pain-pollen, settle downward through a cane-sweet mist and touch the ovaries of yellow flowers. Cotton-bolls bloom, droop. Black roots twist in a parched red soil beneath a blazing sky. Magnolias, fragrant, a trifle futile, lovely, far off.[41]

This scene is foreshadowed by an earlier incident in which Kabnis is overcome with the simultaneous beauty and oppression of the southern land. In fact, Kabnis feels as if he is a slave to the land and history of the South. Lewis has an antithetical reaction to the African American pastoral as he openly "merges with the source," which refers not only to Father John (whom he deems as his living progenitor), but also to the landscape itself. Understanding that his ancestors brutally were forced to work in the fields, Lewis narrates the African American body in terms of the land. Here, Toomer's language suggests that Lewis has faced the complexity of the pastoral—rendering the natural beauty (cane-sweet mist, yellow flowers, and fragrant magnolias) with, in this instance, the sexual abuse that Euro-American men perpetrated against African American women (white faces who touch the ovaries of yellow flowers). Here, as elsewhere in *Cane,* Toomer equates African Americans with the land: African American women are equated with yellow flowers and the black roots in red soil are a metaphor for a southern African American history rooted in the earth. Because Lewis sees himself as a descendant of Father John, he confronts the African American pastoral, gaining strength from the knowledge of those who have gone before him.

The other characters at this gathering also, to varying degrees, recognize the import of Father John to their own life. Stella, a prostitute, makes a literal connection to her elder. Father John evokes memories of Stella's father, a man who became too old to attend church and consequently was carried by members of the community to sit before the pulpit. There, he would lead the congregation in song. Kabnis, as a poet, also wants to transcend pain through song, yet his rejection of his culture belies this desire. Kabnis' reaction to Father John bespeaks the anger and disdain he holds for his racial past.

Kabnis first tries to distance himself from Father John based on his mixed racial heritage. Lewis asks Kabnis, "The old man as symbol, flesh, and spirit of the past, what do you think he would say if he could see you?" Kabnis responds, "he ain't my past. My ancestors were Southern blue-bloods."[42] Although he later admits that there "ain't much difference between blue an black,"[43] Kabnis is attempting to draw a dichotomy between himself and Father John. Kabnis remains fixated on the old man throughout the night, ranting and raving at him. Everyone eventually falls into a deep sleep except for Kabnis, who alone hears Father John mumbling about death throughout the night. Kabnis is attuned to Father John because he is searching, in vain, for answers about his identity and his cultural past.

Early in the party, Kabnis dons a robe found in Fred Halsey's basement. In this garment, Kabnis "is a curious spectacle, acting a part, yet very real."[44] This costume that Kabnis wears can be read as a symbolic shepherd's robe—one which is strange, yet familiar. As Bone claims, "this ritual assumption of the shepherd's garb, is the oldest and most persistent stratagem of pastoral."[45] Traditionally, a member of the elite would assume the shepherd's robe in order to achieve peace and gain perspective on his own life. Toomer rewrites the familiar masquerade and places the act within an African American context. Through the assumption of this identity, Kabnis is attempting to become a member of the African American folk culture and specifically a part of the slave past. Despite his desire to assume that identity, Kabnis cannot reconcile the pain symbolized in the figure of Father John, and his masquerade fails. Indeed, at the moment Kabnis reconciles himself to an isolated and alienated lifestyle, he mournfully and ceremoniously takes off the robe. Ultimately, Kabnis' pastoral journey fails as he will not or cannot reclaim the history and lineage that would redeem him.

Gloria Naylor's first act of signification in *Mama Day* is her characterization of George, who like Kabnis is not only a cultural orphan, but grew up as a literal orphan as well. Thus, George's cultural alienation is evident not only because he is a culturally isolated northern male, like Kabnis, but because he has no knowledge of family or bloodlines which directly connect him to his history. George's journey to the South begins symbolically when he meets Ophelia Day in New York City. Ophelia, known to her family and friends as Cocoa or Baby Girl, is from the island of Willow Springs, a symbolic Sea Islands. George and Cocoa eventually fall in love and marry, and George accompanies Cocoa on her annual visit to Willow Springs. Here, George's immersion ritual / pastoral journey begins. George's presence in Willow Springs sets the traditional pastoral tension in motion. His visit establishes the familiar pastoral contrast between urban North and rural South as well as a patriarchal and matriarchal conflict.

Naylor evokes and elaborates on the southern landscape that Kabnis enters, highlighting the African American folk culture which serves as a backdrop to section three of *Cane*. By focusing on the various aspects of this folk culture, Naylor extends the vista of Kabnis' world, and in so doing provides a more complete picture of the African American pastoral. Typifying Naylor's revision, the nameless women singing folk songs in "Kabnis" move to the forefront of *Mama Day*. The title character Miranda Day (Mama Day) and her sister Abigail Day are the physical embodiment of the folk culture: they inhabit and are representative of this female landscape which George enters and to which he eventually surrenders.

The intimate relationship between the past and the present in Willow Springs is antithetical to George's life perception prior to his immersion journey. As an orphan, George was indoctrinated with the phrase, "only the present has potential." As he crosses over the bridge to Willow Springs, his notions are destabilized. He feels an almost palpable sense of history and family of which he is a part. Unlike Kabnis, who fights his connection to the cultural landscape of the South, George feels like he has come home. In the presence of Mama Day and Abigail, George feels like somebody's child for the first time. This bridge that connects Willow Springs with the mainland holds pastoral significance in Naylor's text. George must cross the bridge to enter the Arcadian landscape which signifies the journey motif. However, the bridge is eventually destroyed by a hurricane and George must abandon much of his educational training in order successfully to rebuild the structure with the townspeople. By literally building bridges with the folk culture, George symbolically is able to embrace his ethnic heritage and reconcile his identity.

Mama Day is the central character in this pastoral community as she is the living embodiment of great-grandmother Sapphira Wade. As her name suggests, she is the matriarch of Willow Springs even though she has never been married and has no children. The title "Mother" reveals Mama Day's position as a conjure woman. Thematically, conjuring is a focus of the text, and the impact of this cultural presence on *Mama Day* again roots Naylor's

Willow Springs in a distinctly African Diasporic tradition.[46] Lindsey Tucker's characterization of conjuring is salient to this analysis:

> Conjurers are said to be closer to their African roots than other, more acculturated African slaves. Also, conjure abilities are found to run in families; the conjure man or woman inherits his / her aptitude and the mantle of power, along with an expertise in herbal medicines. Conjure women often carry the name *Mother* and hold considerable power within their communities, and conjurers are, almost without exception, especially gifted with psychic abilities, or are known to have second sight. Often they are spoken of as being 'two headed.'[47]

Mama Day embodies this description. She is rooted in her people and her land and gains wisdom from this connection. She is the spiritual and physical healer of her community. A descendant of Sapphira Wade ("the greatest conjure woman on earth"), Mama Day presides over her community as a force of good—spiritual healer, midwife and wise woman.[48] Graveyards become signs of life in *Mama Day:* Mama Day is rejuvenated through her family burial site as she communicates with those who have passed on. Here, the pastoral employment of death (as antithetical to the idyllic world) is reconfigured. Naylor uses the spirit world of Mama Day's ancestors as complimentary to the living force in the community.

Naylor creates an authentic folk culture chiefly through the setting of her novel. Tucker elaborates on the significance of Naylor's Sea Island-like setting:

> Naylor's choice of location has obviously been dictated by the historical relationship of the islands to the perpetuation of African culture, for these Sea Islands are, with the exception of New Orleans, the most African of places in America . . . they also became the place where the least acculturated Africans remained. The distinctive Gullah heritage, that is both social and cultural, makes of the Sea Islands an actual and symbolic African presence, one rich with magico-religious beliefs . . . the islands suggest a place of myth.[49]

Therefore, Naylor revises "Kabnis" by creating a male character who greets a distinctly African American cultural landscape. Although it is clear that Kabnis encounters aspects of the folk culture which, in his own words, "torture" him, the reader is given little information about the cultural specificities of the community. Naylor essentially rewrites Toomer's Georgian landscape with a thoroughly African American culture, and in so doing provides an alternative to Kabnis' failed journey.

The focus on geography and cultural identity is established at the outset of *Mama Day*. Naylor's text begins with a map of Willow Springs which reveals that this island community is not situated in Toomer's Georgia per se, but off the coast. Following this topographical text, Naylor includes a bill of sale and a family tree. The interconnection between land, history and culture is presented prior to the actual narrative and thus serves as a lens through which to read *Mama Day*.

Sapphira Wade, the progenitor of Willow Springs and matriarch of the family tree, is also the subject of the bill of sale. Unlike "Kabnis," where the subject of slavery is not addressed until the conclusion, the history of slavery is presented at the outset of Naylor's text and thus the narrative unfolds with this knowledge as a backdrop. Sapphira is a slave who was sold to Bascombe Wade. The preface to the novel includes a bill of sale for Sapphira, a twenty-year-old woman who has "resisted under reasonable chastisement the performance of field or domestic labour. Has served on occasion in the capacity of midwife and nurse, not without extreme mischief and suspicions of delving in witchcraft . . . Conditions of Sale / one-half gold tender, one-half goods in kind. / Final." The Euro-American community has thus defined and circumscribed her identity through an economic transaction. The receipt, as a financial sign, evokes what Houston Baker refers to as an "economics of slavery," which "signifies the social system of the Old South that determined what, how, and for whom goods were produced to satisfy human wants."[50] Negotiating the economics of slavery, Baker argues, "*must be mastered* before liberation can be achieved."[51] Explicating this concept through Gustava Vassa's slave narrative, Baker reveals that "[h]e realizes, in effect, that only the acquisition of property will enable him to alter his designated status *as property.*"[52] Baker continues, explaining how the economic system of slavery has taken hold in female slave narratives through the sexual exploitation of African American women, thus resulting in children who were also considered the property of slave masters. This concept also is reconfigured in contemporary African American literature. For example, Baker argues that, in *Their Eyes Were Watching God,* Janie's grandmother "conflates the securing of property with effective expression . . . . [H]aving been denied a say in her own fate because she was *property,* she assumes that *only* property enables expression."[53] Therefore, Sapphira's receipt of ownership is given as a prologue to *Mama Day* because it illustrates how Sapphira Wade negotiates the economics of slavery. She acquires the land of Willow Springs for her seven sons, ultimately manumitting her children (who were considered the property of Bascombe Wade). Like Janie's grandmother believed, it is through this acquisition of property that the descendants of Sapphira are able to preserve their indigenous culture and are, in a sense, permitted expression.

The narrative voice of Naylor's text establishes from the outset the cultural independence of the residents of Willow Springs, which is intimately connected to their geographical autonomy: Willow Springs is not on a map, is not in a state and is tenuously connected to the United States by a bridge. The citizens of Willow Springs are afforded expression inasmuch as their geographical space creates and maintains cultural identity.

One of the most obvious aspects of cultural independence in Willow Springs is the interrelationship between legend, myth and history, which creates a unique epistemology for the residents. The physical characterization of Sapphira Wade is emblematic of this fluidity: "satin black, biscuit cream, red as Georgia clay: depending upon which of us takes a mind to her."[54] Continuing in this vein, the story of Sapphira Wade's murder of Bascombe Wade reads as follows:

And somehow, some way, it happened in 1823: she smothered Bascombe Wade in his very bed and lived to tell the story for a thousand days. 1823: married Bascombe Wade, bore his seven sons in just a thousand days, to put a dagger through his kidney and escape the hangman's noose, laughing in a burst of flames. 1823: persuaded Bascombe Wade in a thousand days to deed all his slaves every inch of land in Willow Springs, poisoned him for his trouble, to go on and bear seven sons—by person or persons unknown (*Mama Day,* 3).

While there are a number of myths surrounding Sapphira's relationship to Bascombe, there are some generally accepted "facts," namely that Bascombe Wade died in 1823 (evidenced by his gravestone) and that the residents of Willow Springs were given the land that same year (the deeds being proof of that transaction). Unlike George, who during his visit to Willow Springs wants to prove which, if any, of these stories are true, the residents, comfortable with ambiguity, incorporate the myths of Sapphira into their life and gain strength from her legend.

Sapphira is very much a living force in the townspeople's lives, as they evoke her life and her spirit despite never speaking her name: "Sapphira Wade don't live in the part of our memory we can use to form words" (4). Only the narrator is able to call Sapphira by her name, which is unknown to the community at large. Here, Naylor is exposing the inability of language (as merely a sign system) to capture identity. Throughout *Mama Day,* Naylor illustrates the futility of maps, photographs, charts, documents and even words to represent "truth." Rather, reality is a fluid concept in the text as Naylor undermines dualistic thinking that would permit facile compartmentalization: "It ain't about right or wrong, truth or lies; it's about a slave woman who brought a whole new meaning to both them words, soon as you cross over here from beyond the bridge" (3). Because Sapphira transcends the categories that would attempt to delimit her existence, the townspeople are wary of the limitations inherent in language.

Moreover, the community's lack of textual documentation signifies a distinctly oral society. Because they do not have Sapphira's bill of sale (the only document bearing her name), they, in fact, cannot speak her name. Yet, through oral modes of discourse they are able to evoke her presence by invoking the year in which they became the legal owners of Willow Springs. The townspeople do not merely replace Sapphira's name with a year, but endow "1823" with several meanings—all of which signify their specific discourse community. Because the residents recognize that it was the "18 and 23'ing that went down between them two put deeds in our hands," (5) they appropriate this central metaphor in their description of a variety of situations in Willow Springs. Like their foremother, they are in effect signifying on the notion of fixed meaning by implementing a discourse based on fluidity and cultural knowledge.[55]

Therefore, when a son of one of the community's members returns to Willow Springs from college to do "ethnographic research," he is unable to understand the significance of 1823. He believes that the community has inverted the numbers 81 and 32, which are the lines of longitude and latitude situating Willow Springs on a map. Indicative of his reliance on Western epistemology, Reema's boy wants to put Willow Springs on the map. Wedded to textual representation, he is unable to see Willow Springs' cultural autonomy, and thus interprets the island community as an absence. This college educated man is unable to comprehend the significance of 1823 because, in the words of Stepto, he has no tribal literacy. The narrative voice explains that if Reema's son really wanted to understand the meaning of 18 and 23, he could have asked residents such as Cloris "about the curve in her spine that came from the planting season when their mule broke its leg, and she took up the reins and kept pulling the plow with her own back" (8). This statement suggests that without understanding the African American pastoral, one cannot begin to interpret the language of the community. Reema's son, having no knowledge of the land (he "ain't never picked a boll of cotton or head of lettuce in his life"), has no knowledge of his community or its language (7). Knowledge comes from the legends, myths and personal narratives of Willow Springs and as such is dynamic and inter-pretational. The import of narrative is established from the beginning as the reader is positioned as a listener to the story. So as not to repeat the same error that Reema's boy committed, we are encouraged to "really listen this time" to the ensuing narrative told in "the way we know it" (10). Because the reader is positioned in the role of listener, the story transcends the pages of the text and becomes an interactive narrative. Naylor creates an atmos-phere of a griot relating a tale: the narrative is not offered as the truth, but rather as a story told from various subjective positions.

The fluid community that Sapphira creates is illustrated most clearly in Candle Walk, a celebratory ritual which commemorates the community's foremother. Again, there are many stories surrounding the origin of this com-munal event. Although, as the narrative voice confirms, this may be one of the more "far-fetched stories" regarding the origin of this island commu-nity, it is nevertheless the predominant myth:

> The island got spit out from the mouth of God, and when it fell to the earth it brought along an army of stars. He tried to reach down and scoop them back up, and found Himself shaking hands with the greatest con-jure woman on earth. 'Leave 'em here, Lord,' she said. 'I ain't got noth-ing but these poor black hands to guide my people, but I can lead on with light' (110).

Commemorating this encounter between Sapphira and God, every Decem-ber 22 the townspeople take to the streets carrying light. They exchange "any bit of something, as long as it came from the earth and [is] the work of [their] own hands" (110). Throughout this exchange, the townspeople encourage their fellow residents to "lead on with light" (110). Willow Springs' cul-tural autonomy is evident in this ritual, which is a revision of Christmas. This holiday is anathema to the excessive materialism of Christmas, which Naylor critiqued in her earlier novel, *Linden Hills*—a text recalled in *Mama Day* as Willa Nedeed (a main character in *Linden Hills*) is, like Co-coa, a granddaughter to Abigail Day. Through the celebration of Candle Walk, community is formed and harmony is established with nature, ground-ing Willow Springs in the African American pastoral tradition. While this community includes the progenitors of Willow Springs, Naylor describes how the face of Candle Walk is changing. Mama Day remembers how the ritual was enacted when she was a child and how the younger generation is transforming the holiday: rather than carrying candles, they are holding flashlights and even driving their cars with the headlights on. Although some of the older citizens resent the transformation of this sacred holiday, Mama Day believes that communities should not be stagnant: "like them candles out on the main road, time does march on" (111). Mama Day, like her quilt making suggests, believes in the interconnection of past, present and future as much as she does in the symbiotic relationship of pain and joy, which is in keeping with the African American pastoral tradition.

One of Naylor's signifying gestures towards "Kabnis" is her revision of Father John in the characterization of Sapphira Wade. Both figures occupy central positions in their texts, yet unlike Father John, the isolated and re-mote embodiment of slavery in "Kabnis," great-grandmother Sapphira Wade is a very living part of her community. Father John inhabits the cel-lar of a wagon shop (the "hole" as it is referred to in "Kabnis"), suggesting his figurative burial. The near catatonic state of Father John is also evoca-tive of death, as are the candles that illuminate his symbolic tomb. Images of waste surround him and therefore he can easily be disregarded by all but the most perceptive. Father John's female counterpart, great-grandmother Sapphira Wade, presides over the community of Willow Springs. She, too, is the tangible sign of slavery, resistance, and strength in *Mama Day,* yet her persona is configured differently. She creates community for the resi-dents of Willow Springs. Candle Walk, as representative of her essence, sig-nifies vitality and community. The residents do not merely pay homage to an ossified representative of their past, but incorporate the myths of their foremother in the creation of a vital, evolving society. Naylor refigures the symbol of the candles—which create a somber mood in Father John's base-ment—through the ritual of Candle Walk in *Mama Day.* The light from the candles reflects not only a living tribute to Sapphira Wade, but also signi-fies spiritual regeneration: the residents, fortified with the strength and spirit of their cultural heritage, forge ahead in the darkness, which is symbolic of life's uncertainty.

These representations of slavery are positioned as narratives of life and death in their respective texts. In one telling scene, Kabnis inscribes the Georgian moon with the image of an African American woman nursing a Euro-American child. The perverting of the life-giving force of motherhood through the exploitation of women's bodies during slavery, exemplifies Kab-nis' tormented relationship with African American folk culture. Kabnis only understands the African American female body through a narrative of oppression. This imagery also suggests that Kabnis has been deprived of proper nurturing from the African American folk culture—nurturing with-held from him because of slavery. While Kabnis is symbolically starved,

Mama Day is nurtured by her culture. Mama Day, searching for strength and guidance, dreams of her great-grandmother. Sapphira comes to Mama Day in her sleep, claiming her as a daughter. Through this dream, Mama Day is symbolically reborn:

> There's only the sense of being. Daughter. Flooding through like fine streams of hot, liquid sugar to fill the spaces where there was never no arms to hold her up, no shoulders for her to lay her head down and cry on, no body to ever turn to for answers. Miranda. Sister. Little Mama. Mama Day. Melting, melting away under the sweet flood waters pouring down to lay bare a place she ain't known existed: Daughter. And she opens the mouth that ain't there to suckle at the full breasts. . . . (283).

Mama Day, having been denied a nurturing mother (her mother committed suicide after her daughter, Peace, died), is reborn as the daughter of the slave woman, Sapphira. Unlike Kabnis, who is fixated on the oppression that his foremothers endured, Mama Day is able, as Sapphira instructs, to "look past the pain" and embrace the nurturing and love of her great-grandmother. By signifying on Toomer's image of the white child suckling an African American women's breast with Sapphira nursing Mama Day, Naylor is revising and renarrating the bodies of African American slave women.

Only after her spiritual regeneration is Mama Day able to confront the suicide of her mother, Ophelia. Ophelia tried to jump in the well after her daughter, Peace, but her husband could not let her go. Although he nailed the well shut, he was unable to save his wife from committing suicide in the Sound (the Atlantic Ocean), looking for Peace. Although Abigail cannot "look past the pain" to embrace her mother, Mama Day makes peace with her mother and with her forefather, Bascombe Wade (284). Awakening from her dream of Sapphira, Mama Day visits the well where Peace died. The water completes Mama Day's rebirth, as she symbolically is baptized in the history of the Days. Through these waters, she not only understands that her father could not let go of her mother, but that Bascombe Wade could not release Sapphira. Realizing that Bascombe really did love Sapphira, Mama Day understands that Candle Walk may, in fact, be a reenactment of Bascombe's search for her: "Quiet tears start rolling down Miranda's face. Oh, precious Jesus, the light wasn't for her—it was for him. The tombstone out by Chevy's Pass. How long did he search for her? Up and down this path . . . Up and down this path, somehow, a man dies from a broken heart" (118). Through this historical knowledge, Mama Day realizes that she alone cannot save Cocoa, asserting that "'it's more than my blood flows in her and more hands that can lay claim to her than these'" (294). Mama Day is acknowledging all those who have created Cocoa, both male and female, and thus she realizes that she needs George to be a part of her healing ritual. Cocoa's sickness (she is the victim of evil conjuring) prompts Mama Day and George to clasp hands to save her. While George resists the notion that Cocoa is deathly ill because of something supernatural, he eventually succumbs to Mama Day's logic. At this point, he undertakes to perform a healing ritual.

George travels to the "other place"—the original house of the Days, built by Bascombe Wade—and meets Mama Day. Their encounter illustrates the dichotomy between the African American folk culture and the Euro-American culture, as George cannot even understand Mama Day's language. George, steeped in Euro-American thinking, is initially unable to conceive of the African American pastoral and instead casts Willow Springs within a Eurocentric framework. George, like many southern pastoral writers, fantasizes that this southern community is a mythical garden of Eden. George wants to "play Adam and Eve" with Cocoa, arguing that "'we have a chance to sneak among these trees and take advantage of paradise'" (222). George positions Willow Springs as a "paradise" because he, like many Euro-American pastoral writers, is unwilling to confront the realities of slavery that took place in the South.

As noted, unlike Kabnis, George immediately feels at home in Willow Springs; however, it is not until George abandons Western epistemology and surrenders to Mama Day's wisdom, that he accepts this cultural history as his own. By "reaching back to the beginning," Mama Day knows that she must convince George to fulfill his role in saving her grand-niece. Although George initially rejects Miranda, he finally performs the healing ritual, empowered by her sacred objects. Fulfilling Mama Day's ceremony, it would seem that George is reborn into a distinctly female pastoral world, yet Mama Day armors him with decidedly male objects—namely the half-erased ledger of Bascombe Wade (which contains Sapphira's bill of sale) and John-Paul's walking cane.

Naylor's symbolism of the cane signifies on the central trope of Toomer's text. By recalling *Cane,* Naylor is drawing an analogy between Kabnis' and George's journeys. Naylor revoices the symbol of cane as a male object in *Mama Day,* which reveals her implicit criticism of Kabnis' journey, one which failed, in part, because it was dominated solely by men. Naylor reclaims Cocoa's male and female ancestors and as a result, George's journey is empowered by the strength of this complete community. The etching of water lilies on John-Paul's cane also evokes images of water and birth, which foreshadows his own rebirth. This rite that George performs signals his affirmation of the indigenous culture of Willow Springs. He must travel to Mama Day's hen house and bring back whatever he finds under the blood-red chicken. The trope of the chicken recurs in *Mama Day* as Miranda, a midwife, receives power from this symbol of fertility. By contrast, George is frightened of chickens and thus he has to undertake this journey as a sign of his affiliation with Mama Day. After a bloody battle with the chicken, George learns that there is nothing in the nest except for his own battered hands and therefore questions, "Could it be that she wanted nothing but my hands?" (300). George comes to understand that by performing this ritual, he has symbolically joined hands with the feminine.[56]

Also, the blood on George's hands echoes the early scene in "Kabnis," in which Kabnis kills a chicken. Naylor revisits this action of Kabnis'—one based in violence and power—and revises it as a gesture of love and selfless-ness. George's killing of the chicken is the catalyst for life, not death. Call-ing the chicken an "egg laying bitch," Kabnis disparages distinctly female imagery prior to his killing, whereas George's act is a sign of his accept-ance of the feminine and, by extension, the African American folk culture. The blood on both George's and Kabnis' hands is from the same source, but reveals very different realities: Kabnis' action is an attempt to exert power over nature, while George's signifies a complete acceptance of na-ture and its many powers. Indeed, it is through this ritual that Cocoa and George experience a rebirth. George is reborn as a member of the African American folk culture and, symbolically, is no longer an orphan. Ironically, this rebirth also signals his literal death. George's ritual is the catalyst for Cocoa's life, as she is healed (both symbolically and literally) by the strength and love of a cooperative male and female community.

Naylor stresses the vitality of a male/female community in Mama Day's artwork. Mama Day's quilt making is a richly symbolic act in the novel, for it represents the text of her life. Quilting is a trope in contemporary African American female letters, signifying women's creativity and strength.[57] Alice Walker, in *In Search of Our Mother's Gardens,* reclaims the art of her foremothers, manifest, most notably, in gardening and quilt making—both activities in which Mama Day engages. While connected to other African American female texts, this creative expression also signifies on Kabnis' failed artistry. All of Mama Day's art work is grounded in the history of her family and thus in her culture. The garden she tends is located in the "other place" which suggests that she is literally planting herself in the African American pastoral experience. Her quilt making also reconciles this space of contradiction. Prior to George's death, she and her sister quilt a wedding blanket for Cocoa and her new husband out of the material of their life: "a bit of her daddy's Sunday shirt is matched with Abigail's lace slip, the collar from Hope's graduation dress . . . corduroy from her uncles, broadcloth from her great-uncles" (300). By gathering the scraps of wedding dresses and the remnants of gardening aprons, Mama Day and Abigail create art. Although Mama Day understands Abigail's objection to weaving a piece of their mother's dress into the quilt for Cocoa, she also understands the necessity of including their mother and the accompanying pain she represents in the history of their life. Mama Day, through her art work, consciously maintains the stories of her people and preserves them for future generations. She faces the oftentimes painful history of her past, but unlike Kabnis, she contextualizes this knowledge and successfully weaves it with the family's joys and triumphs. This textual sign of the quilt reveals how the Days have evolved and the implication of this collective history on their future survival.

Mama Day's spiritual beliefs about nature are also reflected in her art. Feeling a part of the earth, her spirituality is based in nature and her art is an attempt to capture the love, peace and wisdom she gains from the land of her people. Her description of the wedding quilt—"The overlapping circles start out as golds on the edge and melt into oranges, reds, blues, greens, and then back to golds for the middle of the quilt" (137)—echoes her narration of the sunrise: "It seems like God reached way down into his box of paints, found the purest reds, the deepest purples, and a dab of midnight blue, then just kinda trailed His fingers along the curve of the horizon and let 'em all bleed down. And when them streaks of color hit the hush-a-by green of the marsh grass with the blue of The Sound behind 'em, you ain't never had to set foot in a church to know you looking at a living prayer" (78). Mama Day's family quilt again reveals the interconnection of land, identity and history. Kabnis' failed artistry is based on his inability to ground himself in the people and landscape of the South, "[s]uspended a few feet above the soil whose touch would resurrect him."[58] Because Kabnis is paralyzed by the horror of the southern landscape, he cannot incorporate this reality into the strength and beauty of the folk culture and consequently cannot be a poet of the South.

Both Mama Day and Kabnis' artistic capabilities are symbolized by their reaction to the African American pastoral. Mama Day regards the land as freedom, for it conveys knowledge from her ancestors in the spirit world. Kabnis, too, sees the land as representative of his African American ancestors, yet he fears them as ghosts. The ghosts in the South, he muses, probably drag trees rather than chains with them. This imagery suggests that Kabnis regards the African American pastoral as a symbol of oppression, losing the larger symbol of freedom and identity that is found there. Naylor reconfigures the rustling leaves that Kabnis interprets as ghosts haunting him as an act of ancestral communication that will, by the end of the narrative, enable Mama Day to communicate with her deceased sister, Abigail. Here, Naylor also signifies on the last scene of Morrison's *Sula,* in which communication from the spirit world is expressed through the stirring of leaves. Kabnis, relying on only one way of knowing, cannot frame this gesture as a sign of initiation into the land and spirit of his forebears and thus remains tormented by it.

The connection between the spiritual world and the living world in Willow Springs is symbolized most notably in the ritual of Candle Walk. Just as the community keeps their progenitor alive through this annual event, Mama Day incorporates George into the festivity the year after his death. Mama Day accompanies Cocoa to New York City after George's death and while there buys a number of trinkets—mugs, T-shirts, dolls and ashtrays. While these items might seem out of place in Candle Walk, the following year Mama Day ties her ginger cookies to them and gives them to members of her community, encouraging them to "lead on with light." Bone's analysis of the pastoral sheds light on Mama Day's act: "[i]n its more sophisticated forms, however, pastoral would seem to be less an advocacy of the rural life than a balancing or reconciling force . . . Pastoral is thus a harmonizing force which mediates between the values of the country and the town, the contemplative and active life."[59] Mama Day, in effect, incorporates George into this agrarian ritual which signifies a final reconciliation between the urban and rural; the North and South and the female and male. The overarching structure of *Mama Day*—a conversation between Cocoa and her deceased husband—reinforces this theme of resolving oppositions. Using Bone's language, Naylor's text can be conceptualized as a "sophisticated pastoral" which, in its reconciliation, results in a "gain in balance and proportion, and a greater complexity of moral vision."[60] Candle Walk exemplifies the spirit of Willow Springs—a community not stagnant in tradition, but enriched by it. Because George was reborn in Willow Springs and is now buried in the family graveyard, he is part of the society. As such, Mama Day incorporates a part of his world (New York City) into the celebration. Candle Walk, then, is emblematic of the interconnection between past, present and future. Mama Day keeps memories alive while, at the same time, moving forward, which reinforces the theme of rebirth in the novel.

Images of motherhood dominate section one of *Cane.* In section three, Kabnis' desire to create poetry is rendered in specifically familial and life-giving terms: as a poet, he wants to be the son of the South, yet because he sees himself only as a "bastard son," he cannot create poetry and thus desires for his art symbolically to be lynched (like Mame Lamkins' unborn child) by white men. Toomer uses a great deal of African American pastoral birth images in the text: "Night, soft belly of a pregnant Negress, throbs evenly against the torso of the South. Night throbs a womb-song to the South."[61] These images are balanced by those of lynching, aborted motherhood and dead children. Indeed, the focus on Kabnis' bastard identity is again a sign of incomplete birth. Candle Walk, the central metaphor of *Mama Day,* embodies this theme of death, rebirth and regeneration. Tucker argues that Candle Walk, "[o]bserved on the 22nd of December, the time of the midwinter solstice . . . suggests a recognition of the fact that this longest night of the year also marks the beginning of the return of the sun from its lowest zenith, a rebirth that correlates with the rebirth of the terrestrial world. Thus, the ritual gestures that make up Candle Walk suggest a conjoining of cosmic and terrestrial."[62] Reading Candle Walk, the major symbol of the novel, as a terrestrial rebirth grounds Naylor's text within the tradition of the African American pastoral. To live in sync with the African American pastoral, the community must negotiate their lives in harmony with the land. Having reverence for one's position in terms of nature and history marks the philosophy of Candle Walk. Configuring the land as a source of renewal is central within this context, as it defines Naylor's pastoral text.

The land as representative of history, culture and family (including past and present members) becomes the vehicle with which Mama Day's oracular powers are realized. Perhaps Naylor's most profound act of signification on *Cane* is her creation of a character who personifies the essence of Toomer's text. Mama Day is exemplary of Toomer's yearning in *Cane* as depicted in his epigraph: "Oracular. Redolent of fermenting syrup, Purple of the dusk, Deep-rooted Cane." Mama Day is the oracle of her people, singing the songs of the pastoral through a voice enabled by the land of her ancestors. Indeed, Naylor's choice of title also suggests the conflation of Mama Day and Willow Springs. *Mama Day* is steeped in place, yet is Naylor's only novel not named directly after a geographical location. This suggests that Mama Day is herself a sign of Willow Springs, and thus of the African American pastoral.

Toomer's *Cane* stands as a seminal African American pastoral text.

Toomer's impetus for writing *Cane* was his visit to Sparta, Georgia. After the publication of *Cane,* Toomer explained why he wrote the text:

> 'With Negroes also the trend was towards the small town and then towards the city—and industry and commerce and machines. The folkspirit was walking in to die on the modern desert. That spirit was so beautiful. Its death was so tragic. Just this seemed to sum life for me. And this was the feeling I put into "Cane." "Cane" was a swan-song. It was a song of an end.'[63]

This is a decidedly pastoral sentiment. The primary tension in traditional pastorals is the strong sense of temporality. Toomer, ambivalent about his ethnic identity, saw the African American southern folk culture as beautiful, but passing. While Toomer created a comprehensive African American pastoral, he was not able to sustain his own vision. Toomer strives for the pastoral mode of reconciliation in section three of *Cane,* but ultimately cannot achieve harmony. Toomer's push toward reconciliation is literalized in the format of *Cane:* the arcs preceding sections one and two of the text culminate in the incomplete circle that is found prior to section three. The broken arcs are a sign of imbalance and unrealized reconciliation in Toomer's text. Nevertheless, Toomer's pastoral vision, as embodied in *Cane,* created a space for contemporary writers to attempt to realize more fully the viability of the African American pastoral tradition.

NOTES

Citations in text to Naylor's *Mama Day* are from the New York: Vintage, 1988 edition.

1. For a discussion of the similarities between Naylor's *Women of Brewster Place* and section one of *Cane,* see Michael Awkward, "Authorial Dreams of Wholeness: (Dis) Unity, (Literary) Parentage and *The Women of Brewster Place,*" in *Gloria Naylor: Critical Perspectives Past and Present,* eds. Henry Louis Gates, Jr. and K.A. Appiah (New York: Columbia University Press, 1991), 37–71.

2. Toomer and Naylor, writing within the African American pastoral tradition, celebrate the kinship their characters experience with the South—and the land-based community it engenders for them—while simultaneously examining the brutalities that have occurred on that very terrain. Some critics have rejected the use of the pastoral as an appropriate label for any work of African American fiction. Wolfgang Karrer, for example, has criticized the adoption of a pastoral or picaresque framework for the explication of African American letters, stating "both categories, again, stem from the European tradition and they ill fit the black experience which until the sixties showed little of either classic pastoral or picaresque ideologies." See Wolfgang Karrer, "The History and Signifying Intertextuality of the

African American Short Story," in *African American Short Story 1970–1990: A Collection of Critical Essays,* eds. Wolfgang Karrer and Barbara Puschman-Nalenz (Wissenschaft-licher: Verlag Trier, 1993), 4. Here, Karrer alludes to the omnipresence of pastoral sensibilities in contemporary African American texts, yet remains adamant in his dismissal of this critical framework. Michael Lynch, in his discussion of the city in Naylor's fiction, also writes that "[m]any black writers have focused on the inequities and evils found in the city, yet they have not been able or willing to envision an ideal pastoral alternative." See Michael Lynch, "The Wall and the Mirror of the Promised Land: The City in the Novels of Gloria Naylor," in *The City in African-American Literature,* eds. Yoshinobu Hakutani and Robert Butler (Cranbury: Associated University Press, 1995), 182. Karrer and Lynch do not consider the African American writers' appropriation and revision of the pastoral.

Neither critic considers what Henry Louis Gates in his seminal text, *The Signifying Monkey,* identifies as the predominance of signifyin(g) in the African American canon. Gates explicitly states, "I can . . . introduce . . . examples of Signifyin(g) revisions . . . that help to demonstrate that authors produce meaning in part by revising formal patterns of representation in their fictions. This production of meaning, in all its complexity, simultaneously involves a positioning or a critique both of received literary conventions and of the subject matter represented in canonical texts of the tradition." See Henry Louis Gates, Jr., *The Signifying Monkey: A Theory of African-American Literary Criticism* (New York: Oxford UP, 1988), 113. Using Gates' critical framework, it is apparent that Jean Toomer and Gloria Naylor have indeed thematized the importance of the southern land in their fiction, yet do not envision this landscape from a Eurocentric perspective. Toomer and Naylor, writing in the African American pastoral mode, reject conceptions of the southern land as a virtual Utopia, and powerfully render the brutalities that have taken place on that soil. Nevertheless, both authors highlight the sustaining power of community (including folk traditions, orality, spirituality, culture and family) often associated with the African American southern past.

3. Frank Kermode, ed., *English Pastoral Poetry* (London, 1952), 13, quoted in Lucinda MacKethan, *The Dream of Arcady: Place and Time in Southern Literature* (Baton Rouge: Louisiana State University Press, 1980), 3.

4. William Osborne, "John Crowe Ransom: Toward a Pastoral," in *Southern Literature in Transition: Heritage and Promise,* eds. Philip Castile and William Osborne (Memphis: Memphis State University Press, 1983), 89.

5. Ibid.

6. Jan Bakker, *Pastoral in Antebellum Southern Romance* (Baton Rouge: Louisiana State University Press, 1989), 40.

7. Ibid.

8. Lucinda MacKethan, *The Dream of Arcady: Place and Time in Southern Literature* (Baton Rouge: Louisiana State University Press, 1980), 12.

9. Ibid., 11.

10. Ibid.

11. Ibid., 103. Chesnutt's short stories reveal the inhumanity inherent in chattel slavery. "Po' Sandy," for example, draws attention to the painful familial separation brought about by slavery. Sandy's master's callous selling and trading of human beings calls into question the characterization of slave masters as benevolent, a portrayal popularized in the plantation school of fiction. See Charles W. Chesnutt, *Collected Stories of Charles W. Chesnutt,* ed. William L. Andrews (New York: Penguin, Mentor, 1992), 14–24.

12. MacKethan, 51.

13. Alice Walker, *In Search of Our Mothers' Gardens* (New York: Harcourt Brace Jo-vanovich, 1983), 21. Here, Walker echoes Alain Locke's argument that African American art could realize "a return to nature, not by way of the forced and worn formula of Romanticism, but through the closeness of an imagination that has never broken kinship with nature." See Alain Locke, *The New Negro* (New York: Albert and Charles Boni, 1925), quoted in MacKethan, 109. Neither Locke nor Walker characterizes African American writers as necessarily pastoral; rather, they highlight the material reality of agrarian life in the historical African American Southern experience.

14. Robert Stepto, *From Behind the Veil: A Study of Afro-American Narrative,* 2d ed. (Chicago: University of Illinois Press, 1991), 167.

15. A recent example can be found in Julie Dash's novel, *Daughters of the Dust.* Amelia, a graduate student in anthropology, returns to her ancestral homeland of Ibo Landing to conduct research for her senior thesis, a film project. Visiting this ancestral place, Amelia arrives at a greater understanding of her position in the culture and in the space of the community's memories. Central to this transformation is Amelia's recognition of her own cultural arrogance: "She had winced when she reread her thesis proposal with its distant perspective and cold language that attempted to describe people whose lives were filled with wonder, vibrancy and uncomplicated honesty" (Dash 283–284). While Kabnis, who wants to be the poet who sings his people's songs, is without cultural knowledge, Amelia's artistry manifests her respect for the Sea Island culture.

Amelia does not exploit the interior lives of the community, and her final film project represents an imaginative reconstitution of history. Her film, richly visual, yet bereft of language, powerfully captures the beauty and magic of those who live on Ibo Landing. Like Kabnis, she initially occupies a hierarchical gaze, yet Amelia's film (a symbolic reference to Julie Dash's own filmmaking) displaces this gaze in numerous ways. First, Amelia's sole construction of the film is ruptured by Ben (her cousin, a Sea Island resident), who adopts her tools of filmmaking and shoots a great deal of the footage. Secondly, Amelia herself becomes part of the culture. As discussed later in this essay, Kabnis remains distant and critical of the community. In contrast, Amelia learns to respect and value the culture, exemplified in the following: "When I first came here and saw how hard folks lived and what little they had, I thought to myself, 'Lord, slavery is not that far gone.' But now I'm wondering who's living in slavery, folks down here working their own land or folks up North working to pay that rent and keep the lights on, too. I saw Lucy stop in the middle of her weeding the garden, grab a fistful of dirt, and smell it. You know that look she can get on her face. I wish I could feel that way about something" (Dash 271). In this way, Amelia's journey succeeds, as she is willing to accept the complexity of this geographic and historic space.

16. John Washington, in *The Chaneysville Incident,* can be read as a Kabnis figure, as he is an educated man (a history professor) who resides in a large urban environment. Although he does not travel South per se, he does journey into a familial landscape—rural Pennsylvania. Like Kabnis, he inhabits an intimate family dwelling—a rustic cabin—and by literally occupying that space, he exhumes two hundred and fifty years of absent history, thereby conjoining oral and written discourses of history.

17. Ibid., 68.

18. Ibid.

19. MacKethan, 43.

20. The relationship between place, identity and history is also manifest in Toomer's

Balo—a one-act play set in the post-Reconstruction South, published in 1921. Despite the title of the play, it is place and not character which dominates. The minimal cast of characters—including Will Lee (a farmer), his wife Sally, and their adult sons Balo and Tom—inhabit former slave quarters, which become the stage on which the politics of their lives are manifest. From the beginning, spatial relations dictate the characters' lives, as the Lee family's domestic rituals—working in the fields, cooking, cleaning, and praying—recall the lives of their enslaved forebears. Like Kabnis' quarters, there is an obvious spectral presence haunting the Lee's home. The farmhouse, originally inhabited by Lee's enslaved grandmother, contains second-hand furniture that belonged to the former mistress of the plantation. The immense fireplace, previously used for cooking meals for the "big house," overwhelms the room. The fireplace is a symbol of exploitation and servitude, yet is reinscribed as a communal meeting place, where friends gather to reminisce and pay tribute to the past. One such reminiscence is of the grandmother's skill at keeping the food she prepared in that cabin warm, despite the one-hundred-yard distance she traveled between the cookhouse and the main house. Thus, the family's place of refuge is, like Kabnis' dwelling, a contradictory space of family and slavery.

Toomer underscores the geographies of the farmhouse and the canefields as more than physical representations of place. Although we do not see the family working in the fields per se, there is a great deal of discussion about agrarian labor. Furthermore, the play takes place in Georgia during the cane-cutting season, which creates an obvious link to *Cane*. The constant labor necessary to cultivate the land and harvest the crop is underscored by Toomer's direction that the play takes place on "any week day." Despite the inescapable role that the land and its accompanying hardships assume in their daily lives, the Lee's are deeply spiritual people, praying late into the evening after returning from a long night of boiling cane, or rising before dawn to read the Bible. Here, a familiar chord is sounded: Toomer reinforces his belief that a life lived close to the earth enables spiritual fortitude and sustaining communal ties.

21. Jean Toomer, *Cane* (New York: Norton, 1988), 87. From CANE by Jean Toomer. Copyright 1923 by Boni & Liveright, renewed 1951 by Jean Toomer. Reprinted by permission of Liveright Publishing Corporation.

22. Nellie McKay, *Jean Toomer Artiste: A Study of His Literary Life and Work, 1894– 1936* (Chapel Hill: University of North Carolina Press, 1984), 153.

23. Toomer, 84.

24. Ibid., 85.

25. J. Lee Greene, "The Pain and the Beauty: The South, the Black Writer, and the Conventions of the Picaresque," in *The American South*, ed. Louis D. Rubin, Jr. (Baton Rouge: Louisiana State University Press, 1980), 275.

26. Ibid.

27. Bernard Bell, *The Afro-American Novel and Its Tradition* (Amherst: University of Massachusetts Press, 1987), 26.

28. Stepto, 67.

29. Toomer, 83–84.

30. McKay, 156.

31. Toomer, 111.

32. Ibid.

33. Alan Golding, "Jean Toomer's *Cane*: The Search for Identity Through Form," *Arizona Quarterly* 39, no. 3 (1983): 212–13.

34. Ibid., 212.

35. Toomer, 91.

36. Ibid., 98.

37. Ibid., 97.

38. Ibid., 108–9.

39. The women of part one of *Cane* are connected to the African American folk culture, as symbolized by their embodiment of the Southern land: "[T]he whole countryside seemed to flow into [Fern's] eyes"; Karintha "carr[ies] beauty, perfect as dusk when the sun goes down." See Toomer, 17, 4. Toomer's desire to capture the Southern African American woman's rich spirituality becomes fully realized in his characterization of Carrie Kate, who, in nurturing Father John—and, by extension, the progenitors of the community—locates the source of this spirituality. See Toomer, 83–117.

40. Toomer, 107.

41. Ibid.

42. Ibid., 108.

43. Ibid.

44. Ibid., 107.

45. Robert Bone, *Down Home: A History of Afro-American Short Fiction From Its Beginnings to the End of the Harlem Renaissance* (New York: G.P. Putnam's Sons, 1975), 135.

46. Shange, too, renders the magic of the South in *Cypress, Sassafrass and Indigo*. Indigo is described as daughter of that land and its history: "There was too much magic in the night. Indigo felt the moon in her mouth, singing. The South in her. . . . She had many tongues, many spirits who loved her, real and unreal. The South in her" (14, 28). Indigo's ownership of the moon (notably placed inside her mouth) is a metaphor for her absorption of the South's terrestrial magic. Receiving power from the southern land, rich with the ancestors' spirits, Indigo's voice / song is enabled. The concurrence of the "real and unreal" voices reveals the coexistence of the mystical and the ordinary in the South, and by extension, in the southern community. Although Indigo is already in the South, she journeys deeper into the region, situating herself in the Sea Islands. Like Mama Day, Indigo ("a consort of spirits") becomes a conjure woman, who tends to the community's needs.

47. Lindsey Tucker, "Recovering the Conjure Woman: Texts and Contexts in Gloria Naylor's *Mama Day, African American Review* 28 (Summer 1994): 176.

48. Valerie Lee explains that "the first black lay midwife came to America in 1619, bringing with her a knowledge of health and healing based in her African background." See Valerie Lee, *Granny Midwives and Black Women Writers* (New York: Routledge, 1996), 6. Lee highlights the critical role that these female healers played in their communities, stating that "they were everything from herbal to ritual specialists." See Lee, 6. This characterization resonates with Mama Day's position in Willow Springs.

49. Tucker, 180.

50. Houston A. Baker, *Blues, Ideology, and Afro-American Literature: A Vernacular Theory* (Chicago: University of Chicago Press, 1984), 26.

51. Ibid., 37.

52. Ibid., 35.

53. Ibid., 57.

54. Gloria Naylor, *Mama Day* (New York: Vintage, 1988), 3.

55. Sapphira Wade can be read as representing a poststructuralist's conceptualization of meaning. Eagleton claims that "[m]eaning is scattered or dispersed along the whole chain of signifiers: it cannot be easily nailed down, it is never fully present in any one sign alone, but is rather a kind of constant flickering of presence and absence together." See Terry Eagleton,

Literary Theory: An Introduction (Minneapolis: University of Minnesota Press, 1983), 128. Sapphira is both absent and present in the signifiers used to capture her essence. This deferment of fixed meaning, or "flickering of presence and absence" is clearly manifest in the ritual of Candle Walk, in which the flame of the candle pays tribute to the foremother of the community and simultaneously reveals the inability to articulate the "fully meaningful" sign.

56. Not all critics share this interpretation. In fact, Susan Melsenholder reads George's actions in the chicken coop as a violent reassertion of phallocentrism: "Unable to abandon his intense masculine individualism, however, George perverts this ritual by acting another white male role. Refusing to believe his hands are all he is to bring back, frustrated at what he (like the white world) sees as only 'mumbo jumbo,' subconsciously afraid of what the chicken represents, he reenacts the archetypal white drama of male oppression" (412). Gary Storhoff also develops the argument that George, so unwilling to abandon his masculine will, fails in Miranda's ritual and himself dies. Both of these critics, though, do not acknowledge that George comes to the realization that he need not do anything, but surrender to the island in order to participate in Cocoa's healing. His frustration in the chicken coop dissipates as he realizes that it is only his own hands—not what he can *do* with them—that will help his wife. Although George learns this lesson late, he dies with the realization that he has joined hands with Mama Day.

George's ritual at the chicken coop is also suggestive of an African funerary custom that has survived in America, namely sacrificing a chicken for the dead (Vlach 144). Although the rite is typically performed following the death, George's act in the chicken coop is a harbinger of his own demise. Translated as a prevalent tombstone marking, the image of the chicken "honors the dead and situates their spirits properly" (Thompson 134). Thus, Naylor's decision to pair George's death with this sacrificial act indicates that, buried as he is in Willow Springs, he is an honored member of the folk community.

57. Julie Dash, in *Daughters of the Dust,* also makes use of the quilt as a symbol of artistry, family and culture. The children on the island plead with Miz Emma Julia to tell them a story. As the children settle in to hear the tale, she wraps them with "worn, colorful quilts" (12). Here, Dash signifies on the motif of the quilt as a sign of storytelling and community. As the children wrap themselves in the comforting tapestry, they symbolically are nurtured by the conjure woman's story and its communal impulses. Enveloped in narrative lore, they emerge from their elder's home with a greater sense of their history and culture, which becomes the symbolic light that "leads the children home" (16).

58. Toomer, 98.

59. Bone, 131.

60. Ibid., 133.

61. Toomer, 105.

62. Tucker, 185.

63. Darwin T. Turner, Introduction [to the 1975 Edition of *Cane*], in *Cane* by Jean Toomer (New York: Norton, 1988), 136.

BIBLIOGRAPHY

Awkward, Michael. "Authorial Dreams of Wholeness: (Dis) Unity, (Literary) Parentage and *The Women of Brewster Place.*" In *Gloria Naylor: Critical Perspectives Past and Pre-*

sent, eds. Henry Louis Gates, Jr. and K. A. Appiah, 37–71. New York: Columbia University Press, 1991.

Baker, Houston A. *Blues, Ideology, and Afro-American Literature: A Vernacular Theory.* Chicago: University of Chicago Press, 1984.

Bakker, Jan. *Pastoral in Antebellum Southern Romance.* Baton Rouge: Louisiana State University Press, 1989.

Bell, Bernard. *The Afro-American Novel and Its Tradition.* Amherst: University of Massachusetts Press, 1987.

Bone, Robert. *Down Home: A History of Afro-American Short Fiction from Its Beginnings to the End of the Harlem Renaissance.* New York: G.P. Putnam's Son, 1975.

Bradley, David. *The Chaneysville Incident.* New York: Harper, 1981.

Chesnutt, Charles W. *Collected Stories of Charles W. Chesnutt.* Ed. William L. Andrews. New York: Penguin, Mentor, 1992.

Dash, Julie. *Daughters of the Dust.* Dutton: New York, 1997.

Eagleton, Terry. *Literary Theory: An Introduction.* Minneapolis: University of Minnesota Press, 1983.

Gates, Henry Louis, Jr. *The Signifying Monkey: A Theory of African-American Literary Criticism.* New York: Oxford University Press, 1988.

Golding, Alan. "Jean Toomer's *Cane:* The Search for Identity Through Form." *Arizona Quarterly* 39.3 (1983): 197–214.

Greene, J. Lee. "The Pain and the Beauty: The South, the Black Writer, and the Conventions of the Picaresque." In *The American South,* ed. Louis D. Rubin, Jr., 264–88. Baton Rouge: Louisiana State University Press, 1980.

Karrer, Wolfgang. "The History and Signifying Intertextuality of the African American Short Story." In *African American Short Story 1970–1990: A Collection of Critical Essays,* eds. Wolfgang Karrer and Barbara Puschman-Nalenz, 1–28. Wissenschaftlicher: Verlag Trier, 1993.

Lee, Valerie. *Granny Midwives and Black Women Writers.* New York: Routledge, 1996.

Lynch, Michael. "The Wall and the Mirror of the Promised Land: The City in the Novels of Gloria Naylor." In *The City in African-American Literature,* eds. Yoshinobu Hakutani and Robert Butler, 181–95. Cranbury: Associated University Press, 1995.

MacKethan, Lucinda. *The Dream of Arcady: Place and Time in Southern Literature.* Baton Rouge: Louisiana State University Press, 1980.

McKay, Nellie. *Jean Toomer Artist: A Study of His Literary Life and Work, 1894–1936.* Chapel Hill: University of North Carolina Press, 1984.

Melsenholder, Susan. "'The Whole Picture' in Gloria Naylor's *Mama Day.*" *African American Review* 27.3 (1993): 405–421.

Naylor, Gloria. *Mama Day.* New York: Houghton Mifflin, Ticknor & Fields, 1988. Reprint, New York: Random House, Vintage Books, 1993.

Osborne, William. "John Crowe Ransom: Toward a Pastoral." In *Southern Literature in Transition: Heritage and Promise,* eds. Philip Castille and William Osborne, 87–99. Memphis: Memphis State University Press, 1983.

Shange, Ntozake. *Sassafrass, Cypress & Indigo.* New York: St. Martin's Press, 1982.

Stepto, Robert. *From Behind the Veil: A Study of Afro-American Narrative.* 2nd ed. Chicago: University of Illinois Press, 1991.

Storhoff, Gary. "'The Only Voice is Your Own': Gloria Naylor's Revision of *The Tempest.*" *African American Review* 29.1 (1995): 35–45.

Thompson, Robert Farris. *Flash of the Spirit: African and Afro-American Art and Philosophy.* New York: Random House, 1983.

Toomer, Jean. *Balo. Plays of Negro Life.* Eds. Alain Locke and Montgomery Gregory. New York: Harper and Brothers, 1927. 296–286.

Toomer, Jean. *Cane.* Ed. Darwin T. Turner. New York: Boni & Liveright, 1923. Reprint, New York: Norton, 1988.

Tucker, Lindsey. "Recovering the Conjure Woman: Texts and Contexts in Gloria Naylor's *Mama Day.*" *African American Review* 28 (Summer 1994): 173–88.

Vlach, John Michael. *The Afro-American Tradition in Decorative Arts.* Cleveland: Cleveland Museum of Art, 1978.

Walker, Alice. *In Search of Our Mothers' Gardens.* New York: Harcourt Brace Jovanovich, 1983.

Serving the Second Sun:
The Men in Gloria Naylor's *Mama Day*

R. MARK HALL

> I am a Black man
> An Afrikan man
> My father's son
> My thoughts include his thoughts
> My blood and bone and flesh include his
> My work include his spirit
> I follow in his footsteps
> I continue them—
> and make my own
>
> I am a Black man
> Speak not to me of compromise
> I am straight line i.e. will
> I am upward spiral i.e. growth
> I am circle i.e. fulfillment
> —George Edward Tait,
> "I Am a Black Man"

In his 1986 essay "The Black Woman Strikes Back: Background of The Anti-Male Attitude of Current Female Writers" Arthur P. Davis begins:

When a person my age reads some of the recent works by Negro female writers, he is surprised and intrigued by the anti-black-male sentiments expressed in them. I have in mind the novels and plays of an impressive number of popular and gifted writers, among them: Alice Walker, Gayl Jones, Toni Morrison, and Ntozake Shange. These authors have given us a rogues' gallery of ugly Afro-Americans, such as Brownfield in *The Third Life of Grange Copeland,* who kills his long-suffering wife; of Truman in *Meridian,* a worthless hangover from the Civil Rights Crusade who loves black but marries white; of Macon Dead, Senior, in *Song of Solomon,* a Scrooge-like, thoroughly insensitive husband and father; of Macon, Junior, who mistreats his aunt and cousin; of Sailor in *For Colored Girls Who Have Considered Suicide,* who with diabolical cruelly drops the child from the window; of Mutt in *Corregidora,* whose cruelty causes Ursa to lose her chance for "generations"; and of the stepfather

in *The Color Purple,* whose sexual abuse drove Celie away from men to
lesbian consolation.[1]

Although Gloria Naylor has not received nearly the critical attention of other
African-American women authors such as Toni Morrison and Alice Walker,
it is easy to include many of her black male characters in Davis's "rogues'
gallery" of ugly African-American men. For instance, Charles Johnson, in
Race & Being: Black Writing Since 1970, says of the men in Naylor's *The
Women of Brewster Place,* "except for the old sot Ben [whose skull Lorraine empties with a brick], nearly every black male in this book resembles
the Negro Beast stereotype described so many years ago by white racists
as the brutal, stupid creature of violent sexual appetites."[2] In sharp contrast,
however, women reviewers of *Brewster Place* reflect on the negative portrait
of African-American men in the novel not with surprise or criticism but
with matter-of-fact agreement: "Most men," Annie Gottlieb writes in *The
New York Times Book Review,* "are incalculable hunters who come and go.
They are attractive—but weak and/or dangerous—representatives of nature
and of violence who both fertilize and threaten the female core."[3] Likewise,
in her review for *The New Republic,* Dorothy Wickenden, too, is not surprised by images of black male violence in Naylor's first novel. The men
of *Brewster Place,* she writes, "visit their women like nightmares, leaving
behind them babies and bile."[4] Of Naylor's women she observes, "Their
personal histories share a common theme: violence and abuse at the hands
of men."[5] Unlike Davis, Wickenden argues, "It won't come as a surprise to
readers of contemporary fiction by black women that Gloria Naylor has few
kind words to waste on members of the other sex."[6] Indeed, she and Gott-
leib imply, Naylor is just writing the truth about black men. Naylor's purpose, however, is not to denigrate black men. In an interview with Donna
Perry in *Backtalk: Women Writers Speak Out,* Naylor herself points out that,
as the title of her first novel makes clear, she was not writing about men:
"'This is a book about women,'" she reminds us, women protagonists who
must overcome obstacles, some of which are men.[7]

In *Linden Hills,* women protagonists must likewise overcome the evil
Needed men, all of whom are named Luther or "Lucifer." The original
Luther Needed sells his wife and six children to buy the land which becomes
the black middle-class community of Linden Hills. Like their forefather,
all of Luther Needed's male descendants are both satanic and tormented.
But the portrait of black males in Naylor's second novel is not limited to
making "babies and bile." As Larry R. Andrews observes in "Black Sisterhood in Naylor's Novels":

Naylor places a more balanced emphasis on both men and women. . . .
Furthermore, the hope is more clearly developed in this novel that the
sensitive black male, in the person of the poet Willie Mason, can begin
to bridge the gap of understanding between men and women and to support women in their quest for identity.[8]

The images of African-American men in Naylor's third novel, *Mama Day,*
are even more beneficent, but therein lies the rub: Naylor's good men—like
Ben in *Brewster Place*—finish last. Andrews says of the men in *Mama Day,*
"Naylor does show that the women can transcend men and have power of
their own, but often at the price of tragic loss for men."[9] Bascombe Wade,
for example, frees his slaves as a demonstration of his love for Sapphira,
yet his "male" love for her remains confining. Similarly, Miranda's father,
John-Paul, agonizes over his wife's madness, while at the same time refusing to let her go. Like the sensitive woodcarver and slave owner before
them, George and Ambush also offer their wives boundless love. Nevertheless, George's relationship with Cocoa is repeatedly plagued by gender
miscommunication.

This essay examines the images of African-American masculinity and
attempts to define the role of men in *Mama Day.* Rather than traffic in simple
rogue stereotypes, Naylor offers, instead, an assortment of male characters
who reflect a vast complexity of existence. On the island of Willow Springs,
where Witchcraft prevails and where Mama Day represents the Mother-Earth
Goddess, Naylor's male characters likewise embody various aspects of the
God of the Witches, or the Horned God. Through the beliefs and practices
of Witchcraft, Naylor encourages us to read her male characters not as
"good" or "bad," but as forces which unify these binaries. Such a reading
suggests that the criticism of Naylor's depiction of African-American masculinity results not from her negative portrayal of black men, but from the
discomfort, particularly of male critics, with her placement of male characters on the margins of this woman-centered novel. This essay first explains
how the principles of Witchcraft are defined and deployed in the novel, then
shows how George, Ambush, Little Caesar, and Dr. Buzzard all represent
various aspects of the Horned God. Neither "positive" nor "negative," Naylor's male characters, like the God and Goddess of Witchcraft, embody both
aspects. And like the God of the Witches, Naylor's male characters are not
central, but function always in the service of the Great Goddess. Through
the lens of Witchcraft, Naylor challenges us to avoid masculinist thinking,
which presumes that anything male should be dominant, and instead, to read
the novel through a world view that privileges the feminine. In her review

of *Mama Day* for *The Los Angeles Times,* Rita Mae Brown argues, "the women possess the real power and are acknowledged as having it."[10] Even Miranda herself argues, "'A good woman is worth two good men any day when she puts her mind to it.'"[11] Like *Brewster Place, Mama Day* is a novel about strong women where men are important, but secondary. This power relationship mirrors that of the Goddess and God of Witchcraft.

The legacy of powerful women in *Mama Day* begins with Sapphira Wade, "the Mother who began the Days," a legendary midwife, nurse, and Witch. George puzzles over Cocoa's description of her: "it was odd . . . the way you said it—she was the great, great, grand, Mother—as if you were listing the attributes of a goddess."[12] Indeed, she and her female descendants, keenly attuned to the natural world, clearly represent the Mother-Earth Goddess in the novel. Naylor's Willow Springs narrator expresses the island's awe and respect for this incarnate Goddess:

> Everybody knows but nobody talks about the legend of Sapphira Wade. A true conjure woman. . . . She could walk through a lightning storm without being touched; grab a bolt of lightning in the palm of her hand; use the heat of lightning to start the kindling going under her medicine pot. . . . She turned the moon into salve, the stars into a swaddling cloth, and healed the wounds of every creature walking up on two or down on four.[13]

Belief in such magical powers is, according to John S. Mbiti in *African Religion & Philosophy,* commonplace in African villages. Willow Springs is the descendent of such a community. "[T]he whole psychic atmosphere of African village life," Mbiti writes, "is filled with belief in this mystical power. African people know that the universe has a power, force or whatever else one my call it."[14] As her great-granddaughter, Miranda is the inheritor of Sapphira's mystical powers. Like her, Miranda is a gifted midwife and practitioner of herbal medicine. She is the trusted adviser and healer of the people of Willow Springs; she mysteriously impregnates Bernice Duvall; she aids Cocoa in finding both a job and a husband; and she helps restore her great-niece's health after Ruby's psychic attack of black magic. Miranda, however, is self-deprecating about her own mysterious abilities: "Yeah, she could disguise a little dose of nothing but mother-wit with a lot of hocus-pocus."[15] Nevertheless, the results of her magic—blowing up Ruby's house, for example—are real enough. In *The Spiral Dance: A Rebirth of the Ancient Religion of the Great Goddess,* the author, Starhawk, explains such magical abilities:

Magic is the craft of Witchcraft, and few things are at once so appealing, so frightening, and so misunderstood. To work magic is to weave the unseen forces into form; to soar beyond sight; to explore the uncharted dream realm of the hidden reality; to infuse life with color, motion, and strange scents that intoxicate; to leap beyond imagination into that space between the worlds where fantasy becomes real; to be at once animal and god. Magic is the craft of shaping, the craft of the wise, exhilarating, dangerous—the ultimate adventure.[16]

But even with such powers, Miranda cannot save Cocoa at the novel's end by her own power alone. Cocoa requires George's help too. Even Miranda herself recognizes, "'It's gonna take a man to bring her peace.'"[17] Naylor writes, "She needs his hand in hers—his very hand—so she can connect it up with all the believing that had gone before."[18] This circumstance suggests that George's role in the novel deserves closer attention. Too often his death is viewed simply as emblematic of failed masculinity, failed rational or "masculine" thought. For instance, Rita Mae Brown argues, "George must let go of his rigidity, his 'male' mind."[19] But George's role in saving his wife from Ruby's black magic is more complicated than that. On the island of Willow Springs, where Mama Day represents the Mother Earth-Goddess, George and the other male characters likewise reflect various aspects of the God of the Witches. Miranda herself emphasizes the importance of this "masculine" principle in the description of her own "pure black" complexion: "Me and Abigail, we take after the sons. . . . The earth men who formed the line of Days, hard and dark brown."[20] And it is she who bestows upon George John-Paul's walking cane—a magic wand—and Bascombe Wade's ledger, two "masculine" symbols of magic. Margaret A. Murray describes "that most ancient of all recorded religions, the worship of the Horned God" in *The God of the Witches:*

The Palaeolithic people were hunters, the Neolithic and Bronze Age people were pastoral and agricultural. Among all these races the Horned God was pre-eminent, for alike to hunting and pastoral folk animals were essential for life. After the general introduction of agriculture, the Horned God remained as a great deity, and was not dethroned even by the Iron Age. It was not till the rise of Christianity, with its fundamental doctrine that a non-Christian deity was a devil, that the cult of the Horned God fell into disrepute.[21]

The image of the Horned God was deliberately perverted by the medieval church into the image of the Christian Devil in an attempt to vilify the Old

Religion and replace it with Christianity. Witches, in fact, neither worship nor believe in the Devil. They consider the dichotomy between "Good" and "Evil," God and Devil, a peculiarly Christian concept, for the Goddess and God of Witchcraft each embody both positive and negative aspects. As for the devilish horns of the God of the Witches, these represent the waning and waxing crescents of the Goddess Moon. They also symbolize the God's animal vitality. As Joseph Campbell points out in *The Hero With A Thousand Faces,* the horns also reflect the reverence of primitive peoples for the animal life that both threatened and sustained them:

> For the primitive hunting peoples of those remotest human millenniums when the sabertooth tiger, the mammoth, and the lesser presences of the animal kingdom were the primary manifestations of what was alien— the source at once of danger, and of sustenance—the great human problem was to become linked psychologically to the task of sharing the wilderness with these beings. An unconscious identification took place, and this was finally rendered conscious in the half-human, half-animal, figures of the mythological totem-ancestors.[22]

Such half-human, half-animal figures led the religious and magical ceremonies of the cult of the Horned God. Likewise, the Palaeolithic people also worshiped the female principle, but, according to Murray, this did not develop until much later.[23] This God of the Old Religion survives today as one of the central elements in most traditions of Witchcraft. The Horned God is viewed as the other half of the Goddess, and many of the rites and holidays are devoted to both God and Goddess. It is fitting, then, that the God as well as the Goddess should be represented in the story of the descendants of Sapphira Wade, the great Witch of Willow Springs. Starhawk offers a contemporary description of the God of the Witches:

> The image of the Horned God in Witchcraft is radically different from any other image of masculinity in our culture. He is difficult to understand because He does not fit into any of the expected stereotypes, neither those of the "macho" male nor the reverse-images of those who deliberately seek effeminacy. . . .

The God is both the predatory God of the Hunt and also the Dying God, the Willing Sacrifice whose death serves to renew life. He is sometimes black, but not because he is evil, but because night is a period of regeneration and heightened power. The God of the Witches also represents untamed animal sexuality. At the same time, however, He is gentle and tender. To His worshipers, then, the God's sexuality is not obscene or sinful, but sacred, "a deep, holy, connecting power," natural and vital for the continuation of life.[24]

The many parallels between George and the Horned God are unmistakable. Like the God of the Witches, George has no parents. The Horned God "is born of a Virgin mother. He is a model of male power that is free from father-son rivalry or Oedipal conflicts. He has no father; He is his own father."[25] George is an orphan, the abandoned son of a prostitute, and because he is without a past of family conflicts, George is a somewhat idealized image of African-American masculinity, "a model of male power." He is neither macho nor effeminate; he is strong, yet gentle and tender. In "Here's Looking at You, Kid!" in *The Female Gaze,* Suzanne Moore labels such an image, the "New Man": "he is tough but tender, masculine but sensitive— he can cry, cuddle babies, and best of all buy cosmetics."[26] George is an engineer, a stereotypical "masculine" profession. Likewise, he loves football, but because of his weak heart he could never play. Instead he cooks and reads Shakespeare for pleasure. And sex with George is transcendent. Cocoa recalls, "You'd take me in your arms with such hunger and tenderness, demanding only that I be pleased, that I'd feel a melting away of places in my body I hadn't realized were frozen voids. Your touch was slowly making new and alive openings within me."[27] Like the God of the Witches, George embodies both Logos and Eros. Naylor herself says of George, "I really like George; I think he's a wonderful character. I cried for a whole year, knowing that George was going to die."[28] Spying George from across the road one day, Miranda decides:

> She likes the way that boy walks, kinda free and bouncy. And he holds his head up high. A man should have starch in him, especially a colored man. There's too much out there to mow him down permanent if he ain't got the where-with-all to spring back. But he done made out real well. . . .[29]

George's principle phrase, "Only the present has potential," sums up his family history, his character, and his worldview.[30] Yet Naylor's *Mama Day* emphasizes the importance of balance between the past and present. As Peter Trachtenberg writes, Naylor

> simultaneously explores and effects several kinds of reconciliation: between the black rural past and the black urban present; between myth and history, individuals and communities, faith and logic, the living and the dead. Not the least of all she symbolically reconciles the scattered children of Africa with their first, true home.[31]

This unifying of opposites is a recurring theme in the novel and a central belief in Witchcraft. With his marriage into the Day family, George gains a past rich in African-American tradition and achieves such a reconciliation. On the island of Willow Springs George is reborn in Africa. "God, I was acting like a kid," he says. "But something about this place did that to you, it called up old, old memories."[32]

Most importantly, George represents the Divine Victim, the Dying God of Witchcraft. Murray explains this aspect of the Horned God:

> The underlying meaning of the sacrifice of the divine victim is that the spirit of God takes up its abode in a human being, usually the king, who thereby becomes the giver of fertility to all his kingdom. When the divine man begins to show signs of age, he is put to death lest the spirit of God should also grow old and weaken like its human container.

Until the appropriate time for this fertility rite, no harm could come to the incarnate God, for a premature death to the king meant certain disaster for his people. When, however, the time came for his sacrifice, no aid could be offered to the Divine Victim. Later in the development of the cult of the Horned God, a substitute might be offered in place of the king, satisfying both his duty to bestow fertility upon his kingdom and his personal desire for a long life:

> This, put shortly, is the theory and cult of the Dying God. The belief belongs to all parts of the Old World, and survives in Africa into the present century. It was a fundamental dogma of the pre-Christian religion of Europe, believed in and practiced as ardently as among the Africans of to-day.[33]

Murray, in fact, applies a number of Sir James George Frazer's theories of African Witchcraft to English Witchcraft.[34] For instance, Frazer writes of the killing of the Divine King in *The Golden Bough:*

> If the high gods, who dwell remote from the fret and fever of this earthly life are yet believed to die at last, it is not to be expected that a god who lodges in a frail tabernacle of flesh should escape the same fate. . . . for if the course of nature is dependent on the man-god's life, what catastrophes may not be expected from the gradual enfeeblement of his powers and their final extinction in death? There is only one way of averting these dangers. The man-god must be killed as soon as he shows

symptoms that his powers are beginning to fail, and his soul must be transferred to a vigorous successor before it has been seriously impaired by the threatened decay.[35]

Before George is sacrificed as the Dying God, however, he first enacts the role of the God of Fertility as he and Cocoa share the sacrament of sex for the last time. George says, "I couldn't attain my ultimate desire to get inside and change places with you, but I tried the best I could."[36] Only then is he finally able to see the evidence of the worms that are wasting Cocoa from within. Such wasting maladies are frequently applied, in fact, by evil magicians in many African societies. They are used to "'suck'" or to "'eat away'" the health and souls of victims.[37] Only after his deep, holy communion with Cocoa does George return to offer his help to Miranda. What's more, George's death takes place in August, when Lamastide or Lughnasa, one of the four Great Sabbath's of the Old Religion, is celebrated. In this celebration, the God is sacrificed by the Goddess for the good of the people. George's sacrifice allows Cocoa to move on to a new level of being. As Rita Mae Brown suggests, George "sacrifices himself on the altar of love. Success," she argues, "is a form of surrender: the opposite of the desire to control."[38] George, like the God of the Witches, surrenders to the Goddess, for She is the final arbiter of fertility. We see this principle throughout the novel, in which none of the men impregnates anyone: Cocoa is no longer using her diaphragm, yet she does not get pregnant; Ambush can't impregnate Bernice—it takes Miranda's chicken to do that; Dr. Buzzard presumably has no children; and Junior Lee is seemingly only involved with postmenopausal women.

Not only does George parallel the God of the Witches in both his birth and death, but also his name is suggestive of another aspect of the God. Critics have noted the significance of the women's names in *Mama Day*. "Miranda," for example, comes from Shakespeare's *The Tempest,* while "Ophelia" comes from *Hamlet.* The names of Naylor's male characters, however, have gone ignored. Nevertheless, each male character bears a name which has more than coincidental meaning and which further helps to develop his ties to the Horned God of Witchcraft. George's name, from the Greek, meaning "farmer" or "worker in the earth," suggests his role in saving Cocoa. Before he can help her, he must first sow his seed in her earth. Then he must unite his power with the Earth, with Mama Day, the dark, nurturing mother who brings forth life. Naylor prepares the reader for the image of George as farmer with his fantasy of remaining on the island and making his living as Ambush Duvall does. Cocoa's New York-bred husband is also associated with the North, which in Witchcraft "is considered the most powerful direction." Likewise, "North corresponds to the Earth."[39] Having come to the South from the most powerful direction, George is the most appropriate choice to unite with Mother-Earth, Mama Day. Together they offer a balance of power and love to restore Cocoa after Ruby's attack. George himself recognizes such balance as an essential ingredient in his marriage to Cocoa. He says that living with a woman is "a day-to-day balancing act, and I really enjoyed the challenge. Because the times I got it right, your being different made all the difference in my world."[40] Starhawk explains this principle of balance so essential to Witchcraft:

> The Goddess is the Encircler, the Ground of Being; the God is That-Which-Is-Brought-Forth, her mirror image, her other pole. She is the earth; He is the grain. She is the all-encompassing sky; He is the sun, her fireball. She is the Wheel; He is the Traveler. He is the sacrifice of life to death that life may go on. She is Mother and Destroyer; He is all that is born and destroyed.[41]

Similarly, Ambush Duvall is also linked by his name to both the God of the Witches and to the Earth. His pet name, "Ambush," comes from the Latin verb *inboscare,* which means "to place in a wood, or among the bushes." The "fairies" or worshipers of the Horned God were well known for their ability to conceal themselves, particularly in order to surprise an enemy. As Murray points out, they were "so highly skilled in the art of taking cover that they were seldom seen unless they so desired."[42] Ambush's given name, "Charles," means "strong, manly, of noble spirit, or robust." Kings throughout history have shared the name "Charles," which, like "George," suggests an obvious connection to the Divine King, the Horned God. With deep reverence George says:

> I never realized you were paying me such a high compliment whenever you said I reminded you of Ambush Duvall. There was something so steady and genuinely kind about the man. We were about the same age, but he appeared older than me, perhaps because he was married almost three times as long. But after a while I began to feel that it was due to his infinite patience. He had to have it in order to put up with the temperamental nature of the weather and his farm crops, and he certainly needed a good measure of it with Bernice.[43]

Like George, Ambush adores his wife, offering her a deep, abiding, and supportive love, even though he and Bernice seem, at times, like George and Cocoa, wholly incompatible, or as Naylor herself describes them, "totally incongruent."[44] George and Ambush, then, embody one of the many aphorisms in *Mama Day:* "A woman shouldn't have to fight her man to be what she was; he should be fighting that battle for her." In some ways, these two husbands seem almost too good to be true. In fact, that's exactly what Cocoa's girlfriends insist about George. In this way they serve as sharp contrasts to the rogues, Junior Lee and Dr. Buzzard. But also like the other men in the novel, Ambush is distanced from women, shut out in some ways even from his own wife. For example, George recognizes Ambush's inability to read Bernice's silent response when George asks him if Miranda had delivered their son: there was, George thinks, "something she'd never shared with him."[45] Here Naylor suggests that the bounty—the sexuality—of the Goddess is controlled by no man. Instead, both George and Ambush are "cuckolded," if you will: Cocoa spends a night with an old boyfriend, and Ambush never learns about Miranda's chicken.

Also like George, Ambush serves as a balancing force to one of the women in the novel. Just as Mama Day requires the balancing efforts of George if she is to save Cocoa from Ruby's nightshade poison, so Ambush serves as a balancing force in his relationship with Bernice. He is gentle and unhurried, while Bernice is high-strung, nervous, and impatient. He is the calm and humane disciplinarian of their son, while Bernice hovers over and pampers Little Caesar. As George says, "a lid for every pot." Here again Naylor emphasizes the unifying of opposites as a reoccurring theme in the novel. As parents, Bernice and Ambush parallel Cocoa's grandmother and great-aunt. Cocoa reflects, "But if Grandma had raised me alone, I would have been ruined for any fit company. It seemed I could do no wrong with her, while with Mama Day I could do no right. I guess, in a funny kind of way, together they were the perfect mother." Naylor further develops Ambush's harmonizing influence through his role as farmer. "Walking with Ambush through his fields was to watch the hand of a virtuoso stroke the instrument of his craft," George observes:

An absentminded handful of soil worked between his fingers as the end-less rows melted into the blurred outlines of the horizon. The weight, the texture, the smell, telling him of possibilities I couldn't begin to understand. In the fading light it could have been his own skin flaking gently into the ground.[46]

More than the other men in the novel, Ambush is, as George's metaphor suggests, in complete accord with Mother Earth.

Charles Jr., like his father, is also associated with the Horned God. Again, Naylor demonstrates the significance of naming to make this connection clear. Little Caesar's father recognizes the importance of choosing his son's pet name wisely. Ambush tells George, "'a Charlie Duvall won't be fit for nothing but designing ladies' panties while a Caesar Duvall is gonna be welcome into many of 'em.'" Ambush hopes for his son to be just that, a Little Caesar or "powerful ruler." Like the other men in the novel, this only male child also represents an aspect of the Horned God. Indeed, he lives up to his name, as Naylor's Willow Springs narrator observes, "You couldn't find a king that's treated better than that child. He's almost four now and his feet hardly touch the ground." Later the narrator warns, "When you raise a god instead of a child, you're bound to be serving him for the rest of your days."[47]

But Little Caesar's other pet name, "Chick," (a nickname for "Charles") reflects his connection to Miranda. This link helps to explain Caesar's death and to illustrate how he too serves as a balancing force in the novel. First, Bernice's "Chick" is bound magically to Mama Day. This connection is established when she eats the chicken's egg as she performs the mysterious spell that allows Bernice to become pregnant. Later, like his birth, Little Caesar's death is similarly enigmatic: "Folks is sure to disagree for years," Naylor writes, "about what caused the death of Little Caesar."[48] While we never learn exactly what kills him, this boy-child's death suggests another sacrifice by the Goddess to ensure the continuation of life and balance. Before Miranda can save Cocoa from Ruby's black magic, Little Caesar's death guarantees a return to balance after she takes Ruby's life by blowing up her house. Little Caesar's life is exchanged for Cocoa's recovery. As the sacrificial child, Little Caesar thus brings to mind the Catholic saint Caesarius or Caesar, a legendary African deacon who was killed for protesting the sacrifice of youths to the gods.[49]

Just as Bernice makes a king of Little Caesar, so Ruby makes a king of her young husband, Junior Lee. The name "Lee" may be taken as a diminutive of "Leo," which is derived from the Greek, meaning "lion" or "of lion-like nature." Both names suggest, of course, strength, since the lion is the "king of beasts." This is a fitting name for Ruby's husband. Indeed, Naylor's Willow Springs narrator suggests that Ruby behaves as though she has married not just a king, but "a god." "Lee is eating *royal* at Ruby's," Miranda exclaims. Nevertheless, all the residents of Willow Springs—including Ruby—know that Junior Lee is nothing but a false idol: "Not that Junior Lee got anybody up in heaven worrying about losing their job, but you couldn't tell Ruby that."[50] Again Naylor links the men in the novel to the Horned God. But in Junior Lee's case, he represents an obvious caricature of the God of the Witches. His touch brings death, not life. First Frances is driven mad by his philandering, then his oyster-digging companion, May Ellen, falls victim to Ruby's jealous rage, then Ruby sets her sights on Cocoa, another of Junior Lee's supposed lovers.

While his name implies a "lion-like nature," the "Junior" before "Lee" results in a double diminutive, which more aptly suggests Junior Lee's inferior status among the residents of Willow Springs: "Any man who'd lose more money than you at a poker table and then be happy to turn right back around and drink you under that same table is the last thing you'd bring home to meet any woman you cared about." "Junior" comes from the Latin word for "young" and is most commonly used *after* a person's name to denote, of course, the younger of two bearing the same name in a family, especially the son of the same name as his father. But "Junior" placed *before* the name, as in the case of Junior Lee, suggests not that he bears the same name as his father, but a second meaning of "junior": "of less standing, of lower position." Indeed, his marriage to Ruby only further reduces his already poor position in the community. At her hands, Junior Lee is contaminated, like the poisonous graveyard dirt she uses against Cocoa: "Ain't nobody over seven and under seventy that desperate. No, even the ones who might find it challenging to try to tame a good-looking, no-good man wouldn't come within a mile of Junior Lee." As a result of Ruby's threats, the women of the island understandably avoid Junior Lee. But he is isolated further, emasculated, in a sense, by this phallic woman because she cuts him off even from the company of other men. As Naylor's narrator points out, "Even the men done stopped bothering with Junior Lee." In contrast to the neatly starched George, Junior Lee is limp: "This man was so soft," George observes, "he was eerie" Instead of strong and courageous, Junior Lee is slow-witted, dull, and laughable, the kept man of a powerful and evil conjure woman. In this role, Junior Lee serves, like the other men in the novel, as a balancing force. He is the ridiculous make-believe rival to George, just as Cocoa is a mistaken rival against Ruby. The two couples are repeatedly paralleled throughout the novel. For instance, their marriages nearly coincide. And later, when Cocoa becomes jealous of George's long absence one morning, she warns George that Junior Lee has been "'passing by and admiring what you'd left at home.'"[51] Both Cocoa and George laugh. Even they themselves can't take seriously Cocoa's attempt to make George jealous.

Just as Junior Lee's name suggests his inferior position, so Dr. Buzzard, Naylor's other rogue male in *Mama Day,* also elicits contempt, particularly from Miranda. She calls him a "con-artist, bootlegger. . . . a shiftless, no-good, slew-footed, twisted-mouthed, slimy-backed . . . Oh, the adjectives went on and on." As Miranda's description of Dr. Buzzard suggests, his name too, like the names of the other men in the novel, is a fitting one. A buzzard is a bird belonging to the falcon family. Dr. Buzzard's association with high-flying birds reflects another aspect of the God of the Witches, the Lord of the Winds. Dr. Buzzard, however, is a parody of the God. Though falcons are renowned for their hunting ability, the buzzard is an inferior kind of hawk, useless for hunting and commonly regarded as the coward of the species. Hence, we have the expression "between a hawk and a buzzard," which means between a good thing and a bad of the same kind: the hawk being the true sporting bird, while the buzzard is a heavy lazy fowl of the same species, known not as a hunter but as a connoisseur of carrion. Dr. Buzzard's name, then, reflects his contrast to Miranda. He is the buzzard of Willow Springs conjure, while she is the true sporting bird, the falcon of Witchcraft. Dr. Buzzard's unauthentic "hoodoo" magic balances the powerfully potent magic of Mama Day. He maintains a similar delicate balance with Ruby: "He's got a yin for her yang, a do for her don't." In addition to the bird, "buzzard" may refer to a worthless, stupid, or ignorant person. It is also a euphemism for "bastard." In her frequent tirades against him, Miranda evokes these negative connotations. But Naylor's Buzzard is himself "between a hawk and a buzzard": shiftless, lazy, fraudulent, but certainly not all bad; for this old bird takes George under his wing—like a son—to befriend him, to usher him into the fraternity of Willow Springs men, and to guide him to help Miranda save Cocoa. And like Ambush and the would-be farmer, George, Dr. Buzzard is also tied to the Earth, to Willow Springs. In fact, he sacrifices his marriage because he puts his devotion to the land before devotion to his wife. Dr. Buzzard laments, "'some folks can live here and some can't. And with seventy acres and a house . . . Somebody had to keep it.'"[52]

As the oldest and most prominent member of the male community in Willow Springs, Dr. Buzzard is the don of the poker game, an especially important ritual in the novel, a ritual among men. It is first an outward and visible sign of George's acceptance by the men of Willow Springs. This approval is bestowed upon George, appropriately, by Dr. Buzzard, who later acts as a surrogate father to George: "'You know,'" he says, "'I like you. You got a lot of understanding for a city boy. You play poker?'"[53] George not only accepts the invitation, but wholeheartedly embraces the men of Willow Springs in return. He enters into the male-only barbershop for some guy-talk. Larry Andrews—citing Marjorie Pryse's *Conjuring: Black Women,*

Fiction, and Literary Tradition—argues that "such passing on of the oral tradition with its elements of genealogy, magic, and naming, is a particularly female tradition that empowers the women who inherit it."[54] But genealogy, magic, and naming are important, as we have seen, not only to the women in the novel, but also to the men. At the barber shop, George gets to know the men of Willow Springs, learning their names, their histories, the details of their lives. He discovers

> that Paris had gotten his name from fighting in France during World War II with the Ninety-second Infantry Division, that Winky Browne had batted against Satchel Paige in the bush leagues, [and] that Dr. Buzzard was once married to a dancer on the vaudeville circuit.

Later George proclaims, "'I found out there are a lot of Saints fans in this town.'"[55] This is exceptional praise from George, a man who loves nothing—except maybe his wife—than football.

But Dr. Buzzard's invitation to play poker is only that, an invitation, not yet an initiation. Though the men in the barber shop respond positively to George's genuine interest in their lives, we are reminded that George remains—in many ways—an outsider. Because he does not yet understand the spoken code of Willow Springs, he fails at first to learn how Dr. Buzzard makes his living and the nature of the "professional rivalry" between Dr. Buzzard and Miranda. The confusion over the nature of Dr. Buzzard's "profession" further emphasizes the split between the two. Likewise, when George lays his plans to row ashore in an attempt to save Cocoa, he remains, instead, cut off not only from the mainland but also from the men of Willow Springs because he impatiently resists rebuilding the bridge *their* way. "A week in Willow Springs," George realizes, "was enough to understand that the words spoken here operated on a different plane through a whole morass of history and circumstances that I was not privy to."[56]

To further his initiation into the fraternity of Willow Springs men, George must first undertake a journey—or a quest—to get to the poker game. But this quest, like Dr. Buzzard, is a fraud, a sharp contrast to the genuinely arduous journey George makes earlier that day with Miranda. George reflects, "my thighs and legs were still sore from following Miss Miranda, but the south woods were a playground, considering what I'd been through that morning. Here I only had to follow his instructions and stay on a well-worn path that led me straight to his campfire and still." Likewise, this trek is child's play compared to the quest Miranda sets for George later, when he must face both the setting hen and his own male ego/values before returning to Mama Day. Thus, the "playground" of the south woods is an appropriate setting for the gaming that takes place there. But George's journey is not the issue. His trek through the woods to get to the poker game is more importantly a simple test of his ability to follow instructions. When Dr. Buzzard urges George to go to "the other place" to help Miranda perform the spell that will save Cocoa, he again tests George's ability to follow instructions. When George refuses to believe in the magic that governs Willow Springs, insisting instead that he believes only in himself, Dr. Buzzard challenges George's manhood:

> "That's where folks start, boy—not where they finish up. Yes, I said *boy*. 'Cause a man would have grown enough to know that really believing in himself means that he ain't gotta be afraid to admit that there's some things he just can't do alone. Ain't nobody asking you to believe in what Ruby done to Cocoa—but can you, at least, believe that you ain't the only one who'd give their life to help her? Can you believe that, George?"

While George remains a *"boy"* in their consciousness, we see that Dr. Buzzard serves not only as an intermediary between Miranda and George, but also as a stern father figure and guide. Dr. Buzzard is the father George must kill in order to become. But first Dr. Buzzard must, in a sense, ritually purify himself before he can truly help George. Though everyone—including George—knows Dr. Buzzard is a con artist, he must first acknowledge that himself if he is to gain George's trust. To gain credibility with George Dr. Buzzard confesses that his "'miracle elixir'" was no miracle: "'Ya see,'" he says, "'I've always been an old fraud.'" The result is that Dr. Buzzard not only gains George's trust, but also offers him his most genuine and valuable advice, not merely another of his fraudulent "gambling hands."[57]

The poker game itself involves a series of inversions. For example, because of Dr. Buzzard's cheating, the men play not to win, but to see how much they can get away without losing. As Naylor's narrator says, "Being we was brought here as slaves, we had no choice but look at everything upside down." The poker game is only one of many ways that the people of Willow Springs see the world "upside down." When Dr. Buzzard dances on his hands after the poker game, he enacts this inverted logic of Willow Springs. Here, the former vaudevillian, known as "'Rainbow Dan with the dancing hands,'" is again identified with another aspect of the Horned God, the Lord of the Dance.[58] Starhawk explains, "As Lord of the Dance [the God of the Witches] symbolizes the spiral dance of life, the whirling energies that bind existence in eternal motion. He embodies movement and change."[59] The poker game, then, becomes the passing of the torch, so to speak, from Dr. Buzzard to George. By winning the poker game, George takes on the role of the next Dying God, the role Dr. Buzzard has played (with his repeated humiliations, including his failed marriage, his failed vaudeville career, and the loss of his house). Stretching his feet toward the stars, Dr. Buzzard enacts the symbolic death of the Dying God. Even the campfire, which Naylor describes as "dying," serves to foreshadow not only Dr. Buzzard's symbolic death, but also George's. Neither George nor the other men are happy, however, that Dr. Buzzard has been beaten, and they sing a slow, mournful hymn, a "dirge," to comfort him.[60]

Their song is the "gospel blues" hymn "Take My Hand, Precious Lord," which Michael W. Harris attributes to the famous blues pianist, Thomas A. Dorsey. Like other significant details in this scene, this funeral hymn both mourns the death of Dr. Buzzard and foreshadows George's role as the next Dying God. Written in response to the death of both his wife and child, Dorsey's melody bears a striking resemblance to another hymn, "Must Jesus Bear the Cross Alone," by George Nelson Allen. Allen's hymn asks:

> Must Jesus bear the cross alone,
> And all the world go free?
> No: There's a cross for everyone,
> And there's a cross for me.[61]

Allen's original melody suggests that the sacrificial Dr. Buzzard is, like Jesus, not alone, for George will soon bear the same cross as the next Divine Victim. This hymn also foreshadows George's final union—another unifying of opposites—with Miranda, for it is she who urges him to, in effect, "Take My Hand, Precious Lord": "'I can do more things with these hands than most folks dream of—no less believe—but this time they ain't no good alone,'" she insists. "'[I]t ain't gonna be complete unless I can reach out the other hand and take yours.'"[62] Here Naylor effects another reconciliation, joining images of the Old Religion of the Great Goddess with lyrics of a Christian hymn.

Together, George and the other male characters in Naylor's *Mama Day* represent various aspects of the God of the Witches. And each serves as a balancing force in the novel. As Starhawk writes:

> Like the Goddess, the God unifies all opposites. . . . He is both the bright sun, the light-giving, energizing force, and the darkness of night and death. The two aspects . . . are complementary, not contradictory. They

cannot be identified as "good" and "evil": both are part of the cycle, the necessary balance of life.[63]

This, for me, suggests an alternative view of Naylor's portrayal of African-American men in her third novel, a view which reconciles the binary oppositions of positive/negative. For Naylor, either/or dichotomous thinking is both Eurocentric and masculinist, contrary to the African religious beliefs upon which the novel is based. With her feet planted firmly in the Old Religion of the Great Goddess, Naylor resists evoking a monolithic homogeneous representation of black masculinity. Instead, she weaves together an assortment of truths, a broad range of portraits essential for a full, rich story. She herself responds to the criticism that she has painted "'negative portraits'" of black men by challenging readers to question our own masculinist thinking:

> But that criticism is all about the kind of society we live in. The underlying presumption has always been, until lately, that anything male should be central, and if males are not central, then it's jarring. And if something jars us we tend to think, Well, what is wrong with it? as opposed to, What is wrong with the way we have been programmed to think?[64]

Clearly the male characters in *Mama Day* are not "central" to the novel, and the result, as Naylor suggests, is not defective, but different. In other words, we might well apply the wisdom of Mama Day herself to our interpretation of the novel which bears her name: "everybody wants to be right in a world where there ain't no right or wrong to be found. My side. He don't listen to my side. She don't listen to my side. Just like that chicken coop, everything got four sides: his side, her side, an outside, an inside. And all of it is the truth."[65]

NOTES

1. Arthur P. Davis, "The Black Woman Strikes Back: Background of The Anti-Male Attitude of Current Female Writers," *MAWA Review* 2.1 (1986), 4.

2. Charles Johnson, *Being & Race: Black Writing Since 1970* (Bloomington: Indiana University Press, 1988), 111.

3. Annie Gottlieb, review of *The Women of Brewster Place*, by Gloria Naylor, *The New York Times Book Review*, 22 August 1982, 11.

4. Dorothy Wickenden, review of *The Women of Brewster Place*, by Gloria Naylor, *The New Republic*, 6 September 1982, 37.

5. Ibid.

6. Ibid.

7. Donna Perry, "Gloria Naylor," *Backtalk: Women Writers Speak Out* (New Brunswick: Rutgers UP, 1993), 226.

8. Larry R. Andrews, "Black Sisterhood in Naylor's Novels," in *Gloria Naylor: Critical Perspectives Past and Present,* eds. Henry Louis Gates Jr. and K. A. Appiah, Amistad Literary Series (New York: Amistad, 1993), 286.

9. Ibid.

10. Rita Mae Brown, review of *Mama Day,* by Gloria Naylor, *The Los Angeles Times,* 6 March, 1988, 2.

11. Gloria Naylor, *Mama Day* (New York: Vintage, 1988), 240.

12. Ibid., 218.

13. Ibid., 3.

14. John S. Mbiti, *African Religions & Philosophy,* 2d ed. (Oxford: Heinemann, 1969), 192.

15. Naylor, *Mama Day,* 97.

16. Starhawk, *The Spiral Dance: A Rebirth of the Ancient Religion of the Great Goddess* (New York: Harper & Row, 1979), 109.

17. Naylor, *Mama Day,* 263.

18. Ibid., 285.

19. Brown, 2.

20. Naylor, *Mama Day,* 48.

21. Margaret A. Murray, *The God of the Witches* (London: Faber & Faber, Ltd., 1931), 38 and 14.

22. Joseph Campbell, *The Hero with a Thousand Faces,* 2nd ed. Bollingen Series xvii (Princeton: Princeton University Press, 1968), 390.

23. Murray, *The God of the Witches,* 15.

24. Starhawk, *The Spiral Dance,* 94.

25. Ibid., 96–97.

26. Suzanne Moore, "Here's Looking at You, Kid!" in The *Female Gaze: Women as Viewers of Popular Culture,* eds. Lorraine Gamman and Margaret Marshment (London: The Women's Press, 1988), 45.

27. Naylor, *Mama Day,* 119.

28. Perry, "Gloria Naylor," *Backtalk,* 233.

29. Naylor, *Mama Day,* 194.

30. Ibid., 23.

31. Peter Trachtenberg, *Mama Day by Gloria Naylor: Vintage Books Teacher's Guide* (New York: Random, 1994), 1.

32. Naylor, *Mama Day,* 184.

33. Murray, *The God of the Witches,* 160–61.

34. A. D. J. Macfarlane, "Murray's Theory: Exposition and Comment,"*Witchcraft and Sorcery: Selected Readings,* ed. Max Marwick (Penguin Modern Sociology Readings. Middlesex: Penguin, 1970), 201.

35. Frazer, *The Golden Bough,* 309.

36. Naylor, *Mama Day,* 298.

37. Mbiti, *African Religions & Philosophy,* 196.

38. Brown, review of *Mama Day,* 2.

39. Starhawk, *The Spiral Dance,* 65.

40. Naylor, *Mama Day,* 143.

41. Starhawk, *The Spiral Dance,* 95.

42. Murray, *The God of the Witches,* 51.

43. Naylor, *Mama Day,* 197.

44. See note 28.

45. Naylor, *Mama Day*, 203 and 198.

46. Ibid., 198, 58 and 200.

47. Ibid., 201, 161, and 162.

48. Ibid., 256.

49. Julia Stewart, *African Names* (New York: Carol Publishing, 1994), 27.

50. Naylor, *Mama Day,* 162, 68 and 162.

51. Ibid., 162–63, 290, and 190.

52. Ibid., 191, 163, and 187.

53. Ibid., 186.

54. Andrews, "Black Sisterhood in Naylor's Novels," in *Gloria Naylor: Critical Perspectives,* 298.

55. Naylor, *Mama Day,* 190.

56. Ibid., 196 and 256.

57. Ibid., 208, 292, and 209.

58. Ibid., 8 and 188.

59. Starhawk, *The Spiral Dance,* 99.

60. Naylor, *Mama Day,* 212 and 213.

61. Michael W. Harris, *The Rise of Gospel Blues: The Music of Thomas Andrew Dorsey in the Urban Church* (New York: Oxford University Press, 1992), xvii, 225 and 230.

62. Naylor, *Mama Day,* 294.

63. See note 59.

64. Perry, "Gloria Naylor," *Backtalk,* 225–26.

65. Naylor, *Mama Day,* 230.

Re-Writing Sacred Texts:
Gloria Naylor's Revisionary Theology

SHIRLEY A. STAVE

In *The Signifying Monkey,* Henry Louis Gates, Jr., explores the African-American rhetorical practice of "signifying," which he defines as a "principle of repetition and difference" in which a speaker or a writer revises an original source to "[realign] . . . the signifier,"[1] hence disrupting, complicating, and sometimes unraveling both the original meaning of a text and the intentions of its author. Gates's discussion of "signifying" may be a particularly useful avenue by which to approach Gloria Naylor's two most recent novels, *Mama Day* and *Bailey's Cafe,* both of which are heavily encoded with references to the Bible. However, it becomes immediately clear that Naylor's use of the Bible is oppositional—she "signifies" upon it through her revision of its stories, a revision that particularly highlights the perspective from which a panoply of biblical figures are viewed. Ultimately, Naylor's texts serve to challenge canonical "meaning" and to present an alternative mythology of redemption, one that is configured in terms celebratory of the feminine.

In considering a woman novelist's attempt to create a new sacred mythology, Alicia Ostriker's discussion of what she calls "revisionist mythmaking" is useful; Ostriker argues that such a narrative practice enables women writers "to transform the self and the culture," explaining that "Myths are the sanctuaries of language where our meanings for 'male' and 'female' are stored; to rewrite them from a female point of view is to discover new possibilities for meaning."[2] That Naylor's writing has specifically addressed the issue of women's power and powerlessness is evident in the charges of "male-bashing" that are frequently hurled against her. In considering the position of women in society, in attempting to come to some understanding of the system of oppression at work, one must engage on some level with the Bible, not simply because it is a text frequently cited to justify the oppression of women, but also because it is the source for the overarching myth that governs western thought, ethics, and social mores. Re-reading the

Bible through feminist eyes enables one to see an alternative mythology, a counter-narrative that challenges the privileged interpretation. From Ostriker's perspective, the Bible essentially documents the denial and repression of the Goddess who is the necessary feminine counterpart of the male Jahweh.[3] *Mama Day* can be read as Naylor's exploration of what a theology of that feminine counterpart might entail.

Naylor draws reader attention to *Mama Day's* textual antecedents even before the formal narrative begins. Immediately after the work's title page, the Day family tree appears, revealing a first generation of men bearing the names of Hebrew Bible prophets, followed by a generation of men named after New Testament apostles. Given that the two generations replicate the chronology of the Bible, one would assume one male progenitor to head the family tree. On this family tree, however, the line of descent begins not with a man but with a woman—Sapphira Wade, encoded by the text as the Goddess who has generated not only the folk of Willow Springs but their culture, with its rituals, as well. No male counterpart is cited on the document; hence, the original forebear, the one who was in the beginning and who set into motion the prophets and the apostles, here cannot be read as God the Father, but rather as the Great Goddess, portrayed quite literally as the mother of all human life on the island. Naylor's obvious decision to situate the Goddess at the center of her work is significant in terms of her continual narrative focus on women's lives; as Ostriker states, "Central to women's spirituality is the restoration of the goddess presumed to have been obliterated by male monotheism."[4] Although Naylor's narrative reveals that Sapphira Wade's name is unknown to any of the living residents of Willow Springs, they retain a knowledge of her in a place inaccessible to language and conscious thought—the narrative voice explains that "Sapphira Wade don't live in the part of our memory we can use to form words" (Naylor, *Mama Day,* 4). Beneath the veneer of Christianity in the book, then, lies an earlier mythology, an archetype not transmitted by the word, not about the Word, but prior to it. Furthermore, the family tree reveals no living male members. The youngest of the "apostles" fathered three daughters, one of whom is the novel's title character, configured in the novel as a Goddess-figure herself. Therefore, Naylor's signifying on the Bible returns the Goddess to the locus of origin but also situates Her in the present, suggesting Her return is the inevitable consequence of history.

Naylor introduces Sapphira Wade to the text in such a way that compels a reading of her as the Great Goddess. In the text's third sentence, we learn that Sapphira Wade is "satin black, biscuit cream, red as Georgia clay . . . depending upon which of us takes a mind to her" (3). The text's discussion of her magical abilities is encoded in imagery of Witchcraft, which contemporary scholarship has revealed to be the worship of the Great Goddess: "She could walk through a lightning storm without being touched; grab a bolt of lightning in the palm of her hand; use the heat of lightning to start the kindling going under her *medicine pot.* . . . She turned the *moon* into salve, the *stars* into a swaddling cloth, and *healed* the wounds of every creature walking up on two or down on four" (3) [emphasis mine]. The narrative emphasizes that its story "ain't about right or wrong, truth or lies" (3). Naylor's revision of the Genesis account, then, not only undermines patriarchal authority by switching the gender of the deity (quite an act of signifying in itself), it also challenges a literal interpretation of the Bible which would deny alternative paradigms of spirituality and which would insist on a single truth rather than on multiple truths. Naylor's narrative opens up the Bible to alternative readings, using metonymy to allow for the return of the repressed (i.e., the Goddess). Thus, the theology of the Great Goddess, here configured in the character of Mama Day, is set alongside the theology of the Christian God, represented here in his aspect of Christ the Redeemer by George.

The narrative confusion about origins revealed in the conflicting creation accounts in Genesis as well as in the Kabbala is recreated in Naylor's text. Hence, two versions of the Sapphira—Bascombe story exist in the text. Although the narrative voice insists that Sapphira was never a slave, a "document" appears in the fore matter of the book that appears to be her bill of sale. This written account of the foremother's history, then, parallels the first creation narrative in Genesis. The bill of sale would "prove" that Bascombe bought Sapphira, who bore him seven children in four years before killing him, an account that echoes Eve's being created specifically for Adam and her subsequent "disobedience" which dooms him along with all humankind. The existence of a written text, the document, seemingly possesses the authority to fix and define truth, but Naylor's signifying challenges such a claim to authority. Mama Day's discovery of an alternative version of the story (which the narrative voice, presumably the communal voices of the dead of Willow Springs, validates as legitimate) occurs through revelation after a night of meditation. Her version more nearly parallels the kaballistic account of what happened in Eden, a narrative whose central female figure is not Eve, but Lilith, a being never created by God and never controlled by Adam. According to legend, Lilith, frustrated with Adam's repeated attempts to wield power over her, simply flies away, abandoning him in his garden, at which point God creates a subservient (and flightless) Eve to avoid further rebellion. Mama Day learns that Sapphira also flew away—quite literally—leaving Bascombe Wade, who loved her deeply, to his unending grief; hence his grave, with its phallic marker, is prominent on the island—hers does not exist. All subsequent love in Willow Springs appears tainted by the unresolved Sapphira-Bascombe tension, just as all human love is perceived as flawed by Eve's "sin." On Willow Springs, heart after heart is broken as woman after woman leaves her mate. However, Naylor's revision of the account dispels any concept of sin, positing the source of human discontent as the inability to accept the condition of freedom as a prerequisite to love. The folk of Willow Springs, themselves never literally enslaved because Sapphira Wade bore them freely (in spite of a counternarrative that suggests Bascombe Wade freed the original seven sons, another parallel to the biblical narrative of salvation through a male deity rather than the pagan narrative of always already free), enslave themselves by jealousy, possessiveness, and a desire to wield power over their lovers.

Within the diegetic time-frame of the narrative proper, Mama Day, the incarnation of Sapphira Wade, is an old woman who functions as the healer and midwife to the folk of Willow Springs, who revere her but never underestimate her magical abilities (so for example, when the issue of selling their land to mainlanders is raised, the communal narrative voice explains, "Cause if Mama Day say no, everybody say no. . . . [N]obody was gonna trifle with Mama Day's [magic]. . . . No point in making a pile of money to be guaranteed the new moon will see you scratching at fleas you don't have, or rolling in the marsh like a mud turtle" (6). Although Mama Day's internal narrative would suggest she is simply an intelligent, observant old woman who has acquired a thorough knowledge of nature and human psychology, the scene involving a spring equinox ritual that results in Bernice's conceiving a much-wanted child disallows such a "rational" reading of her character. Helen Fiddyment Levy correctly refers to Mama Day as the "daughter of the Mother Goddess[5] and claims, "Sapphira and her female descendant Miranda guard the gates of birth and death."[6] However, the knowledge of magic is not Miranda's alone. The narrative suggests the practical know-how can be acquired by anyone willing to learn; hence, the island is home to another conjure-woman, Ruby, who uses her power exclusively to hex rather than to heal, but it remains clear to everyone but Ruby herself where the greater power lies.

The disrupted state of human love resurfaces (as, the narrative reveals, it has done in every generation) in the love relationship between Cocoa, Mama Day's great-niece and spiritual heir, and her husband George, a native New Yorker. His geographical "descent" from north to south parallels the biblical narrative of Christ's descent from heaven to earth, while his mysterious parentage—he believes himself to be the child of a prostitute who committed suicide and an anonymous father—aligns him with the cross-cultural type of the hero. George embodies the antithesis of all the values, beliefs, and rituals of the folk of Willow Springs. An engineer by profession, he represents science, reason, and the death of what he would call "superstition," but what the islanders consider magic. One of George's first acts after arriving on the island involves his using mathematics and statistics to subvert one of the island's male rituals, the outdoor poker games held at the site of Dr. Buzzard's moonshine still. In a scene reminiscent of Christ's ridding the temple of the moneylenders, George reveals Dr. Buzzard's magical powers to be sham, oblivious to the psychological need of the men of the island for what magic offers—a sense of awe in something greater than the self along with the possibility of exercising some control over the day-to-day happenings of one's life. However, in signifying on the New Testament scene, Naylor both complicates and clarifies it. After the end of the poker game, when George has clearly won the entire pot, the men, including the old man himself, begin to sing to comfort the young man who experiences a sense of loss and dismay at his transgression. On an August night, the time for the ritual of Lughnasa, when the god (understood to exist in the grain that is harvested) is traditionally sacrificed to allow for the continuation of the human species and the appearance of the new god/seed/crop, Dr. Buzzard divests himself of the symbols of his authority: "[He] took off his feathered hat and the necklace of bones. He emptied his overall pockets of crumpled tissues, bits of stone, a rabbit's foot" (213). He then undergoes a symbolic death, dancing on his hands, thrusting his feet into the sky until George sees the old man's body "stretching up into the stars" (214), ascending to the Great Mother.

While George appears to be "winning" the game and ridding the island of its superstitions, the narrative reveals that, while Dr. Buzzard understands himself to be a charlatan, Mama Day and Ruby work true magic. Furthermore, if George is to redeem Willow Springs completely, he must not merely destroy the belief in "superstitions" but must resolve the issue of disrupted love as well. That issue is brought to a head when Ruby, perpetually jealous of women she mistakenly believes have designs on her worthless husband, Junior Lee, casts a spell on Cocoa that moves the novel's narrative to its telos. Descended from and linked to women who leave by air (Sapphira Wade, who flies away), by fire (Willa Prescott Nedeed, who burns up with her dead child on Christmas Eve, another instance of Naylor's signifying on the Bible in her novel *Linden Hills*), and by water (the child Peace and then her mother Ophelia), Cocoa is hexed to leave by earth, to turn into a worm-eaten corpse even while she lives. However, in bringing the circle of the elements (air-fire-water-earth) to completion, Ruby sets a greater pattern of completion into motion. A ferocious storm blows in, "moving counterclockwise against the march of time" (249)—counterclockwise being the direction known in magic as widdershins, the direction of undoing, of unweaving, of destruction. The storm is narratively linked with Sapphira Wade: as it grows fiercer, Mama Day takes the Bible from her sister's hands and closes it, its named God useless in dealing with "what could only be the workings of Woman. And *She has no name*" (251).

The impact of the storm hits Willow Springs simultaneously with the onset of Cocoa's illness. Both Mama Day and George are determined to save Cocoa's life, although Mama Day, knowing that the illness is not physical but metaphysical, realizes immediately that George's plan, to get Cocoa off the island to a "real" doctor, would solve nothing. The narrative does, however, posit alternative modes of action. The novel suggests that, bound by love to both Mama Day and George, Cocoa is not an individual consciousness, an isolated self, but is fused, shared. If, then, one of the people with whom she is bound emotionally were to die in her place, the conditions of the spell would be met, since a part of Cocoa would die, although her body would live. However, if those same people were to recognize their inherent unity, they could allow their love to override Ruby's hatred and thereby dissolve the death-spell. The first solution bespeaks a kind of rigid justice, a playing by rules established by someone else, to which consent has not been given. It recalls the biblical edenic transgression for which Jahweh demands either the death of the "sinning" agents or the death of Christ in their stead. This solution, then, is predicated on the physical and moral superiority of the sacrificial victim and insists on the discrete boundaries of the self; hence Christ is perceived as superior to and separate from humankind. The second alternative, Naylor's exploration of a Goddess-centered theology, rejects the hierarchy implicit in the first solution for a concept of the self as communal and fused. It unravels the rigid demands of justice through love; hence, no one need die because the conditions of the spell would be erased rather than fulfilled. Such an alternative would re-write the Genesis narrative, rejecting the concept of the necessity of Christ's sacrificial death, again a radical act of signifying on Naylor's part.

Mama Day finds language an unacceptable medium through which to teach George the alternative route, since he categorically dismisses all magic as superstition and assumes her discussion of hexing and the binding of flesh is simply metaphorical. However, ritual, predating the word, effects enlightenment through its use of drama, image, and gesture, which transform consciousness, not in the rational mind, on the level of thought, but in the intuitions and in the unconscious. Arming him with the staff and the ledger (icons of the strength and the wisdom) of the men who have previously been destroyed by the loss of love, Mama Day undertakes to create a labor for George that will allow him to discover if his is the mettle of the hero. Knowing that he is deathly afraid of chickens, presumably because of their role in her magical rites, which he intuits as antithetical to his essence, she sends him into the chicken coop to retrieve what he finds in the nest of a setting hen, a task the narrative has already encoded as fraught with danger (Mama Day indicates that she herself would not attempt to approach a hen in the process of hatching her eggs). He succeeds in facing his fears, but when Mama Day's ritual becomes transparent to him (he asks, "Could it be that she wanted nothing but my hands?" (300),) his ego will not allow him to abandon his individuality to fuse with the feminine, which he perceives as weak and irrational. Rather, he chooses to re-enact Christ's sacrifice. The text encodes his death in the imagery of Christ's crucifixion. His hands are pierced (by the beak of the hen) and he experiences the sensation of wearing a crown of thorns ("glassy needles splintered throughout [his] brain" (301)) from the pain he undergoes while dying of a heart attack; he withstands the pain long enough to allow him to cross the road (which "felt like water under [his] buckling knees" (301), an allusion to the biblical scene in which Christ walks on water) to find Cocoa and die in her stead, thereby resolving the fractured legacy of Bascombe Wade. Released from the spell, Cocoa recovers from her illness and by the novel's end is portrayed as slowly evolving into a Goddess-figure in her own right, one whom, the text reveals, will eventually be more powerful than Mama Day and will learn to speak Sapphira Wade's name. George on the other hand, continues to be referred to as "that boy" by the communal narrator. Having rejected a concept of maleness that would have allowed transcendence of the ego to connect with his anima, the crone aspect of the goddess, here represented by Mama Day, he is never allowed to achieve full maturity.[7]

In *Bailey's Cafe,* Naylor focuses more specifically on the Bible, which she rewrites to provide a narrative voice for characters whose stories it treats summarily or shapes to fit its narrative purposes. Here, Naylor incorporates her extensive biblical knowledge, sometimes in bitterness or anger, sometimes by punning wickedly.[8] The key to understanding Naylor's agenda appears in the introductory narrative of the unnamed main male character, (who as the proprietor of Bailey's Cafe is typically referred to as "Bailey"). Functioning as a kind of inverse St. Peter figure, a keeper of the gate who directs lost souls (specifically women) to sanctuary and salvation, Bailey explains that Nadine, his wife, taught him "a whole different way of looking at . . . women" (19), a perspective the reader is invited to adopt. Naylor's text consists of a series of personal narratives framed by Bailey's contextualizing interludes. Most of the speakers are women who arrive at the cafe despairing, friendless, and emotionally lost. Bailey functions to point them in the direction of Eve's house, the site of the only possible redemption for these women. Eve offers an alternative paradigm to the familiar Judeo-Christian-based one that in each narrative is implicated in the suffering of the victims who arrive at the boardinghouse.

If *Mama Day* demands that the reader accept a magical island on which witches cast spells, heal, use chickens to impregnate women, and call down the lightning, *Bailey's Cafe* posits a restaurant that can only be found by those in the final stages of despair before suicide. Time and space are fluid in this world. Bailey stumbles onto it, when, upon returning from World War II, having suffered the horror of the war in the Pacific, he stands on a wharf in San Francisco considering suicide. He hears Nadine calling him, turns, and finds himself frying hamburgers in the cafe whose proprietor he at that moment becomes, a cafe that is seemingly located somewhere in Manhattan. Eve, who, the text claims, walked away from her home on the delta one thousand years before, discovered the cafe somewhere outside of New Orleans. However, the text also claims Eve's house has "*always* been right down the block from [the] cafe" (80), suggesting that what Eve represents has always existed although it has not been readily accessible to women. Eve's house, with its group of women boarders, is viewed by many as a brothel, although Bailey insists that he "can't find a thing wrong with what goes on at Eve's" (80), another case of his reading women and women's matters through non-traditional eyes—eyes the narrative invites the reader to see through, since Bailey's voice shapes and comments upon the other narratives. However, the narrative provides the reader with a choice. Only women (with the exception of one man who wears women's clothing) live at Eve's; most receive men as callers, men who must first buy flowers from Eve's garden before they can "court." Reading the encounters between Eve's boarders and their visitors as prostitution aligns one with the Judeo-Christian tradition which has continually referred to the ancient practice of women serving the Goddess by engaging in acts of ritual sex as "temple prostitution" in an attempt to denigrate the practice. However, the narratives that follow encourage an alternative reading, since they reveal women who move toward healing through their sexuality, through that part of themselves that the Judeo-Christian tradition has seen as unclean, as sinful, as destructive of spirit.

Eve, Naylor's revisionist reading of the character from Genesis with the same name, reveals herself to be an exile from Eden, having been "thrown out of the world" (85) by the *Godfather* (more of Naylor's punning), a mean-spirited, vindictive preacher who has raised the child who "never had a real mother or father and wouldn't be alive if it weren't for him" (82). That he is Naylor's version of the biblical Jahweh is obvious; that she creates him for the reader to despise as maniacal and dangerous is equally clear. In Naylor's version of the Genesis account, the knowledge for which Eve is punished leads her to claim her sexuality and find pleasure in her body, a practice which frees her from patriarchal constraint but which sets her in opposition to a biblically-articulated definition of gender-appropriate behavior. No serpent tempts Eve to eat of the tree of the knowledge of good and evil. The male figure here more nearly resembles the Pagan Pan, "a crazy man-boy smelling like a goat, kicking up dust, and howling in the twilight."[9] Billy Boy's stomping sets up tremors that cause Eve, lying prone on the ground, to come to orgasm. However, it is not Billy Boy, nor any male, who is the sexual initiator here; rather, Eve explains, "The earth showed me what my body was for" (87). Naylor's revision of the Genesis account of the "fall" insists on the inevitability of human sexual desire and sexual response. However, it also articulates female sexuality as independent of a male partner/presence, which has the effect of diminishing the significance of maleness in general, more of Naylor's radical revisionism. Naylor's Eve is, furthermore, unrepentant, proud, and self-possessed. In an inversion of the words of the Jahweh of the Hebrew Bible, she claims, "what I am-I am" (85), claiming his power and his authority for herself.

However, Naylor's narrative reveals that the female empowerment Eve discovers within herself is not accepted by mainstream society; hence, Eve finds "there was nowhere on earth for a woman like [her]" (91). If, however, knowledge of and empowerment through the Goddess is not readily available to women in the day-to-day reality of their lives, the Goddess remains an archetype that has not been completely eradicated from human thought—in this way, the street at the edge of the universe can be read as the deepest unconscious, the place to which a persona descends, in Jungian terms, when all other avenues to individuation have failed and when the survival of the self is at stake. If the seeker is successful, s/he achieves an integrated self. If s/he fails, disintegration continues until suicide or "accidental death" occurs. The unconscious, according to Jung, is often represented by a labyrinth or a maze. Nor surprisingly, then, the women who seek Eve wander first to Bailey's Cafe, unable to arrive at the boardinghouse directly. As selfhood is achieved for a woman, Jung suggests she often encounters "a superior female figure—a priestess, sorceress, earth mother, or goddess"[10] within herself. Eve here can be read as that archetype. In a culture in which no "superior female figures" occur in the dominant theologies, women must break through a residue of consciousness that would interpret priestesses, sorceresses, and goddesses as evil (an interpretation obviously fostered by Judeo-Christian thought), a consciousness that leaves her incapable of finding her inner strength and thereby achieving wholeness. As Bailey notes, "A woman is either ready for Eve's or she's not" (22). If she remains invested in a discourse that privileges maleness, the text suggests, she will be unable to accept the kind of healing Eve—and all she represents—offers. Only by denying the entire patriarchal paradigm—with its exclusively male deity—can a woman achieve individuation (i.e., salvation). In Naylor's recasting of the biblical narrative, Eve herself has planted the garden with which she is always identified; in its center, one finds, not a lone tree, as the Genesis account would lead one to expect, but rather one tree stump, suggesting the destruction of any source of temptation that would further un-do women already devastated by living in a world that has rendered them powerless and made them the victims of systems of oppression which have been made to appear inevitable and even just. Naylor's Eve, portrayed as a benevolent, if fierce, deity, does not dangle goodness in front of their faces only to withdraw it (as the Jahweh of Genesis has been accused of doing). Around the tree stump grow circles and circles of lilies, the flower of rebirth, but, significantly, the only flower Eve will not sell. The rebirth that Eve offers women who come to feminine wisdom through her cannot be purchased, but must grow from within.

In offering redemption for women, Eve goes so far as to un-do the curse of Genesis that accompanies the expulsion of the woman from the biblical garden. Although the patriarchal god insists it will be her lot in life to bear children in pain, when the young Mariam, genitally mutilated and pregnant although she has never been touched by a man, is due to give birth, Eve announces "there's a way to alter the pain" (224), using her magic to create a rainbow of hope, a play of shimmering, breathtaking light that stuns all the customers in the cafe and overrides Mariam's pain. Eve's power, then, is again articulated as a healing power that can un-do Jahweh's hexing; in that, it is not simply equal to, but greater than, his power. Significantly, the redemption Eve offers is a matter of the body, the flesh, which in Naylor's economy is not understood to be of less significance that the soul, but inseparable from it. Naylor's narrative begins with the premise that, for many women, pain is scripted onto the body. Hence Mary/Peaches has disfigured her face with a beer opener, Jesse Bell is heroin addicted, Mariam has been genitally mutilated, and Esther has been forced to enact sadomasochistic sex scenes by her husband. Naylor's signifying disrupts the body:soul duality evident in the Bible, insisting that the soul can only flourish through its interconnection with the body, not in opposition to it.

The first of Eve's boarders to narrate her history is Esther, obviously Naylor's revision of the biblical good queen Esther who saves the Jewish people through her subtle manipulation of her husband. In the Bible, Esther is chosen for the throne after the king banishes his first wife, Vashti, for disobedience. The king had requested Vashti to appear before his guests in all her beauty; one scholarly interpretation of the phrase suggests she is to appear completely naked—in other words, to be the plaything, the pornographic image, to titillate and arouse a group of men. The first wife suddenly appears less unreasonable; Naylor envisions her as less powerless as well. In her version, Esther is married off by her impoverished brother to an extremely wealthy husband whose wife has deserted him rather than perform in the kinky sex scenarios he scripts. In Naylor's signifying on the biblical account, Esther's sexual torture profits her brother and his family (her "people," as the biblical Esther's people are the Jews), who thrive financially during her enslavement. What the biblical narrative overlooks is the effect on the psyche of marriage to such a man. When Naylor's Esther deserts her husband, she carries with her a hatred of men so intense that it "could change the air" (94), a hatred that threatens to destroy her entire being. At Eve's, she lives in the basement, in a room without lightbulbs, where men come to enact their sadomasochistic fantasies on and through her. But to do so, they must bring Esther white roses, which are difficult to grow and hence costly; their game playing, then, demands a sacrifice on their parts as well as hers, and Esther's desire (for the loveliness of the flowers) is fulfilled even as she fulfills their desires. The narrative remains unresolved on whether Esther ever grows beyond her hatred; however, it does reveal that she is present at the birth of Mariam's baby and that, for the first time, she smiles. The white roses—Eve's strategy for healing—have led to her acknowledgment of joy and beauty, which begins to unravel her devastating hatred and move her closer to the realm of the fully human.

Another of the biblical figures whom Naylor treats is Mary Magdalene, the legendary repentant prostitute of the New Testament, who appears here in the guise of the extremely beautiful and sexual Mary, also known as Peaches. Naylor uses her chapter titles to indicate the shared nature of Mary Magdalene (the Whore) with the Mary the Mother of God (the Virgin): Peaches's narrative is entitled "Mary (Take One)," while Mariam's story is called "Mary (Take Two)." Naylor's paralleling the narratives emphasizes the cultural division imposed on women. It is the "take," the perspective of one player, one speaker, one instrument, that determines and names what is seen, but the subject herself is one and the same: woman. The duality resurfaces in Peaches' own self-concept. From even before her teenage years, whenever she looks in a mirror, Peaches sees a "her" whom the "I" despises. Peaches states, "Everywhere I turned, I could see her. But what was she doing in my room? She was a whore and I was Daddy's baby" (188). Having assimilated the virgin:whore duality that, if not created by the Judeo-Christian tradition is certainly reinforced by it, Peaches cannot integrate her sexual urges into her concept of herself as the dutiful daughter; rather, she bifurcates and lives each stereotype fully. Her sexual self will accept any man as lover, while her virgin self loathes the sexual self, perceiving her as "other," as not-self. Eventually, her self-hatred drives her to scar her face with a beer opener; the "I" has punished the "her", attempting to render "her" unattractive to men so that the acts of sex will end. However "her" pleasure, which the "I", inculcated in the Judeo-Christian tradition, does not acknowledge as legitimate, will also end. At Eve's, the men who wish to spend time with Peaches must present her with a bouquet of daffodils, for which they must pay fifty dollars. Eve has taught Peaches to value herself enough to demand a perfect bouquet at that—if a bouquet has wilted from the wait, the gentleman must purchase another one. Initially, the room is filled with men holding bouquets of daffodils, waiting their turns to see Peaches; each week, fewer men return, and winter, the season when daffodils do not readily bloom, threatens. But Eve has convinced Peaches that "a man special enough to understand what the woman upstairs is truly worth" (114) will continue to buy the daffodils and hence she can promise Peaches's father, "I'll return your daughter to you whole" (114). Eve teaches Peaches a concept of womanhood at odds with the more familiar, biblical one—from Eve's perspective, which we must read as Naylor's speculations about a Goddess-centered definition of gender, a woman enjoys her sexuality, is not possessed as an object, is not obedient or subservient, and loves herself deeply. Such knowledge will allow Peaches to achieve wholeness, at which point she will be neither dutiful daughter nor whore, both categories in which she is positioned in relation to men, but rather woman, interacting with men if and when she chooses but not defined by them.

Naylor's boldest manipulation of biblical narrative probably occurs in the Jesse Bell (Jezebel) section, where she elegantly and dazzlingly incorporates many of the details of the story of the Bible's most wicked woman. A brief summary of the biblical story may perhaps be necessary, in spite of the common cultural association of Jezebel with evil; typically the specific nature of her wickedness is misconstrued as sexual. However, the Bible reveals her to have been a good wife, confidante, and advisor to King Ahab. Jezebel's "evil" lies in her ethnicity; not one of the children of Israel, she worships Ba'al and Asherah, God and Goddess, according to the customs of her people, and she invites her husband to participate in her rituals, which he does. Of course as a follower of Asherah, it is likely that Jezebel served Her in ritual sexual acts, which her husband, as a convert to her religion, would have understood for what they were—sacred rites performed in honor of the Goddess. Annoyed by Jahweh's prophet Elijah's continually haranguing her with public accusations, she attempts to rid her country of all the prophets of Jahweh, an act interpreted as evidence of her "evil" by the biblical narrative. Needless to say, however, the narrative voice does not censure Jahweh's followers when they kill the prophets of Ba'al and Asherah. At her most wicked, Jezebel arranges for a man to be falsely accused and executed to allow her husband to fulfill his desire to possess the dead man's vineyard, but given the bloodbath recorded in the historical books of the Hebrew Bible, her act appears barely significant. Elijah arranges a showdown between the prophets of the two religions, and the Ba'al—Asherah contingent is humiliated when their sacrifice will not ignite. Eventually, Jezebel is thrown from a high window and is devoured by dogs.

The conflicting cultures in Naylor's "signifying" narrative derive from social class rather than ethnicity; Jesse Bell, a poor but proud girl from the docks, marries into the wealthy and prestigious "King" family, (more of Naylor's signifying, since the biblical story of Jezebel appears in the book of Kings), after which, the narrative claims, she "went straight to the dogs" (118). In Naylor's text, as in the Bible, the woman's nemesis is Elijah, here in the guise of Jesse's husband's Uncle Eli, the patriarch of a family that has risen to social prominence by denying its cultural heritage and severing itself from overt associations with Blackness. Uncle Eli despises Jesse Bell both for what he considers her inferior class status and for her acceptance and celebration of her sexuality; he perceives her as degrading the Kings through what she eats, how she dresses, and whom she befriends. Jesse Bell proudly acknowledges her sexuality, but allows the reader to perceive it in a different light. Of her husband, she says, "He wasn't my first man, but he wasn't my fiftieth either. He damn sure was my last" (122) and explains that, contrary to the King family belief that she bewitched her husband by "slip[ping] some kind of secret potion in his drink" (122), she "got him the same way [she] kept him—with the best poon tang east of the Mississippi" (122). Jesse Bell's open enjoyment of her body is part of her greater refusal of the dominant discourse's definition of "woman." She will not be shackled by an obsession with virginity, obedience, or subservience. Simply, she does not perceive herself as inferior by virtue of gender, race, or class. Like her biblical namesake, who serves as advisor to her husband, she knows her own worth. Jesse Bell understands Uncle Eli's hostility as stemming from his deeply-rooted hatred of all women. She speculates that "I don't think he was anybody's uncle cause that woulda meant he had to be somebody's mother's child. A woman wouldna birthed him. A woman woulda seen the hate in his eyes for us the minute he slipped out of her, and she woulda crushed his puny little head between her knees. It didn't surprise me to learn he'd never been married, the things he said about women" (123). The reader must assume that Jesse's assessment of Eli serves as a commentary on the biblical Elijah as well. Like Jezebel before her, Jesse Bell not only continues to resist assimilation to the Kings' values, she encourages her husband to appreciate her—and his—rightful culture. When she learns her husband has no knowledge of traditional Black food, one of the primary markers of Black culture, because Uncle Eli will not allow his family to eat what he calls "slave food," she determines to educate his palate. In the novel's most outrageously funny scene, Jesse Bell teaches her husband how to truly appreciate sweet potato pie; the incident can only be interpreted as a clear case of his worshiping at the "wrong grove."

Reading Naylor's narrative back through its biblical source, which emphasizes Jezebel's devotion to Asherah, one can read Uncle Eli's hatred of Jesse Bell's clan as grounded in its matriarchal structure. When Jesse's mother would come to visit, Jesse would "sit her at the head of the table, where she belonged" (126). Uncle Eli's ranting is, for the most part, ignored by his nephew, as Elijah's is with King Ahab, but it does influence Jesse's' own son, who attacks his grandmother's morals in having birthed children without having married their fathers. The child, in other words, accepts the King's patriarchal sexual ethics, which bind women through the enshrining of virginity and fidelity. In Uncle Eli's version of Elijah's "High Noon" of the prophets, he invites the Bell family to a potluck cookout on a day when rain is predicted. Although he has hired a cook with a propane gas grill and a tent to prepare the kind of food he considers appropriate to such a function—"little bits of grilled mushrooms, smoked cheese, and that kind of shit on silver trays" (129)—when the Bells arrive with their spareribs and their chickens, markers of their culture, they find no room for them under the tent. Their attempts to start their own fires in an open charcoal pit fail. Too proud to retreat, they drink their beer and eat their potato salad in the rain, scorned by the wealthy set whom Uncle Eli has invited to witness their humiliation. Jesse Bell's mother gets wet to the bone, catches pneumonia, and dies, paralleling the destruction of the belief in the Great God-

dess by the patriarchs of Israel, who spend centuries chopping down the sacred groves of Asherah and slaughtering Her followers. In her grief, Jesse
Bell turns from her husband to her long-time woman lover, a fixture in the
lives of the couple, Naylor's encoding of the acts of ritual sex done in honor
of the Goddess. However, the Goddess (the mother) is dead and Jesse's life
has lost its focus and its purpose. Her parallel of Jezebel's fall from the high
window occurs when Uncle Eli arranges to have her arrested while she is
high on heroin in a lesbian bar. Jesse is disgraced, because, as she points
out, "Nobody was interested in my side of the story" (121). Uncle Eli, with
his connections, can control what the newspapers say, just as the biblical
narrative, while purporting to tell the "truth," privileges Elijah's story, skew-
ing the perspective from which the reader sees Jezebel, embedding her in
a pre-conceived paradigm of "evil." However, the Goddess, in the form of
Eve, intervenes for Jesse Bell, allowing for a narrative of redemption denied the biblical Jezebel. Unlike most of the women at Eve's, Jesse does not
receive male callers; having arrived on the street accepting her body and its
desire for pleasure, Jesse does not have to re-learn the sacredness of her
sexuality. Nevertheless, it is her flesh that Eve tends through the two har-
rowing scenes of Jesse's going cold turkey, the flesh that must heal if the
soul is to thrive.

Naylor's strategy of re-writing portions of the Bible to shift the perspective from which they are viewed is predicted upon the powerlessness of certain biblical characters in the face of a paradigm that functions to serve its
own narrative purposes. Naylor does not, however, articulate powerlessness
in exclusively feminine terms, as her inclusion of one male narrative exemplifies. Eve's housekeeper, one of her boarders, is a man who calls himself
Miss Maple and who dresses in women's clothing. As a Black male, he has
been excluded from the dominant discourse, as his narrative amply demonstrates. The grandson of a Black man and a Yuma woman, Miss Maple, who
has a Ph.D. in mathematics from Stanford University, cannot find a position in business because of his skin color; even in the post-war economic
boom of the late 1940s, he is repeatedly rejected for positions even though
he is clearly the most, if not the only, eligible candidate. Living in a society
that denies a Black man full participation in its constructs, he is by extension excluded from societal definitions of manhood. On the one hand, his
color is perceived as a semiotic indicator of his subhuman status. Furthermore, in prison (for refusing the draft) he was raped; his acts of sex (forced
or not) with another man position him outside the dominant discourse's definition of masculinity. In contemporary western culture, the proscription
against homosexual practice can be traced back to the biblical strictures of

Leviticus. There, too, he would find no mercy on the basis of circumstance. Presumably, Miss Maple's response to his attacker, who "was six-feet-two, as broad as he was tall, as ugly as he was mean, a repeat offender serving for three counts of murder with nothing left to lose" (192), should have been to choose death before dishonor, as the prisoner before him did. Furthermore, biblical law would define him as an "abomination in the sight of the Lord" for his style of dress. However, Miss Maple has learned from his father that, excluded as he is from the dominant discourse, he must create his own meaning, his own sign system. His father explains, "You see, to accept even a single image in their language as your truth is to be led into accepting them all" (182). Were Miss Maple to accept the premise that men should not wear dresses, he would be engaging in a cultural construct of masculinity from which his skin color and his prison experience have already barred him. Ironically, then, his clothing functions as the marker of his masculinity; because it is so visible, so inescapable, it continually serves as a reminder of his own system of values, which is predicated upon a rejection of a racist, sexist, homophobic ethos. Miss Maple's definition of maleness does not contain within it the concept of superiority to women; hence dressing in women's clothing and engaging in "women's work" (housekeeping) can in no way demean him, any more than it would demean a woman. Although Miss Maple is revealed as possessing tremendous strength of character, he, too, requires Eve's healing, since the repeated rejection against all reason have led him to despair. The despair has passed, and the narrative reveals he will soon leave the street to return to the world, where he will begin his own business.

The book's final section treats Mariam, the genitally mutilated semi-retarded child who wanders in from Addis Ababa, pregnant yet untouched by a man. Her biblical counterpart is obvious. Mariam's chapter is not a first-person narrative; she never speaks, presumably because she lacks the empowerment to do so. Bailey's wife Nadine and Eve provide a frame for a third-person narration that tells Mariam's story. In this section, Naylor signifies upon the doctrine of the Virgin birth, drawing parallels between the biblical Mary and Mariam. For example, Mariam is brought to Eve by Gabriel, who in the Marian account functions as the angel of the annunciation; here he is an old Russian Jew who runs a pawnshop next door to Bailey's Cafe. Eve, the Goddess who has existed from the beginning and who therefore possesses a knowledge of the ancient ways, becomes Naylor's apparatus for a critique of woman-hating cultures. Eve articulates Mariam's past, making it clear that her circumcision and infibulation (practices that continue to this day) were required to make her acceptable marriage mate-

rial in a culture where marriage is an economic necessity for women; hence
Mariam's mother not only permits but seeks out the torture of her daughter's
flesh, understanding that, simply, the alternative is starvation. Eve explains
that "virgin births" are not uncommon in cultures that engage in such practices: "Even on the wedding night, the *ensaslaye,* with a willing bride and
a cautious husband, the village will hear the screaming. Sometimes it will
take months . . . before the wound he slowly makes allows him to penetrate
her without pain. And sometimes she's not fully opened until her first child"
(152). However, the narrative insists that Mariam is not simply a "technical virgin;" her claim that no man has touched her is borne out by Eve's
examination of her body. When Nadine speaks of miracle in the sense of
"the little girl in Galilee," Eve points out, "She wasn't the first either" (153).
Naylor creates a world that contains within it the possibility of recurring
miracle. Christ, in this economy, becomes then, not the only child of God,
but simply one of many such children. However, Naylor structures this
section of the narrative to focus less on Mariam's history than on Hebraic
articulation of the concept of womanhood, particularly highlighting doc-
trinal tenets that state that women during their child-bearing years are not
permitted in the sanctuary and that after menstruation and childbirth, they
are perceived as "unclean." Naylor's text implicates not merely the debase-
ment of the female body, the hatred of the feminine, through genital mutila-
tion but through the entire religious doctrine as well. For example, Mariam's
mother speculates,

> There is a prayer to be said at this time of day. . . . It is spoken before
> the dawn when the hens cry. And then there is a prayer at dawn itself. . . .
> There are ten prayers alone just for the hours of the day. The Beta Israel
> bless the rain, lightning, and thunder, the sunshine, the olive harvest, the
> wheat. They bless each meal before and even after it is eaten. They bless
> new clothes, new lambs, new roads on which they travel. In this ancient
> faith there is a blessing for everything—except her body (156).

Naylor posits a believable world in which the hatred of female flesh, dis-
guising itself (as it often does) as a concern with "morality," allows the Beta
Israel village to cast out—to a certain death—a partially retarded child because she is pregnant and cannot name the man responsible for her condition. At Eve's, however, Mariam finds acceptance and nurturance; as in
Mama Day, Naylor here articulates a theology of the Goddess that is loving and redemptive. A rigid obsession with justice is abandoned in favor
of compassion. Hence, the birth of Mariam's baby draws the community

together in celebration and affirmation. However, Mariam herself does not survive the implications of the ideology into which she was inculcated. Believing herself unclean after childbirth, she attempts to conjure "a running stream to bathe in" (228) and drowns.

Linking Mariam iconographically with "the little girl in Galilee" (153) determines that the child she bears be read as a Christ-figure, a connection Naylor emphasizes. The boy-child, whom Nadine claims is destined "to bring in a whole new era" (160), is sent to an orphanage run by a Mrs. Jackson and grows up to become the George of *Mama Day*. His version of his origin—that his mother was a prostitute who committed suicide—is a patriarchal distortion of his past that denies him his birthright, the knowledge that he is "the child of God" (160). Nevertheless, as *Mama Day* reveals, while George fulfills his Christ-like role of sacrificial victim, because, unlike Bailey, he never develops "a whole different way of looking at . . . women," (19) he forgoes the possibility of "bring[ing] in a whole new era."

One woman steadfastly refuses Eve's hospitality—Sadie (which is, we recall, the Jewish pet name for "Sarah"), who is portrayed as having throughout her life attempted to play by the rules, to be a good girl, a good daughter, a good wife. Naylor uses the character of Sadie to articulate the hopelessness of succeeding at such a task in a system in which women are inherently perceived as flawed, as well as to speculate grimly on the psychological implications of such an attempt. Like her biblical namesake, Sadie is born to a people in captivity, here, the poor Black folk of the South Side of Chicago. Never wanted (she is born only because her mother's abortion attempt fails), Sadie responds to her mother's physical and emotional abuse in a way that denies her own psychological needs but that is consistent with the Judeo-Christian concept of the ideal child/woman—she is obedient, respectful, and modest, attempting to win the embittered, vicious woman's love by good behavior. As she "press[es] threadbare petticoats until the creases reflected light [and] darn[ed] cheap stockings with stitches finer than the ones put there by machine" (43), the girl denies the reality of her physical world for a fantasy world in which she achieves wealth and success; in other words, she privileges the internal (soul, spirit) over the external (the body, her grim world), just as mainstream religious thought has encouraged its followers to do. Naylor, however, emphasizes the suffering of the body to suggest the dehumanization and disintegration that occur when the physical is overlooked or denigrated. Being forced by her mother to begin to turn tricks when she is only thirteen and to undergo an abortion/sterilization does not deter—but only strengthens—Sadie's denial of her own body and its pain; to survive, she retreats still further into her fantasy world.

After she marries—an older man, an alcoholic who does not love her—Sadie appears to forego her fantasy life, channeling her energies into maintaining and even improving on her husband's home, a rundown little South Side house by the railroad track, of which Sadie is nonetheless proud. Although she engages in some of the same coping strategies she learned from her years with her mother, Sadie does on one occasion stand up to her husband and assert her demands. However, the death of her husband results in his house passing to his hostile daughter, who will not allow Sadie to continue living there. Sadie's desperate prayer to be allowed to keep her house is answered when a mysterious figure with a "palm [as] large as a man's [but with] the touch gentle as a woman's" (65) leaves her a bottle of Five Star wine. Naylor's *deux ex machina* tactic must be read in terms of the novel's overall signifying on the Bible. Summoned by her prayer, the being becomes identified with the God to whom Sadie prayed. The gift of the wine allows Sadie to keep her home, but only in the world of the imagination. For this God, then, Sadie's physical reality is inconsequential, her suffering in the body unimportant, the only significant salvation being that of the spirit. In her dreams, in her soul, Sadie continues to live in her house and to turn it into a lovely, elegant home; in her body, Sadie becomes a homeless alcoholic who prostitutes herself to earn the money for the nightly bottle of Five Stars necessary to allow her fantasy existence to override physical reality.

However, Naylor structures her narrative to allow Sadie the possibility of a salvation that includes the body; a man rare enough to see her worth proposes marriage to her after becoming enchanted by her musical laugh. The biblical Sarah, we recall, laughs when she overhears Jahweh's messenger announcing that she is to become a mother although she is years past menopause. In declining the marriage proposal, Sadie reflects, "She knew this dear sweet man was offering her the moon, but she could give him the stars" (78). In unpacking Naylor's statement, the moon can be seen to function as the metaphor of the feminine, the Goddess, while the man who responds to Sadie's laughter becomes identified with that deity, Her messenger, who, like the biblical messenger, heralds the birth of a new life—in this case, Sadie's own. The Biblical Sarah was the wife of the patriarch Abraham, whose children, that text claims, were to be as numerous as the stars. Hence the stars align Sadie with that patriarchal tradition, which is, of course, antithetical to the concept of the Goddess. Sadie's stars, however, are simply a representation printed on a wine label; they are not real, any more than her alcoholic hallucinations of her pretty little house with its matching china and its window boxes are real. Naylor's play with the biblical Jahweh and Sarah hints at the possibility of his lack of sincerity. His offer to Sarah, Naylor's signifying suggests, is illusory. Her life in the body will be unchanged by his promise, and at least in Sadie's case, belief in the promise of the stars leads to the deterioration of her physical state. In an economy in which the spiritual is privileged over the physical, Sadie's spirit-induced dreams lead to her denial of her own body, of her own pleasure, not to mention her own need for nurturance and shelter. Her survival has occurred because she uncannily moves people with her vision; her ability to dream is so powerful that she can temporarily transform matter— hence the heavy, chipped mug in which Nadine serves Sadie tea becomes a fine china tea cup in her worn hand. Similarly, Sadie transforms herself— a worn, homeless alcoholic street prostitute—to her vision of herself as a gentle modest woman of some means—in Bailey's words, "a lady" (39). However, the crippling limitations associated with the word "lady" are implicated in Sadie's ultimate destruction, even as they are what prevent her from seeking out Eve. A "lady" does not acknowledge her body's desires or its need for pleasure. Hence, Bailey points out "there was no use in directing her [to Eve's]. A woman is either ready for Eve's or she's not. And if she's ready, she'll ask where to find it on her own" (80). In refusing the redemption of the body, in refusing to ever consider her own pleasure, her own desire, in choosing to cut herself off from the power of womanhood by accepting the limitations involved in being a "lady," by playing by the hopeless rules a patriarchal culture has imposed on women to contain their power and imprison their bodies, Sadie is lost from the narrative as she is lost from herself.

NOTES

All citations in text to Naylor's *Mama Day* are from New York: Vintage Books, 1989 edition. All citations in text to Naylor's *Bailey's Cafe* are from New York: Vintage Books, 1992 edition.

1. Gates, Henry Louis, Jr., *The Signifying Monkey,* (New York: Oxford University Press, 1988), 64.

2. Ostriker, Alicia Suskin, *Stealing the Language: The Emergence of Women's Poetry in America,* (Boston: Beacon Press, 1986), 11.

3. Ostriker, Alicia Suskin, *Feminist Revision of the Bible,* (Oxford: Blackwell Press, 1993), 33.

4. Ibid., 11.

5. Levy, Helen Fiddyment, "Lead on with Light," in *Gloria Naylor: Critical Perspectives Past and Present,* ed. Henry Louis Gates, Jr. and K. A. Appiah (New York: Armistad Press, 1993), 278.

6. Ibid., 282.

7. Oddly enough, many readers assume Mama Day forces George's sacrificial death on him. For example, Larry R. Andrews argues in "Black Sisterhood in Naylor's Novels," in *Gloria Naylor: Critical Perspectives Past and Present,* ed. Henry Louis Gates, Jr. and K. A. Appiah (New York: Armistad Press, 1993), 299, that "Only through [George's] sacrificial death can Ophelia recover from Ruby's conjuring." Such a reading ignores textual evidence: Mama Day tells George, "There are two ways anybody can go when they come to certain roads in life—ain't about a right way or a wrong way—just two ways. And here we getting down to my way or yours. Now I got a way for us to help Baby Girl. And I'm hoping it's the one you'll use" (295). After George's sacrificial death, the narrative states, "Miranda knows she got no more reason to stand at that gate. He went and did it his way, so he ain't coming back" (302). Clearly her way would *not* have required his sacrificial death.

8. The best example of such punning may occur in a scene in which Eve signifies on a self-righteous character named Sister Carrie by addressing her indirectly—on matters of Scripture—while she keeps her eyes fastened, not on the Lord, but on the *lard* can on Bailey's shelf. The text refers to her as "holding her conversation with the lard" (135), hardly a flattering portrayal of the Judeo-Christian deity.

9. Naylor, *Bailey's Cafe,* 88. Naylor's portrayal of Eve links her with the possible prototype of the Biblical Eve. Ostriker has found that:

the Eve of Genesis may be related to goddess figures who for millennia throughout the Middle East were associated with gardens, sacred trees, and oracular snakes, whose power over the process of childbirth was appropriated by Jahweh. Her title, "Mother of all Living," was the title of the goddess Araru whose priestess initiates the savage Enkidu sexually in Gilgamesh. . . . (Ostriker, *Feminist Revision,* 37).

Enkidu is aptly represented by the semi-retarded Billy Boy.

10. von Franz, Marie-Louise, "The Process of Individuation," in *Man and His Symbols,* ed. C. G. Jung, et al. (New York: Laurel Press, 1964), 208.

BIBLIOGRAPHY

Andrews, Larry R. "Black Sisterhood in Naylor's Novels." In *Gloria Naylor: Critical Perspectives Past and Present,* eds. Henry Louis Gates, Jr. and K. A. Appiah, 285–301. New York: Armistad Press, 1993.

Gates, Henry Louis, Jr. *The Signifying Monkey.* New York: Oxford University Press, 1988.

Levy, Helen Fiddyment. "Lead on with Light." In *Gloria Naylor: Critical Perspectives Past and Present,* eds. Henry Louis Gates, Jr. and K. A. Appiah, 263–83. New York: Armistad Press, 1993.

Naylor, Gloria. *Bailey's Cafe.* New York: Vintage Books, 1992.

———. *Mama Day.* New York: Vintage Books, 1989.

Ostriker, Alicia Suskin. *Feminist Revision of the Bible.* Oxford: Blackwell Press, 1993.

———. *Stealing the Language: The Emergence of Women's Poetry in America.* Boston: Beacon Press, 1986.

von Franz, Marie-Louise. "The Process of Individuation." In *Man and His Symbols,* ed. C. G. Jung, et al., 157–229. New York: Laurel Press, 1964.

The Maternal Aesthetic of *Mama Day*

Julie Tharp

> Mother I need
> mother I need
> mother I need your blackness now
> as the August earth needs rain
> I am
> the sun and moon and forever hungry
> the sharpened edge
> where day and night shall meet
> and not be
> one.
> —Audre Lorde, *The Black Unicorn*

Two comments in recent critical works form the departure point for this discussion of *Mama Day*. In the first, Helen Fiddyment Levy mentions the emotional costs of the mother's loss in one sentence, only to drop the subject. She goes on to write: "Although Hazel Carby calls for a return to the urban setting for verisimilitude in the portrayal of the lives of urban blacks, Naylor's career suggests that portrayals of black rural communities, even the ideal home place, represent more than a facile 'romantic' vision of the folk. . . ."[1] The connection between the two, the mother and the "ideal home place," are apparent enough for Levy that she offers no transition here. And yet, it is the reduction of the maternal to an "ideal home" that often results in a "facile 'romantic' vision of the folk," the vision which Carby is anxious to replace. By overlooking the complexity of the maternal figure in Naylor's work, a complexity upon which she has insisted from her first novel, we replicate that romance, we gloss over the critique she offers.

Virginia Fowler also seems to slip into this romantic view in her study *Gloria Naylor: In Search of Sanctuary,* where she concludes:

> The possibilities for wholeness and restoration of peace that are so powerfully rendered in *Mama Day* are absent from the other novels. But those possibilities are generated by the economically independent, Afrocentric, female-centric world of Willow Springs—in short, by a utopian universe bearing no resemblance to the actual world.[2]

118

Fowler's very search for a sanctuary, of course, limits her perspective some-what, but Willow Springs is by no means a utopian universe by most defi-nitions. A rival conjurer nearly kills Cocoa out of her own jealousy; George risks (and succumbs to) death to save Cocoa; the original Ophelia commits suicide; men drink too much; women lose babies, families fall apart; and large corporations threaten the community's very existence. The island is like any place in these regards. It differs primarily in its responses to these prob-lems; the responses are not, however, always "ideal": Mama Day is not able to "restore peace." It falls to Cocoa to do that. While Fowler's search for restorative space in Naylor's fiction is certainly sympathetic, seeing Willow Springs as a utopian universe replicates the simplification of Carby's assign-ment of a romantic character to the rural and to the black maternal aesthetic which here guides it.

In a 1992 interview Gloria Naylor offers a slightly different interpretation of this material. "Our survival today has depended on our nurturing each other, finding resources within ourselves. The women in Robinson, Missis-sippi, who dealt with herbs for instance, played a crucial role in our com-munity."[3] These women, who did in fact live outside the world of Willow Springs, were directly responsible for the community's physical and often emotional health, their very survival. Speaking of the novel *Mama Day* Nay-lor says:

> It goes back to the stories I listened to when I sat in the corner of the kitchen, and to the different ideas that my parents had regarding the old women who not only worked as quasi traditional doctors, but who used roots and herbs and had supernatural kinds of powers. My mother be-lieved that there were things that happened in life that you could not questions but my father was very reluctant to accept "superstition." The structure of Mama Day emerged from this dual interpretation. I wanted as well to look at women in history, especially at women connected to the earth who could affect behavior.[4]

There is, for Naylor, a connection between recovering black women's history of the woman as healer and source of supernatural power and the survival of a people with their ethnic identity intact. This is far more true for the urban characters—Cocoa and George—than for the rural ones who have maintained some connection all along. Further, Naylor's kitchen ed-ucation suggests that indeed this maternal culture continues to exist at least in people's memories.

One element of this historical background is developed in Lindsey Tucker's excellent article on conjurers as a context for reading *Mama Day*.

Tucker provides several points worth mentioning in this discussion. The conjurers of the Sea Islands have been thought to resemble African elders and their traditions closely. The skills tend to run in families; individuals inherit both the position in the community and the knowledge. "Conjure women often carry the name *Mother* and hold considerable power within their communities."[5] Practitioners of conjure are both supremely rational in their careful attention to nature and supernatural in that they often have "second sight." Mama Day can see, as several critics have point out, the "whole picture."[6] The power that these women carry is generally practiced for the health and well-being of the community, but Tucker points out that such power is presumed to be benevolent only by choice and could as easily be turned against one. The inhabitants of Willow Springs, for instance, know better than to anger Mama Day or to harm what is hers.

Implicit within Tucker's examination of the conjurer and her relationship to the novel *Mama Day* is an understanding that this figure needs to be understood not just culturally or spiritually but also politically and even economically. What Naylor offers us, and what I will develop later, is no less than a road map for an alternative civilization, one based on a reordering of mainstream philosophy as holistic, spiritual and natural, rather than dichotomous, rational and technocratic. This vision does not guarantee utopian bliss, but it does offer the opportunity for mutual support and personal integrity.

For an appreciation of what Naylor is attempting here the novel should be read against a broader historical understanding of motherhood. Black women have often been prevented from assuming their role as mother to their own children. Even assuming that a woman's children were not sold away from her, the slave system kept women working in the fields from dawn to dusk and spinning half the night. Collective child care, Susan A. Mann points out in "Slavery, Sharecropping and Sexual Inequality," was devised for the slaveowners' benefit, rather than for the women's and was, consequently, another instance of their loss of control over their children's welfare.[7] In more recent years women have had to work similar hours in domestic service and in factories, according to Jacqueline Jones in her detailed study of black women's work in the U.S., *Labor of Love, Labor of Sorrow.*

While the act of bearing children (for a future labor pool) has not been generally discouraged, Jones argues that black women's attempts to sustain family life have amounted to a political act of protest: "Most women had to entrust the care of their offspring to a neighbor, nearby relative, or older sibling (in all likelihood these persons also had other responsibilities during the day), or leave them alone to fend for themselves. . . . More than one observer even suggested that the high mortality rates among urban children were due to daytime accidents or diseases that their overworked, distracted parents failed to detect in time."[8] The dual message imparted by the culture—bear black children but raise white ones—was responded to with equally dual behavior. Women might willingly work long hours at domestic chores for their own families but only do a fair job for a white employer.[9] Mothers were and are torn by their children's needs and by economic necessity, a dilemma that is intensified by a dominant political agenda that demands black women's subordination. Furthermore, "Despite their efforts to care for their own offspring and earn a living wage at the same time, black working mothers were held responsible for a variety of social ills related to family life, from the extraordinarily high black infant mortality rates characteristic of all northern cities to education 'retardation' and juvenile delinquency."[10] Often prevented by socioeconomic circumstances from raising their children, black mothers have nonetheless been blamed for their neglect.

Mother-centered literature by African American women must be understood as commenting directly on this state of affairs. Maya Angelou remarks in her Foreword to *Double Stitch: Black Women Write About Mothers and Daughters,* "Each poem makes me know again as if for the first time that the most moving song created during my people's turmoil of slavery was and remains, 'Sometimes I feel like a motherless child.'"[11] These contemporary women writers are repairing the rend in the historical fabric of motherhood. Writing as daughters, they reinstate maternal love and nurture. Writing as mothers, they explore a variety of pressures—physical, emotional, cultural, even mythical. They are in both cases closing the wounds of the bereft mother and child.

Although Willow Springs depicts an island that is not part of the U.S., that belongs solely to its inhabitants of African descent, loss of mother and child still figure largely in the text. Sapphira "flies to Africa" leaving her children behind; when Peace drowns in the well, Ophelia grieves for years before killing herself and leaving her other children motherless; Miranda's great unresolved grief is the loss of her mother; Abigail's daughters, one of which is Cocoa's mother, all die at very young ages, leaving Cocoa motherless. These scenes of loss invite us to consider the strength of the mother/child emotional bond and to read it against the history of loss figured by Sapphira—enslaved African woman who bears seven sons by her white "owner." We have to read Mama Day and her maternal presence against this loss—both Cocoa's need for that nurturance and Mama Day's need for Cocoa to carry on her traditions.

Like Audre Lorde, Toni Morrison, Alice Walker, and many others, Gloria Naylor writes of her understanding of the mother's role in determining black women's identity and integrity. *The Women of Brewster Place,* for example, problematizes the separation of women by poverty, class and sexuality and illustrates their need for powerful othermothers to nurture a fractured community. Naylor's novels, unlike many others, make no claims to being historical per se, but instead express historical context as a concrete presence within each story. They speak to the issues of the historical construction of black motherhood, but tie those issues more directly to contemporary characters' relationships to them.

Willow Springs is utopian in the sense that it functions as an island of mother love, an island where, for generations, women have raised their children without interference from the mainland culture. Naylor allows herself the indulgence, if you will, of imagining just what such a place would be like. In that sense it also functions as symbolic of a mythic African maternal presence in all of black women's lives. What is so interesting about Naylor's depiction, as well as those of the authors mentioned above, is that the mother is never solely an ideal home. She is demanding, powerful, and at times dangerous. The desperation of Toni Morrison's character Sethe, for instance, drives her to kill her own children rather than have them returned to slavery. Part of the island's danger lies in its threat to the mainland culture, to the men who represent it and to the daughters who internalize it. Cocoa herself is vulnerable to Ruby at least in part because she has not embraced her birthright. When George tries to succeed through masculine dominance, he dies. Only in recognizing his own interdependence with others can he survive and thrive. Mama Day and her world view threaten everything George and his world stand for. As long as he is unable to have faith in the unseen, in the apparently irrational, he and all he stands for an endangered. Even accepting a faith in the natural and supranatural would be destructive to many of the thought structures and institutions existing beyond the bridge. Suzanne Juhasz argues that in *Mama Day* the "world beyond the bridge can never be joined with the magic island of mother love without the radical change to its patriarchal nature, a change that seems impossible."[12]

The two worlds of *Mama Day* are the modern city, subject to every kind of fragmentation of space and time imaginable, and the island which runs on mythic time; the history of the island exists simultaneously in the past and the present. Willow Springs's boundaries too are literally fluid, changing with the tide and with the presence or absence of the bridge, the only connection to the mainland. Naylor's use of dual settings in this novel problematizes the issue of identity broached in contemporary black women's writing, outlining the traditions available to them and seeking a tolerable solution through the character of Ophelia/Baby Girl/Cocoa. The three names given to the central protagonist, in fact, illustrate rather well the individual's triple significance. Named by her grandmother and great aunt, Cocoa's identity is layered. She is all three people at once and yet each name/ identity bears a different significance, Ophelia being the great granddaughter, the bearer of past, of tradition; Baby Girl being the future, the hope for generations to come; and Cocoa being the woman of color who exists and acts in the present. She is all three, and the traditional African and maternal aesthetic which guides this naming anchors her here on earth within her family and community. *Mama Day* links black mothering to a gender and ethnic identity which undermines, if not inverts, the destructive fragmentation of capitalism, racism, and patriarchy It restores memory of the past and hope for the future.

The title character, Mama Day, embodies the healing potential available through the African American mother. Not biological mother to anyone but having delivered most of the island's inhabitants, she is given the title Mama, by right of aptitude and honor. At one point in the novel Mama Day even thinks of herself as "Old's mama." She is also Mother to the island in her capacity as keeper of island health and history.

Mama Day and Abigail embody the historical legacy of the island, a legacy of black female power to survive and thrive in adverse conditions. Their embodiment of Sapphira's significance is key, since Sapphira Wade "don't live in the part of our memory we can use to form words" (4). Understanding that comment is essential to understanding the novel since the significance of the African maternal tradition must be grasped from concrete images, from the bodied presence of signs and signifiers. Mama Day reads and understands the world through material signs, reading storms in the behavior of her chickens. It is also then in Mama Day's response to the lush, sensual detail of the novel that Sapphira and her legacy are expressed. She understands context as crucial to the analysis of any situation, constantly reiterating what she knows about people's pasts and about the island's past in studying a sign, or in attempting to work her magic. She frequently invokes female relatives who have died, almost as a prayer or centering device: "Grace, Hope, Peace, and Peace again" (10). As her younger sister and nieces, these four women should have at least helped her bear the responsibility of the family history and tradition. Mama's repetition of their names is a mournful reminder of the cultural and historical weight she bears on her old, tired shoulders, as well as an invocation of much needed peace. The expectations she and Abigail have for Cocoa are understandable only within an appreciation of this weight.

As a conjurer and as midwife and healer Mama Day also embodies

Sapphira's knowledge, carrying on the African-born woman's traditions of knitting body and soul together, easing people through life and death transitions, respecting the presence of the spiritual world in the material and working with both to effect change. Mama Day has psychic ability; she hears the whispering voices of the island's past that tell her what's gone on before. Miranda's second sight usually comes to her when she's performing traditional women's tasks—tending family graves, quilting, brewing tea—connecting her to "other ways of knowing" with the materially feminine. But she also possesses a large helping of mother wit, busying Bernice with walking, planting, cooking and churning in order to strengthen her and to pass the time until spring, knowing full well that Bernice will think the practices to have magical significance. Mama Day performs all of her roles with the use of common sense and natural substances—plants, seeds, charcoal, bone marrow, eggs—operating squarely within the earthly realm from a broader understanding of the natural. Bernice's impregnation seems to rely as much upon mother wit, exercise and nutrition as it does upon the conjure ritual. Whether the ritual is supernatural or not, Bernice's belief in it predisposes her to fertility.

Ultimately, however, Mama Day is only another mother in a line of them extending back to the near-mythic "great great grand Mother" (208) whose name is not known nor spoken by anyone save the narrator. Sapphira comes to Miranda in a dream, calling her daughter, expressing the Mother's significance through her body:

> Flooding through like fine streams of hot, liquid sugar to fill the spaces where there was never no arms to hold her up, no shoulders for her to lay her head down and cry on, no body to ever turn to for answers. Miranda. Sister. Little Mama. Mama Day. Melting away under the sweet flood waters pouring down to lay bare a place she ain't known existed: Daughter. And she opens the mouth that ain't there to suckle at the full breasts, deep greedy swallows of a thickness like cream, seeping from the corners of her lips, spilling onto her chin. Full. Full and warm to rest between the mounds of softness, to feel the beating of a calm and steady heart. . . . (283).

The dream Mother's body, her arms, shoulders, breasts, heart, is a source of strength, sympathy, serenity, and steadiness in addition to being a source of answers.

Cocoa is herself another woman in the Day line who has the potential to rise up as a great grand mother. Miranda thinks, "**the** Baby Girl brings back the great, grand Mother. We ain't seen 18 & 23 black from that time till now.

The black that can soak up all the light in the universe, can even swallow the sun . . . and it's only an ancient mother of pure black that one day spits out this kinda gold" (48). Cocoa's sensitivity about her light skin implies that she does not understand its significance as Mama Day does. At the beginning of the novel she knows little of this import and cares for it less. That Mama Day may be right is confirmed in Cocoa's cantankerous personality certainly, but also in small ways through her need for Abigail and Miranda's function as "living mirrors" and for their sustaining letters (48). Throughout the novel, even as Cocoa assimilates to her urban environment, she depends upon the letters they send, her occasional visits home and the affirmation they provide that tells her who she really is. They convey to her the knowledge that she is not simply another office drone in a large city but someone with a rich history and cultural background, someone who matters very much to a small family and community. Miranda is, in fact, awaiting Cocoa's decision to take over for her and to provide her with the next generation of the Day family before she will allow herself to die.

Traditions of grandmotherly involvement in child-rearing help to establish a strong sense of heritage. Robert Staples documents the prevalence of multigenerational African-American families and notes in particular the common situation of the maternal grandmother raising the children while the mother works.[13] The grandmother's integral role in child-rearing, while honored in Ashanti culture, has often been an economic necessity on this continent. Collins writes, "Although the political economy of slavery brought profound changes to enslaved Africans, cultural values concerning the importance of motherhood and the value of cooperative approaches to child care continued."[14] Everywhere in black women's writing the grandmother looms as a powerful figure both beneficent and threatening: Maya Angelou's grandmother in *I Know Why the Caged Bird Sings,* Eva Peace, Pilate Dead, and Baby Suggs in Morrison's novels, the Grandmother of Hurston's *Their Eyes Were Watching God,* and here Mama Day herself. Clearly their perceived power testifies to their resistance to mainstream degradation of blacks, women, and the aged, but it also imparts to the young a pride in this most maligned flesh and a sense of historical and familial continuity undermined by mass culture.

The Baby Girl, so named in the African tradition by her grandmother in hopes of her survival, is given the "proper" name of Ophelia and the pet name of Cocoa. In her efforts to establish a separate identity, however, Baby Girl seems driven to New York, a place as different from Willow Springs as Mama Day is different from the rigidly ordered George. The most significant evidence that George is Cocoa's antithesis lies in his lack of a mother, the knowledge of which gives him so much pain. George's nameless mother, a fifteen-year-old prostitute/suicide, clearly expresses the devastating effects of a racist, sexist society, when posited along side of the island's alternative visions of motherhood. Although Cocoa and George share the loss of their birth mothers, Cocoa differs substantially from George in that she has an abundance of love and guidance from her "othermothers," Miranda and Abigail, as well as from the closely knit island community. Cocoa's choice of New York and of this man imply that the strength of the mother's love and attraction necessitates and also makes possible Cocoa's departure, although she ritually returns to Willow Springs to replenish herself. Leaving, she takes with her a "hand-stitched counterpane, jars of canned preserves, a basket of potpourri, and a boxful of paper bags marked chest cold, fever, headache, and monthly" (51). Metaphors for the earthly connection derived from her mothers, the gifts appeal to the senses and ease the body. She also returns periodically to keep faith with her Grandmother and with Mama Day.

Naylor expressly announces through the narrative structure that the novel examines a young African-American woman's struggle to live a life informed and strengthened by her cultural and feminine heritage, but not swallowed up in that heritage in the way that George is and Cocoa almost is when Ruby "spells" her. Cocoa fears the destructive power of the mother, surely because she has not yet claimed it for herself. She cannot, therefore, live permanently in Willow Springs, at least not until she has accepted Mama's legacy. Cocoa's departure from New York after the central events of the novel have transpired and her alternative residence in Charleston express her partial acceptance of her heritage. She ceases to see the world as so split—either New York or Willow Springs—and instead finds a midpoint in the southern city, a place from which she can easily make frequent visits to the island.

There seems little indication within the novel that Cocoa is concerned with social transformation; she is not exporting the island ethos to the mainland. She's a practical, contemporary woman—graduate of a business school. The island, however, represents the converse of American business practices. People work only when they need to, create geographically close, multi-generational families, use medicine and medical practices that respect wholeness, practice traditions that unite the entire community. The "assembly-line nutrition" of New York bears no resemblance at all to the apparently abundant peaches, berries, honey, eggs, collard greens, and chickens that Abigail and Miranda prepare (13). Food comes from truck gardens or chicken coops or Dr. Buzzard's beehives and is eaten in season. Candle Walk resists the Christian influence of the original slaveowners and of the mainland world, as does the funeral service for Little Caesar that George attends, even though there is a church on the island and most of the residents have an active faith. The gifts given at Candle Walk must come "from the earth and the work of your own hands," a giving that embodies connection between hand and heart, culture and nature (110). Candle Walk is also a form of non-institutionalized welfare, although to call it that is to demean its spirit:

> Candle Walk was a way of getting help without feeling obliged. Since everybody said, "Come my way, Candle Walk," sort of as a season's greeting and expected a little something, them that needed a little more got it quiet-like from their neighbors. And it weren't no hardship giving something back—only had to be any bit of something (110).

In this manner, the community can share the wealth with whomever needs it in a healing rather than divisive gesture.

In her essay "Uses of the Erotic," Audre Lorde speaks of healing the split between mind, body and spirit, a split which has been imposed by Western civilization. She argues that this integration—eros—is a source of creativity, of healing, of energy, and ultimately of resistance to forces that would divide us from ourselves and from one another. She argues that claiming "the power of the erotic in our lives can give us the energy to pursue genuine change within our world."[15] The economy of Willow Springs as well as its eating and work habits and cultural traditions express such an erotic vision. They provide healing to the island inhabitants and illustrate a radically different way of operating from the urban world of New York City. Furthermore, the alternative customs are all respectful of the fact that the inhabitants live on an island. In other words, they treat their homes and their people as the nonrenewable resources that they are and therefore respect the circular nature of interpersonal and interplanetary relationships. Naylor draws particular attention to the fact that the island is not a part of either Georgia or South Carolina, although both have vied for it. It is not a part of any country and, as such, is both its own country and a parallel to the planet Earth, inasmuch as Earth is an island within space. It is integrated and unified, like an egg from one of Mama Day's beloved chickens.

The novel's language challenges standard usage in much the same way as other African-American writers have challenged notions of "standard English" as adequate. A lush, tropical jungle of concrete detail, *Mama Day* is composed of language as rich as the island's air: "air that thickens so that it seems as solid as the water, causing colors and sounds and textures to actually float in it . . . no choice but to breathe in lungfuls of oaks dripping with silvery gray moss, the high leaning pines" (175). The language, like the sensual elements of the island, resists categories and instead straddles and embraces them. George's accusation that Mama is speaking in metaphors when she tries to explain her ways provides us with a cue as Mama thinks: "Metaphors. Like what they used in poetry and stuff. The stuff folks dreamed up when they was making a fantasy, while what she was talking about was **real.** As real as them young hands in front of her" (294). While "metaphor" is the only term available to express the doubling of Mama Day's language, it is inadequate to the situation in which the doubleness is "real," not figurative. The name Peace, for example, always means both the children named Peace, who died, and "peace," the abstract concept. In tending the family plot, Mama Day thinks: "Got Peace, Grace, Hope and Peace again. They never found mama's body, although John-Paul and three of his brothers dragged the bottom of The Sound for a week. Mother flew off that bluff screaming Peace. And she coulda been put to rest with Peace—and later on, Peace again" (117).

Closely related to the doubled quality of the words is the quality of the silence on the island. The narrator prepares us to listen "without a single living soul really saying a word" in the beginning of the novel, telling us that one could have heard the entire story as she tells it without a word being spoken (10). It is that kind of listening ability at which Mama Day excels, hearing ancestors' voices in the breeze, a woman's hatred in the rustle of the leaves. The bodies of people, as the body of the island and all of its animals, rocks, trees, and plants speak a language beyond metaphor, decipherable to those who attend it.

Naylor's use of two obvious linguistic devices, however, bear mention in this discussion. Sapphira, in name and person, is certainly a reference to and revision of the Sapphire stereotype, implying that the stereotype deliberately defuses and degrades a powerful, even murderous presence in African American history, responding negatively both to the African and feminine alike. Similar to the black mammy, Sapphire renders the dangerous safe for mass consumption, whereas Sapphira summons an African goddess, threatening both white and patriarchal suppression. More complex, Naylor's creation of the 18 & 23 as a reference to the mythical year in which Sapphira, after having borne seven sons, obtains the island and kills Bascombe Wade, and significant of any act or behavior that resembles such a maelstrom, still defies easy classification, used as it is to describe storms, people, events, etc. Both devices testify to the creative and destructive powers of the great grand Mother. In a sense the power of the hurricane

IS the power of the great mother here, connected as she is to the natural world in all its potential. It "could only be the workings of Woman" (251).

Structurally, the novel within the frame leaps between Cocoa's, George's, and the narrator's retelling of the events, moving back and forth in Part I between the two antithetical worlds of the city and the island, seemingly reinscribing the split. Cocoa and George never actually leave the island in "discussing" the events; however, it is there they must go to find "answers." Part II takes place either on the island or en route to it. That the island's philosophy can encompass and even absorb the city is confirmed by Mama Day's visit there to help Cocoa move. Mama Day meets sandwich shop owners and opera-singing streetpersons. She sees what George called the "real" New York, and then carts home cheap souvenirs of the city landmarks to give as gifts on Candle Walk that year: "Folks lucky enough to get one will be sure to prize 'em. It ain't often you're able to display a genuine product from a place like New York" (305). The genuine products of Willow Springs all come from the earth and the work of two hands, while the "genuine product" of New York is a mass-produced trinket, with no connection to the earth, that seems to degrade the very object it enshrines. The seeming naivete of the remark is undercut by islanders' knowledge of the difference. The items therefore lack the threat posed by commodity culture. Willow Springs is distant in space and time from the "big buildings" of New York, but simultaneously very much like it: "Any city is the people, ain't it?" (306).

Mama Day fleshes out in "metaphorical" terms the maternal aesthetic at work in the lives of contemporary African American, middle class women, even as those women struggle to make it in capitalist America. Willow Springs functions as an independent country where the Mother reigns, and it offers, for Cocoa, a grounding in her own heritage, her own identity. Against that backdrop, her life in the U.S. seems not just unfulfilling but oppressive. It is for Cocoa to decide when and if she will accept the challenge offered by Sapphira.

In John S. Mbiti's groundbreaking work *African Religions and Philosophy* he describes the custom of burying or in some way disposing of the placenta and umbilical cord in some spot close to the birth place soon after a child's birth in order to signify to the community that the child has separated from its mother's body and entered the larger body of human society.[16] Recognizing that nonetheless a child remains in close physical proximity to its mother for some time after that, many groups ritually reenact the child's birth between the ages of six and ten, at which time the child formally leaves "babyhood" behind and becomes a productive member of the community. This ritually enforced movement from the nurturant mother space to the active involvement with community is replaced in *Mama Day* with the tendency for young adults to cross the bridge to the mainland, to leave the island behind. The fact that the mother retains an important psychological place in the adult's world, increasingly so as she contemplates motherhood herself, speaks to the primacy of that bond.

It may also reflect, in this country, a greater need for retreats to a nurturant space in a society which consistency undermines the female and person of color and subverts essentially non-dichotomous modes of thinking. Mbiti writes:

> The traditional solidarity in which the individual says "I am because we are, and since we are, therefore I am," is constantly being smashed, undermined and in some respects destroyed. Emphasis is shifting from the "we" of traditional corporate life to the "I" of modern individualism.[17]

Written in 1969 to describe the changing lives of Africans, it could just as easily describe the transition from a preoedipal state of human interconnection to the overdifferentiating stance of European American philosophy inculcated everywhere in "developed" countries and daily penetrating "developing" ones. Conceivable in both psychoanalytic and socio-economic terms, "modernization," or "civilization" if you wish, marks a movement away from the mother, literally and figuratively. The shifting emphasis on wage-earning rather than domestic production, for example, evident in colonized African countries (and earlier in America as well) has led to a devaluing of the mother's contributions to the household and often to her seeking sources of cash income that have taken her away from her children. The long term effects of that devaluation and mother/child separation can be fragmented, alienated cultures which emphasize differentiation rather than connection.

Novels like *Mama Day* expressly resist that movement through the "development" of alternative communities anchored in traditional African notions of interdependence. The extent to which the female characters of these and other novels can embrace that vision of community provides a measure for successful resistance. The novel ends on an affirmation of community as a source of mothering for the women and men who must, in their turn, embrace mothering for the coming generations. Naylor's exploration of the mother is one of the most fully realized in contemporary African American women's literature but also the one least constrained by outside historical influences, arguing implicitly for a separatist space. Given the difficulties encountered by mothers and daughters elsewhere in this body of work, her argument is certainly compelling.

NOTES

All citations to Naylor's *Mama Day* are from New York, Ticknor & Fields, 1996 edition.

1. Helen Fiddyment Levy, "Lead on with Light," *Gloria Naylor: Critical Perspectives Past and Present,* Eds. Henry Louis Gates, Jr. and K.A. Appiah (New York: Amistad Press, 1993), p. 281.

2. Virginia C. Fowler, *Gloria Naylor: In Search of Sanctuary* (New York: Twayne Publishers, 1996), p. 142.

3. Angels Carabi, "Belles Lettres Interview," *Belles Lettres* 7 (Spring 1992): p. 38.

4. Carabi, p. 42.

5. Lindsey Tucker, "Recovering the Conjure Woman: Texts and Contexts in Gloria Naylor's *Mama Day,*" *African American Review* 28, 2 (1994): p. 176.

6. Susan Meisenhelder,"'The Whole Picture' in Gloria Naylor's *Mama Day,*" *African American Review* 27, 3 (1993): 405–19.

7. Susan A. Mann, "Slavery, Sharecropping, and Sexual Inequality," *Signs* 14, 4 (Summer 1989): 774–98.

8. Jacqueline Jones, *Labor of Love, Labor of Sorrow* (New York: Viking, 1994), p. 129.

9. Jones, p. 9.

10. Jones, p. 184.

11. Maya Angelou, "Foreword," *Double Stitch: Black Women Write About Mothers and Daughters* (Boston: Beacon Press, 1991), p. xii.

12. Suzanne Juhasz, *Reading from the Heart* (New York: Viking, 1994), p. 202.

13. Robert Staples, *Black Woman in America* (Chicago: Nelson-Hall, 1973). More recently Patricia Hill Collins writes about the need for community othermothers in *Black Feminist Thought: Knowledge, Consciousness, and the Politics of Empowerment* (Boston: Unwin Hyman, 1990).

14. Collins, p. 121.

15. Audre Lorde, "Uses of the Erotic, the Erotic as Power," *Sister Outsider* (Trumansberg, New York: Crossing Press, 1984), p. 59.

16. John S. Mbiti, *African Religion and Philosophy* (New York: Praeger, 1969).

17. Mbiti, pp. 224–25.

Talking in Metaphors: Language, Knowledge, and "Signifyin(g)" in Gloria Naylor's *Mama Day*

CAROL HOWARD

Readers of Gloria Naylor's *Mama Day* sense fairly quickly that a series of oppositions or complementary terms is being negotiated: man/woman, young/old, north/south, Western medicine/folk remedy, Christianity/hoodoo, mainland/island, slavery/freedom, and so forth. At first glance, these several terms would appear to fall readily into two larger groups that, if one were to borrow an image Naylor herself deploys so crucially at the end of the novel, one might attempt to enter under two columns of a ledger book, on either side of a long dividing line, perhaps under the headings "Western" and "African," if not "debit" and "credit." But Naylor does not, finally, posit the world in terms of fixed binaries, and any effort to record such categories indelibly in one column or the other would quickly lead to a mess of crossings out. Instead, by exploring the relationships between supposed opposites, often through playful rhetorical maneuvers and fantastic imaginative conceits, Naylor questions the very premise of binaries and challenges the possibility that they constitute an irreducible feature of language and knowledge.

A particular binary that Naylor establishes as a theme of the novel and that she complicates rather self-consciously is the semantic split between literal language and metaphorical language. By self-conscious I mean that she both makes this division an explicit source of tension between characters and uses it to alert readers to the enterprise of storytelling itself. In particular, Naylor's deployment of this binary calls attention to the novel's commemoration of the African-American tradition of "Signifyin(g),"[1] a comprehensive tradition of storytelling, rhetoric, and hermeneutics.[2] The division between the literal and the metaphorical is foregrounded by the way that two characters in the novel, George and Mama Day, explicitly consider, through dialogue and interior monologue, whether the language they use to communicate is "metaphor" or whether it is, by contrast, what Mama Day identifies as "real." My argument is that Naylor's focus on this semantic

132

divide and on her characters' attitudes toward it not only reveals a playfully self-reflexive attention to the functions of storytelling and Signifyin(g), but bolsters her challenge to the divide that separates truth from fiction—and history from story—and exemplifies her concern for the possibilities of communication across and within cultural and epistemic boundaries.

This challenge and this narratorial self-consciousness are not unique to Naylor, but instead represent characteristic preoccupations of certain postmodern novelists (e.g., Graham Swift), postmodern postcolonial novelists (e.g., Salman Rushdie), and postmodern African-American novelists (e.g., Ishmael Reed). The conceptual preoccupations of these novelists are also those of some literary theorists of both postmodernism and postcolonialism, at least, to the extent that postcolonial theory allies itself with postmodern theory.[3] In *The Postmodern Condition,* for instance, Jean-François Lyotard's attention to the epistemological implications of the tension between "scientific knowledge" and what he calls "narrative," and his recognition that the primacy of scientific knowledge reflects the "perspective" or "choice" of the "Occident,"[4] complements the postcolonial critique of the universality of Western metanarratives.[5] Of course, Naylor is writing neither criticism nor theory, not, anyway, according to traditional generic definitions. Nor does she adapt the signal thematic concerns of the postmodern novel, such as fragmentation and chaos, which are typically represented through generic disruption of some kind; to the contrary, through its narrative continuity and its thematic emphasis on spirituality and community, *Mama Day* actively counters the postmodern perspective and aesthetic. Nor, in her presentation of an African-American experience, does she identify a postcolonial experience in the strict or early sense of the phrase, except as she attends to the effects of African diaspora and nationalism. Nevertheless, through her playful self-consciousness—and her self-conscious playfulness—Naylor establishes herself as a novelist-counterpart to such contemporary postcolonial raconteur-culture critics as Trinh T. Minh-ha and Gloria Anzaldúa, writers whose aim is to unsettle and interrogate established cultural, epistemological, generic, and semantic boundaries and norms.

Let me first elaborate upon what I mean by the self-consciousness with which Naylor employs the literal-metaphorical binary by pointing to the novel's climax, a scene in which Signifyin(g) becomes the site of negotiation between two distinct semantic registers and two opposing cultures and world views. We may then consider how this scene is complemented by other self-conscious moments of Signifyin(g) in the text. The scene is that in which the hero, George, has arrived to help his wife Cocoa's great-aunt

Mama Day (Miranda) save her dying grandniece. It is not long after Mama
Day begins to reveal to George the nature of Cocoa's ailment, an ailment
that has been wrought through the jealous and vengeful neighbor Ruby's
conjuring and that therefore traverses the bounds of the physical and the
metaphysical, that communication breaks down. A perplexed George says
to Mama Day:

> "Well, you're talking in a lot of metaphors. But what it boils down to
> is that I can be of some use to you, and I came here for that. So, please,
> what is it, Miss Miranda?"
> It's only in her eyes that Miranda is slowly shaking her head. Metaphors.
> Like what they used in poetry and stuff. The stuff folks dreamed up when
> they was making a fantasy, while what she was talking about was *real.*
> As real as them young hands in front of her.[6]

This moment is one of several in which Naylor draws attention to the division between literal and metaphorical language, although clearly what is
at stake is not simply a function of rhetoric. The disjunction here in the
characters' perceptions of the linguistic register is a symptom of a larger
disjunction between the characters' own epistemic registers. George is the
representative of Western rationalism, while Mama Day is not only a practitioner of hoodoo (*vaudun,* voodoo), but one who has fairly obvious symbolic associations with at least two of the most important *loa* (gods, spirits)
in the tradition: Damballah-wèdo, the serpent god of fertility; and Papa
Legba, the old, physically small, limping god of the crossroads, mediator,
divine interpreter, and seventh son of the primal Fon deity.[7] The diminutive
and elderly Mama Day is a midwife and fertility doctor, as well as a great
reader of "signs," who traverses the crossroads of her island community
with a walking cane designed of wood-carved intertwined snakes;[8] she is
the first-born child of the seventh son of a seventh son of the primal matriarch of her island world, Willow Springs.[9]

In this crucial scene, the tension between the two characters depends on
what appears to be a fundamental rift caused by George's literal-mindedness
and his reliance on empirical reality. Even before the dialogue begins, Mama
Day knows that George's rational worldview will be an obstacle to effect-
ing Cocoa's cure. She awaits George in the mystical "other place," the old
family homestead where the supernatural blends with layers of history and
memory, the place where Mama Day reluctantly undertakes those occult
practices whose effects are sometimes less salubrious and less predictable
than those of her usual fare of healing arts and mundane natural magic. The

reader, in fact, knows that Mama Day has been up the entire previous night enacting a kind of shamanistic ritual. Her incessant burnishing of two relics of the Day family heritage, a walking cane and a ledger book, works as the ritual correlative to what we may assume—the text is suggestive, rather than explicit here—is her communion with and her plea for guidance from the world of ancestral spirits. That she polishes these objects with "Balm of Gilead" (293), an ointment valued for its healing properties, also implies the associative function of this ritual, its function as complement to sympathetic magic.

As George approaches, Mama Day "hope[s] he understands enough to trust her" (294). She describes to George the etiology of Cocoa's ailment and gestures toward its cure:

> "I can do more things with these hands than most folks dream of—no less believe—but this time they ain't no good alone. I had to stay in this place and reach back to the beginning for us to find the chains to pull her out of this here trouble. Now, I got all that in this hand but it ain't gonna be complete unless I can reach out with the other hand and take yours. You see, she done bound more than her flesh up with you. And since she's suffering from something more than the flesh, I can't do a thing without you" (294).

What provokes George's exasperated response—"you're talking in a lot of metaphors"—is precisely Mama Day's esoteric description of the problem. Mama Day speaks wise-woman language, the language of the African *griot,* that esteemed bard figure whose lessons in truth and meaning and history come in the form of "story" or "fiction" or "poetry," at least from the perspective of Western rationalism. What this amounts to, at the level of the sentence, is that Mama Day conveys information through semantic indirection. That is, she enacts the language of Signifyin(g), which, insofar as it is a technique, is a "'*technique* of indirect argument or persuasion,' 'a language of implication,' 'to imply, goad, beg, boast, by *indirect* verbal or gestural means.'"[10] Mama Day tells George indirectly that she has special healing powers that he may not be able to comprehend, that she has consulted history and ancestry for guidance, and that Cocoa's cure can be effected only through George and Mama Day's spiritual union.

This union, Mama Day suggests in this passage and elsewhere, is a merging of strength and belief, the ritual counterpart of which is a joining of hands, the symbolic (from George's perspective) building of what Mama Day identifies variously as a "chain" or "bridge":

> She needs his hand in hers—his very hand—so she can connect it up with all the believing that had gone before. A single moment was all she asked, even a fingertip to touch hers at the other place. So together they could be the bridge for Baby Girl to walk over (285).

By this point, the reader recognizes literal and figurative hands and bridges as central and recurring images in the novel.[11] Both hands and bridges represent community, connectedness, and human creativity and ingenuity. But George, in his distress, has little patience for spiritual bridges and hand-holding, and there is tragic irony in his frantic, futile efforts to save Cocoa by using his talented hands—George is a mechanical engineer with practical skills in construction—to reconstruct the storm-wrecked wooden bridge that links the island community to the mainland. What the people of the island know, and what Mama Day must try to teach George, is that he is building the wrong kind of bridge: this wooden bridge would allow him to rush Cocoa to a modern medical facility on the mainland, but such a rescue attempt would only remove her from the island people who can help George build the *human* bridge that would cure the spiritual disease.

The problem that defeats the possibility of connection between George and Mama Day is both epistemic and rhetorical. For George, to dismiss Mama Day's speech as "metaphor" means two things. First, "metaphor" has a cast of unreality to it. That is, its value as a mode of conveying knowledge in George's empirical world is slight. It is for this reason, this problem of epistemology, that Mama Day thinks, "Metaphors. Like what they used in poetry and stuff. The stuff folks dreamed up when they was making a fantasy, while what she was talking about was *real.*" The point here is that Mama Day is beginning to realize that George perceives a qualitative difference in language that she does not, in this instance, intend. The irony is that her response suggests she places less value in the concept of metaphor than does George. George, at least, a great lover of the classics—Shakespeare, Hemingway, Ellison (60)—is sympathetic to literary language, but such language has a time and a place, which happens not to be here and now. As for Mama Day, there is an endearing philistinism both in the way that she regards metaphor as a thing to be "used" in poetry, as if it were an ingredient in one of her herbal remedies, and in the way she opposes "poetry" to the "real." If Mama Day is in one sense a *griot* figure, she certainly carries no pretensions about her own elevated status as poet-historian, nor about the worth of the activity of storytelling. This attitude sets her apart from, for instance, one contemporary griot, Djeli Mamoudou Kouyaté, of the classic Malian epic *Sundiata,* who celebrates his own role and that of his griot forebears: "without us the names of kings would vanish into oblivion, we are the memory of mankind."[12] It also sets her apart from another character in Naylor's novel, the buffoonish, if sympathetic, hoodoo man Dr. Buzzard, a consummate performer who manufactures mystery around himself and his stories.

Mama Day tellingly opposes "metaphor" not to the "literal," but to the "real," because she identifies the difference as having to do principally with the distance between two distinct systems of knowledge. But it is worth noting that the rift between Mama Day and George is clearly also a problem of rhetoric. Mama Day's language is not simply unbelievable; it also lacks an economy of expression. For George, at a time of crisis, Mama Day's "metaphor," in its indirection, is inefficient and impractical. It is wasteful language, lacking in expediency. There are, of course, both rhetorical and etymological ironies in George's immediate distaste for metaphor. Rhetorical, because the phrase, "you're talking in a lot of metaphors" is itself an indirect, idiomatic way of stating dissatisfaction with rhetorical indirection. Etymological, because the very word "metaphor," which derives from the Greek "meta," meaning "over," and "pherein," meaning "to carry,"—"to carry over" an aspect of one object to another—works as yet another bridge, a semantic bridge, that George chooses to reject.

In the end, George dismisses Mama Day's advice and language as "mumbo-jumbo" (295), thereby suggesting that it is both irrational and, if one were to pursue a stricter sense of the phrase that George does not intend, too African in its use of circumlocution, in its Signifyin(g) play.[13] The ultimate frustration for Mama Day is that, despite her best efforts to convey information in as succint and rational a manner as possible, the face of the unrelenting "stone city boy" (9) has, like one who defies the Medusa, "turned . . . to stone" (295). The despairing George has secured himself emotionally and intellectually against Mama Day's privileged knowledge; he now regards himself as having wasted precious time indulging the idiosyncrasies of a dotty old woman. The moment brims with the tragedy of regret: Mama Day is a reluctant Medusa, but George will die when, like a voodoo initiate,[14] he mechanically and slavishly fulfills her instructions to search the chicken coop "and come straight back here with whatever you find" (295), discovering the meaning of that task only too late.

Mama Day, too, is in despair. When her efforts to communicate go awry, she resorts to mimicry, or "motivated repetition,"[15] a primary exercise of the Signifyin(g) tradition:

"You're a crazy old woman!"
"Yes, I'm a crazy old woman."
"And I was a fool to come here!"
"Yes, you were a fool to come here."
"There's nothing you can give her!"
"There's nothing *I* can give her" (296, emphasis in original).

Mama Day begins to repeat what George says to her, although with slight variations that produce new meanings, that Signify, through the disjunction from his own language. This mimicry is her final effort to make him understand, this time through his very own words, as she attempts to build a semantic bridge that will make those words belong to both speakers. But because George is not a willing participant in this call-and-response operation, the operation fails.

It is important to consider that George's resistance to Mama Day's lesson in humanity, community, and alternative ways of knowing does not bespeak a failure of imagination and outlook that is integral to George's character. Rather, George forges his resistance out of the fear and desperation that come with the circumstances of Cocoa's disease and his lack of familiarity with the ways of Willow Springs. I make this distinction because there is a tendency among critics to overlook the complexities of George's character and to see him as an unflagging agent of Western patriarchal culture. Ralph Reckley, Sr., for instance, writes that "George Andrews is an intelligent man, but his mind is regulated by and hence limited by the rational. To him, the reality of anything could only be known through its physical existence."[16] Virginia Fowler, in the context of a discussion of the relationship between George and Cocoa, writes that "In Naylor's vision, it is the black male who has been corrupted by the value system of the white world, not the black female."[17] The danger of these perspectives on George's character is that those very cultural and epistemic binaries that Naylor challenges appear, instead, to be reaffirmed through the representation of characters whose values and actions are made to seem to fit snugly into one culture or another. The danger in Fowler's argument, in particular, is a perpetuation of a false dichotomy between the southern, rural, matrofocal community of Willow Springs and George's urban world. The implication is that the former is the more authentic African-American experience. But such romantic celebrations of the "folk" have a tendency to risk delegitimizing urban black culture[18] entirely and reducing the black professional classes to a caricature embodiment of racial pathologies.[19]

Naylor's novel avoids such dichotomies and simplifications: George's

resistance to Mama Day's alternative ways of knowing is clearly circumstantial, rather than inherent to his character. We know this because George's
response to Mama Day—"you're talking in a lot of metaphors"—creates a
peculiar echo to a line he has uttered nearly two hundred pages earlier: "I'm
not talking in metaphors" (124). The circumstance is his explanation of what
he identifies as his "passion" for football, a passion he distinguishes from
a mere "pastime," and his sense that a relationship with Cocoa could only
work if she were able to understand that passion. Such an assertion might
aggravate or amuse the reader who recognizes in George's statement only
the adolescent enthusiasm of the male sports fanatic. But I would argue that
George's description of football to Cocoa anticipates his later conversation
with Mama Day, except that in the first instance it is he who tries to convey a sense of the miraculous and of the power of a shared human spirit that
exists outside the bounds of rational experience:

> Since I couldn't be out on the fields in high school, I would help the
> coach design plays, and he often listened to my suggestions because he
> said I had a very rational mind. But there was nothing rational about what
> happened when I became part of the crowd—and the bigger, the better.
> Unless you've been there, you can't understand what it's like. Yet, even
> being there for someone like you wasn't enough—you'd only see twenty-
> two men on a field and seventy-odd thousand screaming people. So why
> tell you what you couldn't believe? The crowd became a single living
> organism—one pulse, one heartbeat, one throat. I've seen it bend down
> and breathe life into disheartened players. I've seen it crush men with its
> hate. And *I'm not talking in metaphors*—it could create miracles (124;
> my emphasis).

George's attempt to convey the power of the collective human will and its
ability to affect, for better or worse, and through no empirically discernible
procedure, a struggling player forms a suggestive counterpart to Mama
Day's own attempt to explain that same phenomenon to George at the climax
of the novel. It is striking that here, too, George identifies the epistemic
problem in relation to the rhetorical problem. The reference to metaphors
again implies an inadequacy of language, a failure of verbal communication across epistemic boundaries. Moreover, just as Mama Day will later
justify explaining Cocoa's ailment to George so that at least he will "know
what he ain't believing" (271), so George in this scene wonders rhetori-
cally, "why tell you what you couldn't believe?" Both fear their interlocutor's skepticism, yet both continue to hope that their efforts to communicate
may not be in vain.

George's insightful, expansive moment describing football should not be regarded as an aberration in a character who is otherwise trapped by bourgeois, urban, alienated norms. We know, for instance, that George, despite his shortcomings, and despite the extent to which he has benefitted from his contact with the African-American island community of Willow Springs, has in his turn taught an initially fearful and defensive Cocoa to appreciate the vibrant cultures and neighborhood communities of his own island world, Manhattan, and the other four boroughs that make up New York City. In other words, if this novel is a *Bildungsroman,* it is one that operates in two directions: George and Cocoa educate one another. He teaches her to look beyond the undifferentiated and alienating crowds of midtown Manhattan and to look beyond her own racial and ethnic prejudices to see the many distinct cultures of New York folk (100). As George explains it: "My city was a network of small towns, some even smaller than here in Willow Springs" (61).

* * *

George's earnest encounters with Mama Day and Cocoa are not the only instances in the text in which Naylor mediates the literal-metaphorical divide, nor are those moments when Signifyin(g) becomes the site of urgent cultural negotiation the only situations that render Signifyin(g) a motif. Such serious efforts to communicate complement Mama Day's less serious Signifyin(g) repartee, which reminds us of the unaffected pleasure of language and storytelling that this novel celebrates. And yet even the exchanges that seem purely incidental moments of linguistic play and comic relief serve a didactic function: scenes of playful Signifyin(g) between Mama Day and other members of the Willow Springs community allow readers to feel the texture of that community, to gain a sense of its social hierarchy and strong communal bond.

One such scene worth examining closely is that in which Mama Day playfully teases Dr. Buzzard, her pretended medical rival, outside the barbershop as the townspeople look on. This scene suggests the way that Signifyin(g), here in the form of ritualized public humor, reinforces the community's social ties and the unofficial hierarchy of its citizens. The situation unfolds this way: Dr. Buzzard brags to a gathered crowd that he has heroically and effectively wielded his "mojo hand" against "haints" in the local woods (92). As the resident snake-oil salesman, Dr. Buzzard uses the occasion to hawk his "mojo hand"—a kind of hoodoo insurance policy against troublesome spirits—to the gathered crowd. Peddling his wares for money, however, is only one reason for the event. A primary function of the gathering is to provide the occasion for Dr. Buzzard's epic boasting about a battle well fought. It is a community ritual: Dr. Buzzard entertains the crowd, while the crowd obligingly lends the benign Dr. Buzzard a feeling of pride. If they pay money for his "mojo hand," they are also clearly paying for his entertainment, for his story.

Mama Day's arrival on the scene complicates the performance. She knows the details of the actual incident that gives rise to Dr. Buzzard's vaunting, since it was she herself who hid in the woods impersonating the very haints against whom Dr. Buzzard wielded not his mojo, but his shotgun (80–81):

> "Sure you ain't used no silver bullets?" Miranda says, coming by on her way from the grocery store. The crowd parts to let her move toward the front, and gets real still to listen.
>
> "What's that, Mama Day?" Dr. Buzzard kinda squints his eyes.
>
> "Silver bullets. See, I was over at the Duvall's the night you talking about, and I heard gunshots coming from them woods and an awful lot of yelling. So I'm just figuring that maybe you put some silver bullets in your shotgun to use on them haints—everybody knows regular bullets won't do no good."
>
> "No, I never bothered to use that remedy myself." Dr. Buzzard starts sweating, and it ain't a bit hot. "But if you heard a gun go off, could be somebody was shooting at coons."
>
> "Or a coon shooting."
>
> Miranda leaves the crowd laughing and stamping its feet. Dr. Buzzard's sales was certain to fall off a little this afternoon (92).

Mama Day holds a special position in Willow Springs: she is a healer and a custodian of history, culture, and story. She is also the undisputed, if unofficial, community leader; as the neighborly narrator puts it: "if Mama Day say no, everybody say no" (6). But Mama Day's authoritative speech is not always prophetic, didactic, or wise. Like the principal god with whom she is associated, Papa Legba, Mama Day is also a trickster, which is to say that she plays practical and rhetorical jokes or "signifies" upon others, especially upon those who appear to need humbling. It is clear, moreover, from the way her exchange with Dr. Buzzard unfolds that Mama Day's wit is dispensed through her position of authority, which tells us something about how humor works in relation to social hierarchy. If there are two models of literary tricksters—one the king's jester, the other the king himself—Mama Day is a version of the latter, Odyssean model.

The dialogue between Mama Day and Dr. Buzzard is a ritual exchange.

It is immediately clear to the entire audience (which is why everyone "gets real still to listen") that Mama Day's initial question inaugurates a contest of wits. Mama Day's opening gambit, like her entire delivery, is so skillful that Dr. Buzzard cannot possibly expect to gain an advantage. By mentioning silver bullets, the common folkloric remedy against werewolves, it is clear to everyone that she is baiting Dr. Buzzard. Silver bullets are universally recognized as a Hollywood cliché, and by alluding to them, Mama Day implies, through the Signifyin(g) strategy of indirect analogy, that Dr. Buzzard's story of the haints is similarly contrived. It is also apparent that, given the personalities involved, the contest is one that Dr. Buzzard is destined to lose, which is why he breaks into an anxious sweat in the middle of the exchange. What creates suspense is that no one knows exactly how Mama Day will deal the final blow or how much humiliation Dr. Buzzard will be forced to suffer.

The punch line, "or a coon shooting" displays Mama Day's rapidity of wit, since the rhetorical play forms an instantaneous response to Dr. Buzzard's own sentence. The line is clever Signifyin(g) play on several counts. First, it deploys its elements through chiasmus, a rhetorical balancing pattern in which the main terms of a phrase are reversed: shooting coon/coon shooting. Second, it employs a variation of zeugma, a rhetorical device in which a word stands in the same relation to two other words, but with different meanings, typically one literal and one metaphorical. Here Mama Day's play on the literal and metaphorical meanings of one word, "coon," allows her to imply two different semantic and syntactical relationships at once. The punch line is funny because the dexterous arrangement of the pun accompanies an appropriation and deployment of a racist slur, the humor of which depends on the very conventionalism of Mama Day's speech. First, "coon shooting" cleverly revitalizes a dead metaphor, the "coon" epithet being a well-worn racist cliché. Second, Mama Day's mimicry of the white racist slur is itself a theatrical staple of Signifyin(g): one black actor's humorous playing out of a racist challenge indirectly signals her actual sympathy for and intimacy with the other black actor. The situation here is similar to the even more conventional moment later in the text when Cocoa confronts George with a *"Nigger—please,"* and George responds that "I didn't marry you because only you could call me a nigger. It's just that you'd never feel the need to explain" (145). The principle here is the same: Cocoa, like her great-aunt Mama Day, initiates a trust game, confident that her partner will not be offended.

Having brought down the bragging Dr. Buzzard a notch or two, Mama Day completes the scene by turning her Signifyin(g) talents on Pearl, another townsperson, whose holier-than-thou posturing, middle-class affect, and somewhat archaic and entirely disingenuous interest in "racial uplift" deserve to be subdued:

> "Ain't it awful," she says to Miranda, nodding toward Dr. Buzzard's crowd. "It makes you downright embarrassed being part of the Negro race, with all them ignorant superstitions. Reverend Hooper says we all should get together and run Dr. Buzzard out of Willow Springs—this is a Christian place and he's doing the devil's work."
> ... "Well, Pearl, the devil—like the Lord—works in mysterious ways. And maybe he's using Buzzard to let folks see the *big* difference between the way he's living his life and the way you're living yours."
> "Why would the devil do that? It would only bring disciples to the Lord."
> "Maybe the devil don't see it that way."
> Pearl stands there kinda puzzled; she ain't got the reputation of being the quickest mind on the island (92–93).

Mama Day uses innuendo to expose Pearl's hypocrisy. Not only does Pearl exploit other people's foibles to congratulate herself on her own sense of righteousness, but, as Mama Day knows, Pearl, despite her pretense to uphold Christian virtues, has been less than charitable toward her emotionally and physically distressed daughter-in-law. The ingenuity of the rejoinder— "Maybe the devil don't see it that way"—is both that Mama Day works from a premise Pearl herself has supplied and that its indirection shields Mama Day against further protest. Pearl is unable to respond partly because of her own dim-wittedness, partly because the statement is conjectural and enigmatic, but also because the authority for the sentiment is projected onto a third party who happens to be a supernatural agent and is therefore incapable of being opposed. The insult, aside from being humorous, is also intended to serve a didactic function: if the rebuke ever sinks in, Pearl may begin to abandon her disdainful airs.

✳ ✳ ✳

In the scenes discussed thus far, Naylor's self-conscious attention to the entertainment and didactic purposes of Signifyin(g)—self-conscious because we hear not only the Signifyin(g) exchange, but the audience's response and the narrator's commentary—raise questions of communication across and within cultures. Such moments are not simply isolated incidents, but constitute part of a motif that runs throughout the text, and to which the

narrator explicitly draws attention in the very opening of the novel, the section that establishes the geographical and historical setting, as well as the
mythic scope of Willow Springs. One particular anecdote the narrator tells
during the *mise en scène,* the story of "Reema's boy," anticipates the later
difficulty between George and Mama Day and serves as a parable of communication across and within cultural boundaries. It is also intended as a
cautionary lesson in communication for the reader, an instance of "schooling"[20] in which we readers are asked to consider our own relationship to
the stories and conversations we encounter in the text and to reflect on the relationships between speaker and audience, between narrator and listener:

> Think about it: ain't nobody really talking to you. We're sitting here in
> Willow Springs, and you're God-knows-where. It's August 1999—ain't
> but a slim chance it's the same season where you are. Uh, huh, listen.
> Really listen this time: the only voice is your own. . . . Pity . . . Reema's
> boy couldn't listen, like you . . . or he woulda left here with quite a story
> (10).

The passage is an unsettling one, for any reader who is "really" listening
recognizes that he or she is indirectly implicated in the round of Signi-
fyin(g) play that has ostensibly been directed at "Reema's boy" and in which
the reader has complacently been taking great pleasure.

The anecdote of "Reema's boy" is generated through the peculiar relationship between narrator and subject. The narrator, in this case, is neither
George nor Cocoa, the two characters who hold a dialogue of monologues
with one another through much of the novel. Rather, we hear the collective
folk voice of the town, a limited-omniscient voice cast in the first-person
plural who surfaces periodically in the text, and whose distant closeness
resembles that of Faulkner's neighborly narrative voice in "A Rose for
Emily."[21] This narrator tells the story of "Reema's boy," the unnamed scholar,
presumably a cultural anthropologist, who has been educated in "one of those
fancy colleges mainside" (7), and who decides to embrace his heritage by
conducting an appreciative study of Willow Springs. The problem is that
for all the young man's enthusiasm for his culture of origin, he is so caught
up in his own scholarly method that—as the narrator sees it—he fails to
learn how to communicate with the people of Willow Springs and ends up
both alienating them and compromising the results of his research. Like
George, this young man senses how special Willow Springs is, but his elite
university training and his newly adopted middle-class values impede his
ability to interact with the very people whose culture he seeks to embrace.

The folk narrator expresses "pity" (7) for the young man's benightedness, but it is clear to the reader that the "pity" is ironic and that the narrator is actually expressing dissatisfaction with the anthropologist's youthful arrogance. By willfully misconstruing the young man's use of language, the narrator enacts Signifyin(g) play to undermine his academic pretensions. When the young man desires to "put Willow Springs on the map," he means that he wants his research to make the island community have consequence in the world at large. The narrator Signifies at the young man's expense by taking the idiomatic expression literally:

> We was polite enough—Reema [his mother] always was a little addlebrained—so you couldn't blame the boy for not remembering that part of Willow Springs's problems was that it got put on some maps right after the War Between the States (7).

The context for the actual map "problem" is that Willow Springs, having been charted at least by some American map-makers (although later George becomes frustrated when Willow Springs fails to appear on a standard map), has become coveted territory to Georgia and South Carolina, both of which states would like to claim the island as their own, not for its cultural heritage, but for its prime real estate. By intentionally mistaking metaphorical language for literal language, thereby creating a gap of miscommunication, the narrator is able to make the intellectual, university-educated young man seem particularly dull, and to heighten the cultural differences the young man would like to minimize. Further, by strategically confusing the activity of the anthropologist with that of the cartographer, the narrator deflates the attribute of which the young man seems most proud.

In another instance of Signifyin(g), the narrator deliberately mistakes the young man's technical language for something much more commonplace. When the young man earnestly records in his book that he has conducted "'extensive field work,'" the narrator responds "ain't never picked a boll of cotton or head of lettuce in his life" (7). The pun, obviously, is to confuse two senses of the anthropologist's phrase; the effect is a skillful insult across class boundaries. The pretensions of the middle-class academic who never engages in manual labor are bathetically construed as effeteness by the rural, working-class narrator. This playful insult is reinforced by the narrator's refusal to name the young man, except in relation to his mother. "Reema's boy" can be regarded simply as a southernism, but, given the context, it also thwarts any self-aggrandizing impulse the anthropologist might possess, and effectively infantilizes him. The conflict, it seems, is generational as well as cultural.

Instructive though they may be, these instances are isolated one-liners. Far more significant and wide-ranging is the narrator's complaint that the anthropologist fails to conduct his research effectively because he is unable to communicate with the people he interviews. At the center of this miscommunication—and central to the question of Signifyin(g) in this novel— is the anthropologist's search for the etymology and definition of "18 & 23," a phrase that is peculiar to Willow Springs vernacular and that the anthropologist enthusiastically seizes upon in his examination of the culture's "'unique speech patterns'" (7). Alternately used as noun, verb, and adjective, the phrase is a wandering signifier whose exact meaning shifts with each articulation and each new context, but whose connotations are roughly the same in each instance. "18 & 23" implies actual or potential brazen behavior, and the narrator defines the phrase by way of several illustrations:

> But ain't a soul in Willow Springs don't know that little dark girls, hair all braided up with colored twine, got their '18 & 23's coming down' when they lean too long over them back yard fences, laughing at the antics of little dark boys who got the nerve to be 'breathing 18 & 23' with mother's milk still on their tongues. . . . [And] who don't know that old twisted-lip manager at the Sheraton Hotel beyond the bridge, offering Winky Browne only twelve dollars for his whole boatload of crawdaddies— 'tried to 18 & 23 him,' if he tried to do a thing? (4).

In lieu of arriving at a fixed definition for contemporary vernacular usage, the anthropologist cleverly hits upon a plausible etymology: he concludes the phrase "was really 81 & 32, which just so happened to be the lines of longitude and latitude marking off where Willow Springs sits on the map" (8). According to the narrator, the anthropologist accounts for the reversal of the numbers in everyday speech as the community's way of "'asserting our cultural identity,' 'inverting hostile social and political parameters'" (8).

The narrator ridicules this explanation for its presumptuousness, and this ridicule seems warranted, in part because the anthropologist appears to have glibly mistaken a temporal marker for a spatial one, and in so doing has overlooked an empirically unverifiable indigenous history in favor of the scientific safety of geographical measures that are universally recognized. That he does so lends irony to the narrator's Signifyin(g) play over the idiomatic line "put Willow Springs on the map," since it seems the anthropologist does, in the end, try to fix the meaning of this dynamic signifier "18 & 23" through the cartographer's terms. In fact, "18 & 23" derives not from the coordinates on the map, but from the events of the year 1823, the originary moment in Willow Springs history, events that are not, for the most part, recorded on paper, but in the collective unconscious of the community (4). And yet the reader, who, through a narrative conceit, paradoxically possesses an approximate knowledge of the unknowable events, recognizes that 1823 is the year that the African-American community won its independence through the audacious "18 & 23" exploits of the Day family matriarch, Sapphira Wade, a conjure woman who successfully resisted slavery and gained legal ownership of Willow Springs. But in contemporary vernacular usage, it is the mood or spirit of "18 & 23" that lingers, rather than any historical incidentals. The name of Sapphira Wade and the details of her history "don't live in the part of our memory we can use to form words" (4).

One could adduce rational explanations for the way this tradition reveals itself. One could argue, for instance, that the peculiar manifestation of the revelation can be attributed to the fact that Willow Springs history has been disseminated primarily through oral, rather than literate, means, and that oral transmission works differently from literate transmission. One could point out that the impulse of the anthropologist, the man of letters, is to stabilize for literate posterity that which has semantic dynamism in an oral culture. And since orality alone cannot account for the obscurity of the details of this history, one could add that all romantic creation myths of cultural and national origins account for the genesis of a people in ways that allow that people to experience a sense of pride and patriotism, despite the fact that the details of such stories may be cryptic or may seem scientifically or historically implausible. In fact, the anthropologist's own explanation of the etymological inversion is not so very wrongheaded, given that the phrase, as it happens, represents a way of "asserting our cultural identity."

But such rational explanations seem to be beside the point. The narrator implies that the anthropologist misses what is most important about the history and the usage of the phrase "18 & 23," which is its vibrancy, its ability to allow each speaker to Signify, to create meaning anew with each usage and to claim Sapphira's history as his or her own. The point of the phrase is not to secure a definition, for the effect of such stability is that the very culture the anthropologist embraces as his own willy nilly becomes a museum piece, an object of anthropological inquiry. The anthropologist should learn, instead, why the nature of the phrase is to elude fixed definition. As the narrator describes it: "He was all over the place—What 18 & 23 mean? What 18 & 23 mean? And we all told him the God-honest truth: it was just our way of saying something" (7). The anthropologist's persistence, and his likely exasperation with such enigmatic responses as "it was just our way of saying something," anticipates George's mood during the miscommunication with Mama Day. Both men evince an immediate frustration with, rather than a willingness to understand, semantic indirection:

> If the boy wanted to know what 18 & 23 meant, why didn't he just ask? . . . He coulda asked Cloris about the curve in her spine that came from the planting season when their mule broke its leg, and she took up the reins and kept pulling the plow with her own back. . . . (8).

The "boy" had indeed been asking what "18 & 23" means, but the narrator's point is that he had been asking the wrong way, and that the way he asked indicated that he did not know how to understand any response he might receive.[22] Of course, one can approximate a meaning for "18 & 23" based on the common elements of its usage, and one does not need to hear the narrator's recounting of the travails of townsfolk to gather that the currency of the phrase had something to do with the possibility of survival through adversity. But this again misses the point that "18 & 23" is the manifest linguistic trace, paradoxically the sign and the signifier, of a history whose signified object is by its nature obscure.

At the center of this miscommunication is Willow Springs cosmogony itself. "18 & 23" is the trace of the life of that mythic matriarchal Presence, Sapphira Wade. Each enunciation of the phrase is a reinvention of that life; it is an affirmation of the speaker's connection to that life. That "18 & 23" is a wandering signifier should come as no surprise, for Sapphira Wade herself is a wandering signifier, as is her act of genesis, which is worth quoting at length:

> Everybody knows but nobody talks about the legend of Sapphira Wade. A true conjure woman: satin black, biscuit cream, red as Georgia clay: depending on which of us takes a mind to her. . . . And somehow, some way, it happened in 1823: she smothered Bascombe Wade in his very bed and lived to tell the story for a thousand days. 1823: married Bascombe Wade, bore him seven sons in just a thousand days, to put a dagger through his kidney and escape the hangman's noose, laughing in a burst of flames. 1823: persuaded Bascombe Wade in a thousand days to deed all his slaves every inch of land in Willow Springs, poisoned him for his trouble, to go on and bear seven sons—by person or persons unknown. . . . The wild card in all this is the thousand days, and we guess if we put our heads together we'd come up with something—which ain't possible since Sapphira Wade don't live in the part of our memory we can use to form words (3–4).

The narrator poses the events of the cosmogony, the "thousand days," in several forms, as a way of representing their indeterminacy. The variance of detail reinforces the status of the events as wandering signifier, or, as the narrator puts it, as "wild card." Sapphira's floating racial identity and the difficulty of naming her suggest that she, too, is fundamentally unrepresentable; she is a wandering signifier, never quite signified, the creator of meaning and history and genealogy. She, therefore, may be even more fundamentally associated than her great-granddaughter Mama Day with Papa Legba, "the wild card of Fon metaphysics, the wandering signifier" (Gates 23). Or, to put it in terms of the other major theological tradition that informs the novel, Sapphira Wade is the Logos, the Living Word, rather than the dead letter of the text.

Even the name the reader has access to, Sapphira Wade, is ultimately a kind of intertextual joke, a Signifyin(g) ruse. A "Sapphire" is one of the most pervasive stereotypes of African-American women and derives from the domineering, emasculating character of that name in the *Amos 'n' Andy* radio series beginning in the 1920s; the actress who played Sapphire was Ernestine Wade. "Sapphira" is also the name of the abusive white mistress in Willa Cather's *Sapphira and the Slave Girl*,[23] while "Wade," the surname bestowed upon Sapphira by the Norwegian slave owner, is the name borne by the mid-ninteenth-century abolitionist senator from Ohio who denounced the fugitive slave laws and other proslavery measures. ("Bascombe," the Norwegian slave owner's given name, recalls another abolitionist Ohioan, Henry Bidleman Bascom, the Methodist minister whose outspoken abolitionism resulted in a fundamental split in the Methodist church in 1844.)

In Biblical currency, the name Sapphira is synonymous with "liar," Sapphira being that woman, who, with her husband Ananias, is struck dead for withholding from the apostles part of the proceeds of the sale of a parcel of land, thereby, as Scripture construes it, "lying" to the Holy Spirit (Acts 5:1–10). This association of Sapphira Wade's name with that of the summarily smote Biblical liar is ironic, since it is through her seductive "lying" (her conjuration, her persuasive language, her creation of stories) that Naylor's Sapphira, like the legendary Scheherazade, not only survives the thousand days—and perhaps a thousand and one nights—but triumphs over adversity and the man who owns her.[24] In Naylor's text generally, "lies" does not signal a morally reprehensible act, a "falsehood," as it does in standard (white) usage, for "lies" in the Signifyin(g) tradition connotes "figurative discourse, tales, or stories" (Gates 56). In Sapphira's moral order, the truth is in the telling, in the Signifyin(g) act. But so is the lie. As the narrator confidently explains it: "It ain't about right or wrong, truth or lies; it's about a slave woman who brought a whole new meaning to both them words" (3).

Sapphira's creationary moment, the thousand days, might be said to authorize the festival of language and story that obtains throughout the novel. There is a great deal of inventive rhetorical play that attests to Naylor's sheer love of language and text, and that comes in the form of clever negotiation between the literal and the metaphorical, as well as through the thickly spun web of allusion that covers this narrative. Such play is sometimes epic in scope, as, for instance, when Naylor reprises the cosmic storms of Shakespeare and Hurston. Other times it occurs at the level of the sentence, often poignantly, as when Naylor recasts Morrison's plangent "circles and circles of sorrow," for Sula Peace, as "circles and circles of screaming" for Peace Day (284). The most resonant single instance of such play, one that manipulates the literal-metaphorical divide, is also the most obvious—the "heartbreak" motif, which culminates when George's metaphorically heartbreaking passion for Cocoa leads him to ignore the medical condition, a heart murmur, to which he otherwise devotes such scrupulous care, thus allowing his heart literally to break for love of her. These provocative instances of Naylor's self-conscious literariness complement those scenes of Signifyin(g) between characters. The combined effect of these celebrations of language and story is to honor and to elucidate the culture and the myth of Naylor's imaginary world, and to foster the possibility of connection to the fictional and non-fictional worlds that exist "beyond the bridge."

NOTES

1. This tradition has been accorded full theoretical, historical, and literary critical investigation in Henry Louis Gates, Jr.'s watershed *The Signifying Monkey: A Theory of African-American Literary Criticism* (New York: Oxford University Press, 1988). I employ Gates's representation of the term as "Signifyin(g)," the capital "s" marking the distinction from standard white usage, the parenthetical "g" registering the black vernacular tradition's conventionally oral usage of the word. For a thorough explanation of this practice, see Gates, p. 22.

2. This is not to assume that Naylor is closer to or more closely informed by the African-American tradition than by the Western European tradition that clearly also informs her work; this is only to suggest the novel offers an appreciative presentation of the tradition of Signifyin(g).

3. For a lucid discussion of both the oppositions and allegiances between postmodern critical theory and postcolonial theory, see Bill Ashcroft, Gareth Griffiths, and Helen Tiffin, *The Empire Writes Back: Theory and Practice in Post-Colonial Literatures* (London: Routledge, 1989), pp. 155–65.

4. Jean-François Lyotard, *The Postmodern Condition: A Report on Knowledge*, trans. Geoff Bennington and Brian Massumi (Minneapolis: University of Minnesota Press, 1984), pp. 7–8.

5. See the discussion of the implications of theories of postmodernism—especially that of Lyotard—for a postcolonial critique of Western epistemologies in Ashcroft, Griffiths, and Tiffin, pp. 165–66.

6. Gloria Naylor, *Mama Day* (New York: Vintage, 1988): 294. All subsequent in-text citations will be to this edition.

7. Gates, p. 23. Gates offers a comprehensive treatment of the complexities of Legba's character, and his relationship to language, story, and the production of meaning. Gates traces the Legba figure through several incarnations in Africa, the Caribbean, and the United States, and establishes the relationship between Legba and the Signifying Monkey figure of African and African-American tradition.

8. Lindsey Tucker describes some of these associations, as well as the representation of hoodoo in *Mama Day*. See "Recovering the Conjure Woman: Texts and Contexts in Gloria Naylor's *Mama Day*," *African American Review* 28.2 (1994): 173–88, esp. 181–84. Also, see Gates, who demonstrates the fundamental relationship between African-Caribbean-American socio-religious traditions and African-American literary and linguistic practices and epistemology (pp. 3–43).

9. See Tucker for a discussion of the relationship between Naylor's mythical Willow Springs and the actual Gullah Islands, p. 180.

10. Quoted in Gates, p. 54; his italics. Roger D. Abrahams, *Deep Down in the Jungle: Negro Narrative Folklore from the Streets of Philadelphia* (Chicago: Aldine Publishing, 1970), pp. 66–67, 243.

11. For a discussion of the significance of hand imagery, especially in the context of healing and conjuring in *Mama Day*, see Virginia C. Fowler, *Gloria Naylor: In Search of Sanctuary* (New York: Twayne, 1996), p. 119.

12. *Sundiata: An Epic of Old Mali,* ed. D. T. Niane; trsl. G. D. Pickett (1960; Essex, Eng.: Longman, 1994) p. 1.

13. Gates discusses the meaning and etymology of "mumbo jumbo," pp. 220–21.

14. Tucker reads this scene as a metaphorical initiation rite, pp. 182–83.

15. Gates, p. 66.

16. Ralph Reckley, Sr., "Science, Faith and Religion in Gloria Naylor's *Mama Day,*" in *20th Century Black American Women in Print: Essay by Ralph Reckley, Sr.,* ed. Lola E. Jones (Acton, MA.: Copley, 1991), p. 94.

17. Fowler, p. 103.

18. For an excellent discussion of the romantic mythology surrounding the southern, rural black folk experience and its relationship to the black urban experience, see Hazel V. Carby, "The Quicksand of Representation: Rethinking Black Cultural Politics," *Reconstructing Womanhood: The Emergence of the African American Woman Novelist* (New York: Oxford University Press, 1987).

19. This is not to suggest that Naylor does not identify a collective malaise among the black middle class. In an interview with Fowler, Naylor describes her refiguring of Dante's *Inferno* for *Linden Hills:* "I just saw that it would be a perfect fit for what I wanted to say about the black middle class, and to say about life in America for the black middle class" (Fowler, "Appendix," p. 149). My point, nevertheless, is that the lives and values of Naylor's middle-class characters defy quick judgments.

20. See Gates for a discussion of the black tradition of "schooling," p. 84.

21. Faulkner's presence can be felt in much of Naylor's work. Naylor herself acknowledges the importance of *As I Lay Dying* to *Mama Day* (Fowler, "Appendix," p. 152). Also worthy of note is Naylor's choice to link together her several novels through a continuous fictional geography, a device that recalls the one employed by Faulkner in his creation of Yoknapatawpha County.

22. Fowler notes that Naylor "repeatedly read" Zora Neale Hurston's *Their Eyes Were Watching God* "while she was working on the storm scene in *Mama Day*" (Fowler, p. 104). It may be worth considering the possibility that Hurston's autobiography provides an intertext for the anthropologist episode. *Dust Tracks on a Road* tells of Hurston's own inept beginnings as a cultural anthropologist (1942; New York: HarperCollins, 1991). Like the anthropologist of *Mama Day,* Hurston is from the rural South, but ends up at an ivy league school, Barnard College, where she studies with the renowned anthropologist Franz Boas, who is on the faculty of Columbia (George's alma mater in *Mama Day*). Boas sends Hurston back to the South on an anthropological mission. As Hurston describes it:

My first six months were disappointing. I found out later that it was not because I had no talents for research, but because I did not have the right approach. The glamor of Barnard College was still upon me. I dwelt in marble halls. I knew where the material was all right. But, I went about asking, in carefully accented Barnardese, 'Pardon me, but do you know any folk-tales or folk-songs?' The men and women who had whole treasuries of material just seeping through their pores looked at me and shook their heads. No, they had never heard of anything like that around there. Maybe it was over in the next county (127–28)

Hurston relates her failures as an anthropologist from the perspective of one who has learned a difficult lesson. Unlike Naylor's anthropologist, Hurston later learns how to communicate with the people she wants to interview.

23. Helen Fiddyment Levy has argued for thematic similarities between Naylor and Cather. See Levy's "Lead on with Light," *Gloria Naylor: Critical Perspectives Past and Present,* ed. Henry Louis Gates, Jr. and K. A. Appiah (New York: Amistad, 1993), pp. 264–84.

24. In her interview with Fowler, Naylor announces that "you know Sapphira is Scheherazade" (Fowler, "Appendix," p. 152).

This Mumbo-Jumbo: Magic and Vocabularies in Gloria Naylor's *Mama Day*

JOHNNY LORENZ

> Piece the world together, boys, but not with your hands.
> —Wallace Stevens, "Parochial Theme"

> The mind is everything.
> —Gloria Naylor, *Mama Day*

Gloria Naylor's use of the fantastic in *Mama Day* functions as part of the novel's general strategy to take—as well as to encourage—an approach to history that is reverent and engaging. The presence of conjure in the book might make a case for conjure's own extra-textual possibility, but more importantly it functions as the manifestation of legacy and inheritance and, consequently, as a means by which characters recuperate histories and forge communities. By constructing overt and subtle binaries involving Willow Springs and anywhere "beyond the bridge,"[1] the novel creates situations wherein characters—most notably George—must reconstruct their realities to account for, if not accommodate, the new and the other. George readily admits to a personal philosophy of living in the *now,* believing, as he was taught in the boys' shelter, that "the present is *you*" (26). His stubborn independence is challenged not only by Cocoa's love, but—more specifically— by the prospect of her death and by the unusual demands placed on him by Mama Day to save Cocoa's life. Cocoa's assertion midway through the novel can be read as a challenge to George's construction of individual identity: "A person is made up of much more than the 'now'" (127). We are not the sole authors of our life stories; our communities and our histories do not simply constitute a backdrop within which an individual performs. I will argue that George's authorial pretensions limit his ability to deal with the outside forces that actively shape his life.

In addressing the motif of the quilt, Susan Meisenhelder suggests that Mama Day self-consciously weaves the past into the present, thereby confronting history and making meaning:

This notion of history as a quilt, more than simply a way of chronicling the past, is a complex weaving of past, present, and future. The quilt Mama Day stitches is, for instance, not just a historical "document" of a dead past, but a tangible bridge between herself, Abigail, and the children of Cocoa's . . . The result of weaving individuals, past and present, pain and joy together is not simply aesthetic beauty but also spiritual strength, psychic health, and social vitality.[2]

The result is also a heightened degree of agency. What Mama Day does with her hands, she does with her mind; she does not simply accept the night-mare of history to which Joyce referred, she transforms it. Assembling the old scraps of fabric for the quilt awakens painful memories, but she brings the suffering into the pattern as well: "It was too late to take it out of the quilt, and it didn't matter no way. Could she take herself out? Could she take out Abigail? Could she take 'em all out and start again? With what?" (138) The quilt is document and expression. While making meaning of experience, Mama Day is also a student of history. She lives in the "now," but her mind leans on the past in order to shape the future. As George enters the chicken coop, only Mama Day appreciates the magnitude of the situation; this appreciation, however, does not keep her from feeling helpless. She feels the moment resonate with the force of her family's history, and she reads the shape of two possible futures. But everything now depends on George. The course of events does not run like a thread through her hands.

The novel manifests itself as a sort of quilt, an assemblage of pieces, of different voices. The design of *Mama Day,* in fact, is a powerful expression of Bakhtin's understanding of the kind of writing in which a novelist nec-essarily engages:

> The novelist does not acknowledge any unitary, singular, naively (or conditionally) indisputable or sacrosanct language.
> . . . the human being in the novel is first, foremost and always a speak-ing human being; the novel requires speaking persons bringing with them their own unique ideological discourse, their own language.[3]

Much as Faulkner does in *As I Lay Dying,* Naylor stitches together the voices of various "speaking human beings" (. . . Cocoa, George, an unidentified resident of Willow Springs). This tactic draws attention to the fact that these characters speak different languages within one language; each character constructs a discrete reality built with words. And by offering different ac-counts of the same event, the novel reveals that any account of the past is necessarily fictive. Naylor's book embraces Trinh T. Minh-ha's insistence in undermining the imagined division between history (privileged as truth-writing) and story; we cannot ignore the "transformation, manipulations, or redistributions inherent in the collecting of events."[4] As Cocoa says, "there are just too many sides to the whole story" (311). Indeed, the "whole story" is an impossibility. In his *Tropics of Discourse,* Hayden White reminds us that historical facts "are not so much found as constructed by the kinds of questions which the investigator asks of the phenomena before him."[5] When Mama Day discovers the "Conditions of Sale" for Sapphira Wade, she recognizes that official truths—often written truths—are one more kind of fiction: "The paper, itself, means nothing to Miranda. All Willow Springs knows that this woman was nobody's slave" (280). Competing histories also make an appearance in the conflicts that arise between lovers. Recall how George and Cocoa declare separately, "Our worst fight ever. And it was all your fault" (230, 232). Each, of course, goes on to give entirely different accounts of what happened that night, accounts that can be both "true" and conflicting because they pursue different questions. In weaving together the threads of distinct personal narratives, *Mama Day* moves away from giving an account of the truth; the text privileges not truth but experience.

While George finds strength in himself and in the opportunity to define that self in the *now,* Mama Day's strength comes principally from "reach[ing] back" (294) to her past and her ancestry. Larry R. Andrews comments in "Black Sisterhood in Naylor's Novels" that "female power is *there* in the legendary past for the females of Willow Springs to learn, to accept, and to draw strength from in their own lives."[6] I would like to re-frame Andrews' "female power" not in terms of what is *there,* waiting to be used, but rather in terms that privilege the *act* of retrieving and using what is "there." By doing so, we might approach memory more as a creative act than an act of recognition. It would be naive, however, to address history and emphasize its fictiveness at the expense of blunt historical facts; but a historical "fact" must be situated within individual or collective meanings. I do think, however, that Andrews' discussion of female power as being "there," in wait, accessible through memory, finds its basis in moments within the text. Sapphira's visitation in Mama Day's dreams might suggest Mama Day's receptiveness to historical knowledge, but it implies a certain passivity in the act of acquiring that knowledge. The text suggests that the knowledge imparted to Mama Day is "a gift" (280); it is a ghost's gift. As her mind searches for Sapphira's name, Mama Day begins cleaning the abandoned house, as though removing the dust would wipe away the accumulation of years to reveal something lost in time. But the "Conditions of Sale" document that Mama Day discovers is too damaged to make sense of; what written history cannot furnish, Mama Day finds in familial and racial memory. In her dreaming mind, she meets Sapphira. Her comment to Abigail, that "[s]ome things can be known without words" (267) holds true; yet herein we discover a paradox: she needs a word, Sapphira's name, but she must circumvent language in her search. In a similar way, the people of Willow Springs come to know the legend of Sapphira without the need to do research or to even speak: "Everybody knows but nobody talks about the legend of Sapphira Wade" (3); ". . . nobody here breathes her name. You done heard it the way we know it . . . you done heard it without a single living soul really saying a word" (10). I do not mean to suggest that Naylor's book privileges telepathy over language; nevertheless, the characters in this book have the luxury of a history that exists both within *and* outside of the memory of individuals or even a collective.

History, in fact, resides in the land, in the place itself. Willow Springs is its own speaking book. For example, the wind that blows across Willow Springs is a voice, sometimes imparting strange knowledge to those, like Mama Day, sensitive enough to hear (118). The wind, or maybe the old house itself, "speaks" to Cocoa as she and George sit on the porch, revealing to Cocoa that her story is part of a larger narrative of broken-hearted men: *"you'll break his heart"* (224). Willow Springs is a place that speaks history into the present, a place that holds its own kind of power. As Cocoa says to George: "Your maps were no good here" (177). Why?—not only because Willow Springs belongs to no state (neither South Carolina nor Georgia), but because maps offer the "now." Maps locate geography in a fixed frame. But Willow Springs cannot be located simply in the "now": it exists in all time. By giving strange agency to the very soil of Willow Springs and to ghosts, Naylor offers a world in which history never dies. This kind of world, this kind of history, manifests itself in the language of Sethe, in Toni Morrison's *Beloved:*

> Places, places are still there. If a house burns down, it's gone, but the place—the picture of it—stays, and not just in my rememory, but out there, in the world. What I remember is a picture floating around out there outside my head. I mean, even if I don't think it, even if I die, the picture of what I did, or knew, or saw it still out there. Right in the place where it happened.[7]

History exists "out there"—and just as Sethe suggests that a place resonates with history, so does *Mama Day* offer us a world wherein history continues to breathe, to resonate, "right in the place where it happened."

Such a world may (or may not) be fictive, but the imagining of such a world is a strategy for suggesting the agency of history. Naylor's use of the fantastic draws attention to something that is not fantasy: history is not dead. And while the recuperation of histories is an invaluable project to various communities under siege, Naylor's book reminds us that history is not passive. It acts on us. It is not the shipwreck held in the eyes of Walter Benjamin's angel. In her approach to history, Naylor offers us a haunted landscape. And towards the end of the book, we discover that George's voice is another ghost's voice haunting Willow Springs. In the book *Ghostly Matters: Haunting and the Sociological Imagination,* Avery Gordon discusses haunting as a "way of knowing"[8] that occurs when we "admit" ghosts into our vocabularies.[9] But she also suggests that haunting is an expression of history's agency; a ghost might "seize you"[10] and demand to be reckoned with. I would emphasize that the importance of the fantastic in *Mama Day* cannot be appreciated fully if we become enamored of this "other" world we suppose Naylor has constructed. The active hand of history, the haunted imagination—these are not aspects of some "other" world.

I hope I do not contradict myself by arguing that the text does acknowledge, in fact, the damage inflicted by time on cultural memory. The most overt expression of this damage is the gradual dissolution, through generations, of the original idea behind Candle Walk—not only the emphasis on sincere charity, but also the idea of borrowing and creating from the earth. Mama Day recognizes, however, that although Candle Walk changes as newer generations spend more time on the other side of the bridge, the change is not a recent phenomenon: "[Mama Day] says that her daddy said *his* daddy said Candle Walk was different still. But that's where the recollections end—at least, in the front part of the mind" (111). (And once again the text appeals to another kind of memory, one that moves beyond individual experience to include the memories of generations past.) The erasure of histories is touched on, more subtly, by the relationship between Mama Day and Sapphira, a great-grandmother and visiting spirit. The opening page immediately takes us into the past, to Sapphira Wade, a "true conjure woman" (3). The spiritual strength and the extraordinary abilities we associate with Mama Day find their source in Sapphira, but the text makes it clear that Mama Day's self-knowledge and her historical sense are not enough to reclaim parts of her cultural history abandoned by time's progress. She will never know Sapphira's name: "a missing key to an unknown door" (280); "I can't tell you her name, 'cause it was never opened to me" (308). In "Cultural Identity and Diaspora," Stuart Hall discusses the importance of this kind of loss:

Who has not known, at this moment, the surge of an overwhelming nostalgia for lost origins, for 'times past'? And yet, this 'return to the beginning' is like the imaginary in Lacan—it can neither be fulfilled nor requited, and hence is the beginning of the symbolic, of representation, the infinitely renewable source of desire, memory, myth, search, discovery—in short, the reservoir of our cinematic narratives.[11]

Mama Day's and Naylor's own attempts to recuperate a cultural legacy reveal the desire for ancestral knowledge as a motivating force behind the ways in which individuals and communities construct myth—like the myth of Sapphira Wade, a figure whose importance to the community stems as much from what is not known about her life as what has been handed down as certain. Sapphira certainly represents defiance, but she also represents shadowy histories—the ruins and absences of time that complicate our memories and our stories. For the people of Willow Springs, such myth-making becomes an essential tool in the construction of personal and collective identities.

Lindsey Tucker suggests in "Recovering the Conjure Woman: Texts and Contexts in Gloria Naylor's *Mama Day*" that much of the creative power we associate with Mama Day comes out of her own historical sense:

[C]onjure is never far from oaths, entreaties, invocations—from calling up and spell casting. Nor is language, especially the language of the gods, as the myths of Esu Elegbara show, ever far from "making," from creation. Thus, the intertextuality that so characterizes not only Naylor's novel but African American discourse in general is crucially involved in making . . .[12]

Words form the organic, intertextual structure of our consciousness. Gary Storhoff, in his article "'The Only Voice Is Your Own': Gloria Naylor's Revision of *The Tempest*," touches on these same issues of historicity and making, arguing that the text's central theme is "the necessity of establishing narrative authority . . . That her own voice be heard, it is necessary for Naylor to clear a space for 'her own story,' a text among texts."[13] This issue of narrative authority transcends authorship in the sense of writing books to include something much wider—authorship in writing one's own life. If our lives are "texts among texts," then an appreciation for our own historicity—an acknowledgment of legacy and repetition—leads to a heightened degree of agency. George refuses to admit Mama Day's story into the writing of his own story, but only she can appreciate George as a repetition— a manifestation of those men in the Day family, men like John-Paul, who

"*believed*—in the power of themselves, in what they were feeling" (285).
George's failure to appreciate the intertextual resonance of his own life—
to allow Mama Day's story to inform his own—dooms him to repeat tragedy.
George becomes "another one who broke his heart" (308).

Naylor's text suggests that words function as vessels infused with power
through their own historicity, through their own palimpsestic layering of
significance. But it also reveals that "really listening" is an activity wider
than the immediate context of language. I would like to return to the unidentified voice that opens the book:

> Think about it: ain't nobody really talking to you. . . . Really listen this
> time: the only voice is your own. But you done just heard about the leg-
> end of Sapphira Wade, though nobody here breathes her name. You done
> heard it the way we know it, sitting on our porches and shelling June peas,
> quieting the midnight cough of a baby, taking apart the engine of a car—
> you done heard it without a single living soul really saying a word. (10)

In her essay, "Lead on with Light," Helen Fiddyment Levy offers an insightful reading of this passage: "With the insistence on the oral nature of
the printed narrative and its direct, immediate, even telepathic transmission,
the writing daughter Naylor attempts to transcend the limits of modern language and summon the connecting strength of myth."[14] Even so, we know
that the unidentified voice is offering us something that is not entirely true;
we do not hear of Sapphira in the way the people of Willow Springs know
her story, even if, as readers of the printed text, no one is "really saying a
word." Regardless, the point is made: there is a kind of listening that does
not require an audible voice, one that establishes sympathy and allows understanding. I am not speaking of "telepathic" communication. It is the kind
of listening George asks of Cocoa as she walks through New York City,
and, upon "really listening," she begins to appreciate and open up to the
cultural communities she had once commodified. As George explains,

> And best of all, you'd stopped calling people food. You were learning
> the difference between a Chinese, a Korean, a Vietnamese, and a Fil-
> ipino, that Dominicans and Mexicans weren't all Puerto Ricans. You
> could finally pick out German Jews, Russian Jews, Hasidics, and Israelis.
> And when the old Bajan woman took a flower from her cart and pinned
> it in your hair—"'Cause de child, she pretty some"—your eyes got a
> little misty . . . (100)

But it is also the kind of listening that George himself is unable to do when
Cocoa's life and his own are in danger.

What do you do when someone starts telling you something that you just cannot believe? You can walk away. You can stand there and challenge him. Or in my case, you can fight the urge to laugh if it wasn't so pathetic . . . I had stopped listening . . . (286)

George resembles Reema's boy, the cultural anthropologist who, despite all his questions, never knew how to listen (10). George fails to listen because of a failure to believe, but also because of a failure to imagine.

To return to the issue of words and repetition, if language forms a web that ties us to the past, Naylor's use of repeated names in *Mama Day*—names such as Ophelia and Peace—functions not to suggest fate as a vicious, inescapable cycle, but rather as a conscious strategy for remembering and re-constructing legacy. George's admiration for Cocoa's knowledge of her own ancestry is genuine, but also self-serving: "You had more than a family, you had a history" (129). By implying that he lacks a history, George reinforces his own misguided sense of authorship, figuring himself as a hero who is completely self-constructed. Moreover, he is unable to see that Cocoa's life is tied to a long and painful history of women who died young. Mama Day, however, finds strategies for saving Cocoa's life by understanding her suffering in terms of a larger story, "in terms of the whole tradition of suffering women, from Sapphira's slavery to Miranda's mother's grief."[15] George never fully understands Mama Day's commentary—that Cocoa "done bound more than her flesh up with you. And since she's suffering from something more than the flesh, I can't do a thing without you" (294). Through his love for Cocoa, George, although unaware, involves himself dangerously in the troubled and extraordinary history of the Day family.

Much has been written about the novel's construction of two different "worlds"—Willow Springs and New York City. George himself asserts that crossing the bridge to Willow Springs meant "entering another world" (174). One might read Naylor's treatment of this binary opposition as something much more complex than an attempt to hierarchize the rural, Black experience as more "authentic" than the urban lifestyle associated with George. As Gary Storhoff argues, "Manhattan is not the antithesis of Willow Springs but its complement."[16] I would also suggest that we should not adopt a condescending attitude towards George's fit of anger and his failure in the chicken coop. George establishes himself as a sympathetic figure, in part, because of his understandable disbelief, worry and rage. I would argue that he lives in the same world most of us do—a world where lightning *never* strikes twice, a world where a husband would want to find a doctor for his sick wife. The cause of George's death is a tricky issue to re-solve; the simplest explanation is the most literal: that George's rage and physical exertion in the chicken coop make him vulnerable to his congen-ital heart condition. He literally "dies from a broken heart" (118).

Such an explanation is hardly satisfying, for the text gives every indica-tion that George's death is occasioned by much more than a weak heart. Mama Day, in fact, already understands that George might die trying to save Cocoa's life. She knows that George's love will save Cocoa, so she shifts her attention to saving George: "she could guide him safely through that extra mile where the others had stumbled" (285). George does not survive, but neither does he sacrifice himself, for a sacrifice would suggest a degree of understanding on George's part that the text does not support. He fails to realize that what has immediately transpired in the chicken coop is mean-ingful; he thinks it was a "wasted effort" (301). Even as George is dying, he is unaware that his life has been exchanged for Cocoa's: "I didn't know that I was dying" (301).

I would like to frame a discussion of George's death in terms of Mama Day's own declarative: "The mind is everything" (90). I do not think it would be appropriate to read her assertion as solipsistic, but rather as an indica-tion of her own understanding of the fictiveness of our individual realities and of the mind's agency in that continuous act of construction. Naylor's fictive Willow Springs might ignite our belief, or our desire for belief, in the supernatural, but, for the purposes of this discussion, we might use the di-chotomy of Willow Springs and the "world beyond the bridge" in order to appreciate the text's complex treatment of the ways in which individuals operate within and between communities. It is almost too easy to read *Mama Day* as the juxtaposition of two contradictory worlds. As much as the char-acters of the novel tend to construct and refer to this binary of different "worlds," we might adjust the terms of our discussion. Indeed, to speak of two "worlds" is to beg the question, for the language employed suggests contained systems. And when we speak of George's entrance into the "world" of Willow Springs, we are speaking, or should be speaking, of his entrance into a new community, a new culture.

In his introduction to *Writing Culture,* James Clifford asserts that culture is "always relational, an inscription of communicative processes that exist, historically, *between* subjects in relations of power."[17] Furthermore, he states that culture is not a "unified corpus of symbols and meanings."[18] Shift-ing our focus away from binary "worlds" and toward the dynamics that "cul-ture" implies, we might better appreciate Naylor's metaphor of the bridge— for the conceptual bridge George should construct between Willow Springs and the "world" beyond is not merely a means of finding a way back home; it is not even a matter of getting across. A bridge can be imagined as a means of connecting two points or, on the other hand, as a means of measuring the distance between them.[19] For George, a bridge would signify the latter; it is merely a way to "make it back to the real world" (274). I think a more fruitful engagement of this metaphor of the bridge would be to understand the act of connection as necessarily involving a re-constitution of those very "worlds." In other words, the act of "bridging" (as opposed to the "building of a bridge") should transport us away from the construction of "world" binaries and towards something much more complex. This act of bridging, then, necessarily lacks—or immediately destroys—a discrete "bridge." If, as Clifford asserts, culture is not a unified corpus, then it cannot be definitively located. Kenneth Burke's definition for "Bridging Device" offers a useful analogy for our discussion: "When objects are not in a line, and you would have them in a line without moving them, you may put them into a line by shifting your angle of vision."[20] I would like to complicate this analogy by suggesting that a shift in one's angle of vision—in the context of cultural reckoning—might dissolve, or at least undermine, the very metaphor of geography. By casting a cynical eye on the notion of a culture map, we might appreciate more fully the ways in which cultures speak to each other. They are constantly created and re-created, negotiated and re-constituted. Such an appreciation allows us to recognize that when Cocoa shares a laugh with a New York City Greek pastry maker, something is changing that is larger than either one of them.

If cultures construct vocabularies, so do individuals. George's failure in the chicken coop reveals either an unwillingness or an inability to believe in Mama Day. But it also reveals something else—George is a man caught between two vocabularies. I should define "vocabularies" more clearly; by "vocabularies," I mean, loosely, Richard Rorty's name for ways of "describing things."[21] According to Rorty, the vocabularies we use are the words with which we construct our realities. Confronted with an experience that threatens to refigure the character of the "real," George fails to negotiate between the familiarity of his past and the inexplicability of the present. He cannot successfully rationalize away the extraordinary nature of what has taken place in Willow Springs, but he is unwilling to translate this new experience into a usable language for describing the world around him. With Cocoa's life in jeopardy, George prefers to react against this cultural other that demands to be acknowledged. The chicken coop scene manifests itself as a test for George—a test of faith, perhaps, but also a test of the imagination; it is the latter which most informs my discussion here.

While accepting the strange task laid out by Mama Day, George no longer has the equipment to make sense of the world. His philosophy that "the present is *you*" (26) allows for a certain self-sufficiency, but his refusal to trust in anyone but himself prevents him from acquiring an education that only Mama Day can offer—an education that would open the way to new vocabularies. His inability—or unwillingness—to trust in Mama Day renders her instructions meaningless; George can hear only "mumbo-jumbo" (295). These failures—not reconciling his own philosophy with the demands of Willow Springs, not accounting for the supernatural with the limited vocabulary of physics, not allowing interchange between experience and the way in which he speaks—all these failures of the imagination rob George of a strength he needs to withstand Ruby's magic. He slips between the pieces of a reality he has constructed, but that can no longer sustain him.

The one thing that George must surrender to Mama Day is his hands: "She needs his hand in hers—his very hand—so she can connect it up with all the believing that had gone before" (285). Meisenhelder[22] and Donlon[23] both suggest that George's real test in the chicken coop is to bring back his own hands. The surrendering of hands to Mama Day does not necessitate George's complacency or resignation; rather it would signal a shift in attitude and role—to see himself not as the solitary hero, but rather as part of a larger community of love and mutual support. But George cannot believe in Mama Day's mumbo-jumbo, or, to borrow from Mama Day, perhaps George is not "ready to believe" (99). He looks not to the subtle strength of imagination, but to the overt strength of his hands: "I went through that coop like a madman, slamming the cane into feathery bodies, wooden posts, straw nests" (301). It is useful to read these lines alongside Rorty's explanation of the challenge an individual faces when skating on the edge of his/ her "final vocabulary":

> All human beings carry about a set of words which they employ to justify their actions, their beliefs, and their lives. . . . I shall call these words a person's "final vocabulary."
> It is "final" in the sense that if doubt is cast on the worth of these words, their user has no noncircular argumentative recourse. Those words are as far as he can go with language; beyond them there is only helpless passivity or a resort to force.[24]

And George indeed resorts to force. George's failure is his refusal to do anything productive with the doubts he has cast on the worth of his own vocabulary. To return to the motif of hands, it gains an added significance when, referring to Cocoa, George asserts: "these were *my* hands, and there was no way I was going to let you go" (301). By the end of the novel, this strategy—that of holding on—manifests itself as understandable but misguided. Again addressing Cocoa, George says, "And now you were all I had, and with you needing me, I had to hold on to what was real" (291). "Holding on" is a strategy; its limitations are obvious. It precludes any possibility of expanding "what was real." It is in this paradoxical sense that George, a man who freely admits to living in the now, nevertheless fixes himself in the past and refuses to engage the future. He desperately tries to hold on.

NOTES

1. Gloria Naylor, *Mama Day* (New York: Random House, Inc., 1989), p. 7. [All subsequent quotations from this source will be cited in text.]

2. Susan Meisenhelder, "'The Whole Picture' in Gloria Naylor's *Mama Day*," *African American Review* 27 (Fall 1993): 413.

3. M. M. Bakhtin, "Discourse in the Novel," in *The Dialogic Imagination,* ed. Michael Holquist, trans. Caryl Emerson and Michael Holquist (Austin: University of Texas Press, 1981), p. 332.

4. Trinh T. Minh-ha, *Woman, Native, Other* (Indianapolis: Indiana University Press, 1981), p. 120.

5. Hayden White, *Tropics of Discourse: Essays in Cultural Criticism* (Baltimore: Johns Hopkins University Press, 1978), p. 43.

6. Larry R. Andrews, "Black Sisterhood in Naylor's Novels," in *Gloria Naylor: Critical Perspectives Past and Present,* eds. Henry Louis Gates, Jr. and K. A. Appiah (New York: Amistad, 1993), pp. 296–297.

7. Toni Morrison, *Beloved* (New York: Penguin, 1987), p. 36.

8. Avery Gordon, *Ghostly Matters: Haunting and the Sociological Imagination* (Minneapolis: University of Minnesota Press, 1997), p. 8.

9. Ibid., p. 24.

10. Ibid., p. 164.

11. Stuart Hall, "Cultural Identity and Diaspora," in *Colonial Discourse and Post-colonial Theory,* eds. Patrick Williams and Laura Chrisman (New York: Columbia University Press, 1993), p. 402.

12. Lindsey Tucker, "Recovering the Conjure Woman: Texts and Contexts in Gloria Naylor's *Mama Day*," *African American Review* 28 (Summer 1994): 183.

13. Gary Storhoff, "'The Only Voice is Your Own': Gloria Naylor's Revision of *The Tempest*," *African American Review* 29 (Spring 1995): 35.

14. Helen Fiddyment Levy, "Lead on with Light," in *Gloria Naylor: Critical Perspectives Past and Present*, eds. Henry Louis Gates, Jr. and K. A. Appiah (New York: Amistad, 1993): p. 278.

15. Andrews, "Black Sisterhood in Naylor's Novels," p. 298.

16. Storhoff, "'The Only Voice is your Own,'" p. 38.

17. James Clifford, Introduction to *Writing Culture: The Poetics and Politics of Ethnog-*

raphy, eds. James Clifford and George E. Marcus (Berkeley: University of California Press, 1986), p. 15.

18. Ibid., p. 19.

19. Alan Friedman, Class Lecture from "Backgrounds of Modernism," University of Texas at Austin, 1993.

20. Kenneth Burke, *Attitudes Toward History,* 3rd ed. (Berkeley: University of California Press, 1986), p. 224.

21. Richard Rorty, *Irony, contingency, and solidarity* (New York: Cambridge University Press, 1989), p. 53.

22. Meisenhelder, "The Whole Picture," p. 412.

23. Jocelyn Hazelwood Donlon, "Hearing as Believing: Southern Racial Communities and Strategies of Story-Listening in Gloria Naylor and Lee Smith," *Twentieth Century Literature* 41 (Spring 1995): 26.

24. Rorty, *Irony,* p. 73.

Return to Sender: Correspondence(s) in Gloria Naylor's *Mama Day*

KERRY REGAN

A gift is not signed.
—Jacques Derrida

With the establishment of the London penny post in the 1680s, correspondence by letter was reinvented and personalized. Jay Fliegelman notes that the personal letter became a means of conversation among private citizens of the Commonwealth, and that the letter "affirmed the importance of the individual voice."[1] Removed from epistolary England by three hundred years and the Atlantic Ocean, Gloria Naylor's *Mama Day* reformulates this traditional means of communication and correspondence. In Naylor's text, the different narrative voices speak like letters, one sent out to another, a catalogue of replies. But the structural and thematic correspondence in *Mama Day* expands concepts invoked by the formal letter or epistolary novel that Fliegelman depicts as being a mark of rising individualism. For Naylor, each individual voice that makes itself heard is only important *in relation* to its interlocutor, to the community which sustains the individual. Even as the potential of the individual's manipulation of signs and language is acknowledged, spiritual discourse practices such as call and response and other sermonic legacies draw this conversation toward orality, toward communal or collaborative speakers and responders.

Irene Tucker's essay "Writing Home: *Evelina,* the Epistolary Novel, and the Paradox of Privacy" outlines some general paradigms of epistolary fiction. "Letters," Tucker notes, "are identifiable by certain material forms (salutation, address, stationery, seal, etc.)," and in fiction, fabricated letters carry at least some of these signifiers, such as salutation and address.[2] These material markers point to the substantive differences a letter makes in constructing narrative: narration is specifically authored and always directed toward a recipient imagined and noted by the addresser. A letter "is addressed by [the] author (even if at times only implicitly) to an identifiable person or collectivity," Tucker notes (423).

Mama Day's various narrators (the voice of the community of Willow Springs which opens and closes the novel and revisits the reader time and again throughout; the first-person speakers, George and Cocoa) rely heavily on the second-person "you" in their epistles. Though ostensibly not addressed—not written—the segments of prose authored by each voice are very clearly owned by the characters who speak them in first person. Each speaker has a listener: George and Cocoa direct their talk toward one another, and the communal narrator calls out to the reader. All are asking to be heard, and all require participation in order to enact their narratives. They are not, however, mere conversations: the structure of the utterances invokes written narrative, as they form lengthy statements of position rather than an expected interchange of dialogue between two characters. While traditional letters also call upon an addressee, also desire a second party, these dispatches seem to do so more vocally. The insistent second-person demands response; because the utterances are not written (within the bounds of the novel; the novel itself is obviously a written text), not sent off to wait for a response which may not come, these addresses hinge more immediately upon their recipients, both the characters within *Mama Day* and its readers.

While not conversations *per se,* these "spoken epistles" invoke the kind of linguistic dialogism imagined by Mikhail Bakhtin, whose work has been linked to the readerly tradition in African-American literature. Utterance in Bakhtin's Russian [*vyzkazyvanie*] "literally denotes the active process of speaking out and having one's say, of (ex)postulating, to or with an interlocutor."[3] The articulation, the speech act, "orients itself toward an anticipated respondent. In Bakhtin, speaking out, or self-expression, is ever mindful of the already spoken and necessarily attentive to the internalized other, the co-respondent" (763). African-American writers present instances of dialogic relation between margin and center, between what dominant culture refuses to say and the already-said, the authorized. The double-talk of the signifying monkey, a concept discussed by Henry Louis Gates, is a way of talking which remains conscious of its interlocutor while attempting to play a trick or two. Like W.E.B. DuBois's doubly-conscious subject, the speaker in a dialogic text such as *Mama Day* must be simultaneously conscious of what he is and how he is seen; what he says and how it is heard, who hears his utterances. The speaker, like the author of epistolary correspondence, tailors his address to the anticipated response of the person or collectivity to whom his words travel.

While Bakhtin provides a technically compelling way to read the interchanges of dialogue and the formulations of speech in *Mama Day,* the novel's investment in what lies beyond language, the role of conjuring magic and otherworldly forces within the legend of Willow Springs which the novel is charged to tell might require a more spiritual exegesis. Maggie Sale's 1992 article "Call and Response as Critical Method: African-American Oral Traditions and *Beloved*" lays the ground for an interpretation of literature by way of an examination of the call and response style of preaching. Sale notes, "Call-and-response patterns provide a basic model that depends and thrives upon audience performance and improvisation, which work together to ensure that the art will be meaningful or functional to the community."[4] Epistolary individualism is replaced here by a community of verbal utterances. These utterances are read, brought into being, by a community of recipients or respondents, including both the characters within the text and the reader, who receives and responds to all correspondence.

Hortense Spillers concurs that sermons or other religious discourse requires a reader to propagate its legends and history.[5] Sermons require supplicants, an audience to whom utterances travel and who might and must return those calls, must give responses in order to constitute the whole exchange and gesture toward the sacred subject of the discourse. The influence of sermons in *Mama Day* might be seen not only as an oralization of epistolary dialogue, but also a specifically religious structure of speaking and writing, invoked in Naylor's novel in conjunction with its mystical and magic-realist subjects. Spillers sees in the sermon a "*symbolic form* that not only lends shape to the contours and outcomes of African Americans' verbal fortunes under American skies, but also plays a key role in the psychic configurings of their community."[6] The exchanges between characters in *Mama Day* draw upon call and response in order to signal the connection between the tactile reality of narrative and event, and the community of legend or utterance which underlies the apprehensible surface.

Mama Day's opening section puts the reader in its debt: the legend of Sapphira Wade, founder of Willow Springs, is known by all but "nobody talks about" or names the events of 18 & 23. But the communal narrator goes on to detail what happened upon that year of Willow Springs' founding. Sapphira "smothered Bascombe Wade in his very bed and lived to tell the story for a thousand days . . . persuaded Bascombe Wade in a thousand days to deed all his slaves every inch of land in Willow Springs, poisoned him for his trouble," and thus set the strange history of the community in motion.[7] The narrator's disclosures deed to the reader the never-spoken: no one may talk about these events, but now you have been told, you know, you are responsible for keeping these secrets. The rest of the preface is sent off like a letter, a tract meant to convey the un-writable, a tale to be listened to. The narrator concludes,

Think about it: ain't nobody really talking to you. We're sitting here in Willow Springs, and you're God-knows-where you are. Uh, huh, listen. Really listen this time: the only voice is your own. But you done just heard about the legend of Sapphira Wade, though nobody here breathes her name. . . . you done heard it without a single living soul really saying a word. Pity, though, Reema's boy couldn't listen, like you, to Cocoa and George down by them oaks—or he woulda left here with quite a story (10).

The rhythms of this passage—the repetition of "really," "listen," the vocal uh-huh—draw the reader into the narrative in the tradition of sermonic calling. The injunction to the reader is direct and unyielding. You must really listen, though Reema's boy couldn't, in order to hear the legend and receive the narrative. In exchange you will receive "quite a story," a narrative which transcends representation by mere living souls, which can make only "your own" voice appear to speak the language of many. "You" become suddenly and solidly responsible for the narrative which is to follow: the narrative voices of George and Cocoa and the dialogue transcribed which seems to belong to other characters within the narrative are only your own voice speaking in rhythms you are not used to hearing.

As Spillers notes of sermons, "No narrative genre appears to depend so soundly upon the cooperative agency at work in others. The sermon seeks to *inculcate* its words; to make them enter the hearer. . . . [A sermon] cannot execute its program without a hearer, in this case, a 'reader'".[8] The reader must give her/himself up to the story; must go beyond what is "real" in order to listen to the never-told. The legend will cease to be, the sermon will fail to serve its function, without the active participation of a reader/hearer whose listening-as-belief (speaking in the voices of other believers) fixes the truth-value of the narrative. Success comes not when the message is sent (the letter mailed, the tale told, the sermon delivered) but when it has been received, when the cycle of call and response, of speaking and listening, has been completed. The call functions here like a gift: it bestows a message upon its recipient while this offering produces a certain debt (the need for response).[9] The call "demands that one give oneself over to the call as such—to answer the call, in the double sense of abandoning oneself to it and of going toward it."[10]

To give oneself to the call (with *abandon*), the reader in *Mama Day* must listen to her or his own voice and hear the stories of the community s/he may find there. From the prefatory material spoken by the communal narrator to "you," the reader enters Cocoa's first-person narrative: "You were picking your teeth with a plastic straw," she comments, and "you" no longer means you ("I was *not . . .*") but means someone else, a character who suddenly occupies the second-person subject position formerly held by the reader (13). "But, George, let's be fair," Cocoa continues, fixing the new occupant of the pronoun with a name. "You" continues to effect intimacy with the reader—the sense of eavesdropping upon a particularly private conversation between lovers who feel free to remark upon each other's quirks of personal hygiene—while opening up room for movement within subject positions. Formerly, you were courted by the communal narrator's address, and now you are differently brought into confidence by hearing (or being given) something you would expect to have been kept from you.

The reader, as Spillers suggests of the reader of sermons, "is *given* a history at the same time that s/he seeks to fabricate one."[11] The reader's role is no less crucial (s/he must still really listen to the narrative), but part of the task of making or fabricating the narrative will involve receiving what is given. The reader of *Mama Day* may bring her own voice to the text, but the basic outlines of the story of Sapphira and Cocoa and George and the history of Willow Springs are *given.* The reader must find in her/his own voice other voices—Cocoa's, George's—who tell a tale the reader might not be able to imagine but now must both hear and speak. This process of learning to hear and speak through other voices is familiar to most readers; any work of fiction requires some version of response from its recipients. All narrative, to a greater or lesser extent, rests on and in the belief of its addressees. Naylor's text differs from other works not in kind but in degree; the call here for participation is shouted outright, to "you," an imperative. "Really listen," because you *must,* to voices which you have not imagined or heard before. As they speak to "you," they address *you* as well as each other.

The communication between Cocoa and George—from "I" to "you"— shares the "implicit doubleness" Irene Tucker ascribes to the epistolary novel. "Along with the writer and addressee of any given letter within the novel," Tucker argues, "there exists a second writer and addressee—the author of the novel and the novel's readers."[12] The reader first finds him/herself in the "you," in the address, and then relinquishes that position to George (but not, perhaps, with a complete surrender; at least in the first instance of Cocoa's use of the second person, the reader must remember thinking of him/herself as "you," must think that s/he is being spoken to). This *trompe l'oeil* makes the reader realize the illusory nature of the second person, the traps of easy self-identification. You are being addressed— you are part of the cycle of call and response—but who "you" are at any given moment awaits discovery.

As Cocoa continues her narrative, this duplication opens beyond the merely double. She describes the coffee shop in which she and George first glimpsed each other, characterizing the Formica tabletops as "a bit too slippery for your elbows" and the "you" here is not easily ascribed to any one figure known to the narrative (George, Cocoa, reader), but rather seems a generic you, any you who might happen to rest its elbows on the counter (13). This "you," this second-person, is precisely not singular in nature, but rather comprises a host of possible people, any one of whom may or may not actually enter the diner being invoked.

Within this introduction to the narrative, then, the reader finds her/himself both courted and spurned. The continuation of the legend depends upon having an active hearer to "really listen" to the story's permutations, but that listener must not think of him/herself as an individual, autonomous and irreplaceable subject. The narrator of *Mama Day* is clearly communal, and thus introduces the possibility, indeed the necessity, of embracing multiple voices in order to tell the "true" story. There must be a "you" to address the story to, but the bounds of that "you" can, and must, change. The legend must invite more than one listener, must reach out toward a community of listeners as the story attempts to narrate the events of a community of tellers.

To give oneself (with *abandon,* to excess) to the legend of Willow Springs, the reader must first of all cease thinking of him/herself separately from the narrative. The only voice is your own, the reader is warned, but your own voice here goes beyond the cadences an individual subject is able to produce. "By giving," Marcel Mauss indicates, "one is giving *oneself,* and if one gives *oneself,* it is because one 'owes' *oneself*—one's person and one's goods—to others."[13] The reader, as recipient of the address by Cocoa, George, and the communal narrator, owes a debt to the narrative, must give up in return the luxury of thinking him/herself separate from (owing nothing to) the legend of Sapphira Wade and her descendants. You, reader, might be God-knows-where, but that location is not nowhere, is not unknowable (higher beings than you and I might find you); wherever you are your presence is needed to maintain the collective history.

As *Mama Day* continues, the reader sways in and out of its address. Sections authored by Cocoa and George, spoken to one another, intertwine with segments spoken by the communal narrator who speaks to the reader. Lest the reader forget his/her importance to the narrative, the necessity of his response, at the novel's midpoint the boundaries of the second person, the recipient of the call, are once more unsettled. Before the break between sections one and two, the last narrative voice is Cocoa's. She speaks to George about the journey to Willow Springs they are about to make (or have made; does Cocoa talk from 1999, like the narrator? is her speaking voice her voice in 1985?): "At what point could we have avoided that summer? . . . I don't think it would have mattered if we had come a year before or a year after. You and I would have been basically the same, and time definitely stands still in Willow Springs. No, any summer we crossed over would be the summer we crossed over" (165). Cocoa intends her speech for George, wonders at what point they could have changed events so that the tragedies which were to come would not have taken place. Finally, though, she decides that the events transcended their individual participants: any summer they crossed over would be the summer they crossed over. But the reader, turning the page after Cocoa's words, endures a similar crossing.

The narrative is interrupted by the section break which follows Cocoa's address. The reader must cross into the next part of the novel, must journey with Cocoa and George to Willow Springs, and the leap which will be made is marked by the physical gap in the novel, the blank page which separates the story's two halves. You and I are no longer basically the same: the referents of these pronouns have shifted. The "we" who cross over now includes the reader as well as Cocoa and George. Any time the novel is read, in God-knows-what location, the page break will always press the reader to cross over, to pause for a moment before entering the section of the novel where George and Cocoa travel to Willow Springs (and beyond). Continuity of narrative transcends the individual reader, just as the events of Willow Springs prevail over whatever choices Cocoa and George may have made about their travel. Wherever you are, whatever you bring to the story, the moment of crossing will remain basically the same. Your part in it is no less important, but it is no less a part over which you may not have complete authority or control.

The reader has a purpose in the narrative, but the role requires a disavowal of particular identity. The reader becomes *any* reader, becomes the function he or she performs as reader, becomes the crossing that must be made. Georges Bataille remarks, "for the individual making [a contribution], it is a loss of his substance. The giver will find himself again in the gift, but he must give first of all; he must first of all renounce more or less completely whatever is needed for the growth of the whole."[14] The narrative requires the reader to become a giver, to release his/her substance, his actual location and particular self-definition, in order to receive the legend and ensure that it will be carried on. The legend itself responds to its changing readers, gives up the security of solid definition: Sapphira Wade is "satin black, biscuit cream, red as Georgia clay: depending upon which of us takes a mind to her. She could walk through a lightning storm without being touched; grab a bolt of lightning in the palm of her hand . . . : depending upon which of us takes a mind to her" (3). The truth of Sapphira, what she "really" is, is made manifest only through the interaction of her legend with its specific listeners. Within this relationship between caller (Cocoa, George, narrator) and respondent (Cocoa, George, reader), a narrative forms, the story of a community which reaches beyond the individual voices whose utterances mark its borders.

The centrality of community to the narrative—the need to give and take beyond oneself, for a group larger than oneself—is indicated by the failure of singularity and possessiveness. Reema's boy, the ethnographer whose story helps introduce the reader to Willow Springs, produces a false version of the legend of 18 & 23 because he values book knowledge over the kind of knowing one has to ask for. He "came hauling himself back from one of those fancy colleges mainside, dragging his notebooks and tape recorder and a funny way of curling up his lip . . . all excited and determined to put Willow Springs on the map" (7). Unable to listen to, or properly ask about, 18 & 23, he determines through his research that the residents had it all wrong: 18 & 23 is really eighty-one and thirty-two, the coordinates of Willow Springs on the map. The communal narrator sighs, "If the boy wanted to know what 18 & 23 meant, why didn't he just ask?" (8). He would have heard, then, what the reader hears, the legend of Sapphira Wade and the events of 1823 which form part of the larger narrative of the community. This kind of asking requires its interlocutor to know "to stand back a distance calling *Mama, Mama Day*, to wait for her to come out and beckon him near" (9).

The supplicant call, the patience of waiting for a response: these requirements are beyond Reema's boy's school-taught capabilities. He produces a closed and finite text about Willow Springs, bound and signed, and in so doing proves that he has failed to listen, really listen, to the narrative around him. If he had been able to call Mama Day, to call all the voices who speak together and with one another about the legends of his birthplace, he would distrust the sanctity and coherence of a singular text, of simple definition. He would know that there are many sides to this story, most of which exceed his individual comprehension even if he thinks he "knows" where he came from.

George has less advantage than Reema's boy from the outset, approaching Willow Springs as an outsider, much like the novel's reader. His role in the narrative becomes crucial at the penultimate moment of crisis: Cocoa is stricken by the forces of Ruby, a woman with powers approaching Mama Day's and a very jealous mind, who suspects Cocoa of trifling with her husband Junior Lee. Ruby weaves nightshade into Cocoa's hair and sends the young woman slowly toward a painful demise. To save Cocoa, Mama Day cryptically tells George to go to the chicken coop and return with whatever he finds in the back of the nest of an old red hen (295). All she wants from George is his return with his empty hands, which will signal his connection with the community of Willow Springs and his knowledge that he cannot save Cocoa alone: that his hand must be joined with other hands in order to effect the recovery. The communal narrator explains that Mama Day "needs that belief buried in George, of his own accord he has to *hand* it over to her. She needs his hand in hers—his very hand—so she can connect it up with all the believing that had gone before" (285).

George must enact Bataille's injunction, must give up his substance of his own accord and hand it (give his hand) over. Language is demetaphorized in Willow Springs' magic landscape; to succeed, George must hear different meanings behind "handing" over belief. "She" needs that buried belief: Mama Day, to connect it with that which has come before; Cocoa, to live; Sapphira Wade, to ensure the continuation of her legend (for Cocoa must give birth to the next generation of Days). Sensing George's inability to reach beyond himself for help, Dr. Buzzard warns him, "a man would have grown enough to know that really believing in himself means that he ain't gotta be afraid to admit there's some things he just can't do alone" (292). A man needs to call out, to seek a response, outside of the self, outside of the known or knowable. To make this move, one must trust what lies beyond logic, and for George this proves impossible. "I might take a deep breath," George confesses late in the novel, "and say, God help me, really meaning, Let the best in me help me. There wasn't a moment when I actually believed those appeals were going beyond me to a force that would first hear, secondly care" (251).

George saves Cocoa, but fails to save himself, because he fails to see *all* that lies beyond the self, fails to transcend his own individualism. The call he issues is patently fraudulent; he does not expect or believe in the response, cannot conceive of the purported subject of his address as an active participant in the exchange. George imagines for an instant, "Could it be that she wanted nothing but my hands?" but then becomes distracted by the hen's claws in his shoulder and focuses instead on his individual ability to heal or, in this case, kill (300). He goes "through that coop like a madman," or like a lover prematurely bereft, killing chickens in frustration (301). Afterward, George laments, "All of this wasted effort when these were *my* hands, and there was no way I was going to let you go" (301). The highlighted possessive, George's fixation upon the ownership of "his" hands, marks his separation from the community of Willow Springs. As long as George's hands belong only to him, as long as he retains a hold on his substance and keeps it thus separate from those around him, he may only effect partial salvation. Cocoa lives because George can make an individual sacrifice, his contribution to her existence. George dies (at least his body does; his voice lives on in the narrative as received by the reader) because he was unable to link up the individual gift of himself to the larger community of call and response, of gift and countergift, of exchange which comes together to speak to and about what lies beyond language, the legends which constitute Willow Springs.

If the inability to seek community, to believe that a response will come to the call, has brought about George's failure, then an investment in forces larger than the self has ensured Mama Day's success. In trying to prevent Cocoa from slipping away from her, Mama Day must voice a call, call upon the name of the one who preceded her, who founded Willow Springs and enables its continuance. This name: "Sarah, Sabrina, Sally, Sadie, Sadonna—what? A loss that she can't describe sweeps over her—a missing key to an unknown door somewhere in that house. The door to help Baby Girl" (280). Mama Day's continued efforts lead her only to scold herself "for not knowing better: a gift is something that's given, not demanded" (280). Even Mama Day's knowledge here remains only partial: she knows enough to know that help must be sought from outside of herself, from outside of her time, but she slips up, demands what must be freely given, the name which escapes her. Perhaps here the reader's importance to the narrative is again made manifest, for the reader knows, from the narrator's opening disclosures, the name which Mama Day looks for, and thus holds the missing key she needs.

The incomplete nature of Mama Day's knowledge helps unsettle easy binarisms (George as outsider will always fail; Mama Day, as Sapphira's inheritor, holds all answers) and suggests that no one character (no one reader) can ever hold the whole story. The narrative only happens when the individuals who make it up come together and exchange their knowledge—call out and respond to one another. As Maggie Sale argues of Toni Morrison's novel *Beloved,* the elements of the story of Willow Springs (in 1985 and for always) "are presented in such a way that any one of them constitutes only part of the whole, each needing to be balanced by a consideration of all of the others."[15] The reader only knows what Mama Day needs to save her grand-niece through words which Mama Day has not, cannot utter, but which have and must come from another voice.

Looking at the novel more globally, the entire narrative of Willow Springs is only made through the conjunction of the various voices who call to one another, call out to the reader. Each prose section provides one side to the story, which the reader should not take as the final word but only an inflection in a greater interchange. As Mama Day notes, in response to a fight Cocoa and George are having, "everybody wants to be right in a world where there ain't no right or wrong to be found. My side. He don't listen to my side. She don't listen to my side. Just like that chicken coop, everything got four sides: his side, her side, an outside, and an inside. All of it is the truth" (230). Using the physical structure of the coop as her metaphor, Mama Day suggests that truth would collapse, like an edifice without a supporting wall, without all of its components. Unlike a pile of truths or a grab-bag of possible options from which one may be absent without upsetting the whole, the small building precisely needs all of its sides in order to stand, intact.

In her examination of *Mama Day,* Susan Meisenhelder stresses that the separate narratives do not bleed into an undifferentiated master discourse. Instead, "the individuality of people in . . . the community of Willow Springs is not lost—the pieces can be readily identified, but stitched together they create something whole," a whole which outshines its individual components.[16] The voices do not blend together to become one third-person voice, the objective tone of a history book. Cocoa's words, George's, retain the individuality of their speaker; the communal narrator maintains its plurality; the remaining narrative occurs in silences and whispers.

Like the idea of correspondence (which includes congruity and harmony between answering sides but resists the collapse of difference into a unified and equivocal whole), these words and gaps constitute the novel as an aggregate rather than a totality. Just like the chicken coop, the sides of the novel are still seen separately, in relation to one another (left/right, outside and inside), as they comprise the whole structure. In the give and take of the story's different sides, giving and taking are, as Derrida has argued, posed as "equivalent . . . but on the basis of their opposition or at least their distinction" (67). Each side is just as crucial to the whole as each other side, but no two sides are the *same.* Midway through the novel, George and Cocoa explain an argument they had in parallel narratives. Each begins with the same two sentences ["Our worst fight ever. And it was all your fault" (230, 232)] and moves from this shared point of origin to its own conclusion. The grammatical link between the two versions places them upon equal ground: the reader cannot conclusively affix fault or blame upon any one party, but rather must negotiate the conjunction of the two narratives to understand what happened.

In Cocoa's final address to George (to "you"), she further complicates singular ideas of narrative, instead depicting a legend as multiply-figured. "When I see you again, our versions will be different still. . . . You see, that's what I mean," she concludes, "there are just too many sides to the whole story" (311). Who sees? George might know enough to know that he and Cocoa have different versions of their narrative, that when they see each other again the variations will be even more complex. The reader of *Mama Day*, though, is the only participant in this litany of calls and responses who "sees" all of the letter-like dispatches from one character to another. There are "too many" sides to this story, so many sides that they exceed the comprehension of any single character within the novel, so many that they may in fact go beyond even the many sides the novel expresses.

The legend of Willow Springs, after all, does not start and end in Cocoa or George's time; as the communal narrator more fully explains, "it ain't about chalking up 1985, just jotting it down in a ledger to be tallied with the times before and after. We figure it'll all even out in the end," a finality which remains perpetually deferred (305). The whole story contains "too many" sides for any one subject to hear, receive, and respond to them all. Making the history of a community requires that one give up the desire for conclusion. Spillers terms the community described by sermonic discourse as "a content whose time and meaning are 'discovered'. . . . In other words, 'community' . . . becomes *potentiality; an unfolding to be attended.*"[17] Community here never *is*, is never stagnant, but always *becomes,* is always in process, being made. All the sides to the story, all of the voices who call, can never be present in any one place at one time.

The story's end is always suspended as it travels from speaker to listener, as the various narratives are given and reinvented. The legend of Sapphira Wade awaits hearing, being heard. In this manner, "[*Mama Day*] affirms the staying power of the oral tradition . . . although listened to the way the communal voice has demanded . . . it must also be 'read' . . . , must be accompanied by a knowledge that includes the ongoing processes of seeing, hearing, and making."[18] The reader must receive the story in written form and literally "read" the novel in order to hear its call.

Within the novel, characters read each other, receive each other's communication, in a perpetual process of discovery. Mama Day's power as healer, as a knowledgeable member of the community, stems from her ability to read signs accurately. Lindsey Tucker contends that the "concept of divination—the ability to read signs . . . is crucial to the construction of the novel."[19] In the first section of communal third-person narration—the reader's first introduction to Mama Day—she is caught in the process of reading her grand-niece's impending arrival. "A little drop of vapor beads up on the tip of an apricot leaf and shines there in the morning sun," the narrator observes, "Miranda smiles as the bead of water turns golden in color—my, what a pleasant surprise. She must ring up Abigail and tell her Baby Girl is coming in today . . . and on the airplane to boot" (34).

While the narrator cannot, or will not, detail for the reader the process of interpretation which has driven Mama Day to read an airline flight in the water droplet, the result of that reading has been clearly marked, and Cocoa's arrival confirms that Mama Day's perception was accurate. Mama Day later discerns that "Baby Girl was seeing New York with someone" by reading between the lines of Cocoa's letter: why else say she is *now* seeing New York, when she's lived there seven years? Miranda's response to this reading is to leave off her usual P.S. ("Find yourself a husband") and this absence speaks quietly to Cocoa, who (finally) does just that.

Other signs, other calls, which Mama Day must read convey far less favorable news. With the assistance of her hen Clarissa, Mama Day discovers a bag of tricks underneath her trailer. This letter of sorts [appropriately found by the namesake of one of literature's most prodigious correspondents?] is a dirty flannel bag "holding a tablespoon of dirt mixed up with a few white specks of something, little purplish flowers and a dried sprig," as the narrator tells us (171). This charm is "a sign that Miranda reads," as Tucker notes: by spitting on the white specks she determines that they are salt; the purplish flowers, upon examination, are classified as verbena; the dust from a graveyard; further thought about these newly-identified components (verbena's colloquial guise as the "herb of grace") reveals their total meaning, a hex working against the daughter of Grace, Cocoa.

Once Mama Day has read the sign, has heard this call, she intuits its source and executes her response. She heads down to Ruby's house, charm in hand, empty basket under her arm for collecting peaches from Ruby's orchard (the official reason for her visit). Placing the bag upon Ruby's fencepost, "she watches Ruby watching it as the breeze draws it into her yard. They both talk to the grayish dust and purple flowers spilling out around the foot of the gate" (172). Miranda says nothing to Ruby of what she has read in the charm. They talk to each other, their words passing through the flannel bag which lies between them, but neither talks *about* the charm. The conversation about the spell-casting goes on in the breeze which carries the dust over the fence rather than being spoken directly by the human participants. This charm, this letter, has been opened and read, and its contents spill out past the red stamp: Return to Sender.

Mama Day's silence about Ruby's apparent treachery (to trouble what does not belong to her) might suggest that in this exchange, this call and response, judgment is not being passed. Both Miranda and Ruby have their roles to play in the transaction, and while Mama Day may not embrace the contents of Ruby's address, she does not fully negate or condemn Ruby. Ruby's side of the story might counteract (or in this case directly wage war upon) Miranda's side, but, like the walls of the chicken coop, both are needed to compose the legend. The narrator has told the reader from *Mama Day*'s outset, after all, that "It ain't about right or wrong, truth or lies; it's about a slave woman who brought a whole new meaning to both them words, soon as you cross over here from beyond the bridge" (3). At least, it isn't about a fixed notion of truth or justice: the novel is about the way in which exchanges of dialogue, moments of correspondence, come together to create a changing, progressive narrative truth.

Crossing into Willow Springs, the reader of *Mama Day* leaves behind simple binaries of good/evil, truth/lie, right/wrong. Ruby's venom is as necessary to the legend as George's sacrifice, as Cocoa's continued life, as Mama Day's skill at healing. Each point of utterance within this correspondence—this assemblage of communication, this connection—remains essential as well as distinct within the whole discourse of which it forms a part. As is true for *Beloved*'s various calls and responses, "the point is not simply to judge, but to move, as readers, through the many positions that make up this complex situation."[20] Judgment, like a solid conclusion, is eternally deferred. The point is not to "chalk up 1985," call the year complete and move on to the next, nor is it to mete out punishment and reward to the occupants of Willow Springs who lived through that year. Rather, *Mama Day* bids the reader to put together a narrative which may answer to, call toward, and correspond with the community who circulate in and through the legends, with all their many sides.

NOTES

1. Jay Fliegelman, *Prodigals and Pilgrims: the American Revolution Against Patriarchal Authority, 1750–1800* (Cambridge: Cambridge University Press, 1982), 29.

2. Irene Tucker, "Writing Home: *Evelina,* the Epistolary Novel, and the Paradox of Privacy," *ELH* 60 (1993): 424.

3. Dale Peterson, "Response and Call: the African-American Dialogue with Bakhtin," *American Literature* 65 (1993): 763.

4. Maggie Sale, "Call and Response as Critical Method: African-American Oral Tradition and *Beloved,*" *African-American Review* 26 (1992): 41.

5. Hortense Spillers, "Moving on Down the Line," *American Quarterly* 40 (1988): 90.

6. Ibid., 86.

7. Gloria Naylor, *Mama Day* (New York: Vintage, 1988), 3. All quotations taken from this edition.

8. Hortense Spillers, "Moving On Down the Line," 95.

9. I draw my ideas about the gift primarily from the work of Marcel Mauss [*The Gift: the Form and Reason for Exchange in Archaic Societies*] and Jacques Derrida [*Given Time I. Counterfeit Money*]. While Mauss and Derrida disagree on particular aspects of gift exchange, both share common tenets: that there is a gift; that to give a gift produces a debt or requires a countergift (one may not simply keep or hoard a gift); that this intercourse generates a type of economy that supersedes or transcends usual commerce.

10. Jean-Luc Marion, quoted in Jacques Derrida, *Given Time I. Counterfeit Money,* trans. Peggy Kamuf (Chicago and London: Chicago University Press, 1992): 51 n.10.

11. Spillers, "Moving On Down the Line," 90.

12. Tucker, "Writing Home," 422.

13. Marcel Mauss, *The Gift: the Form and Reason for Exchange in Archaic Societies* Trans. W.D. Halls. (New York: Norton, 1990), 46.

14. Georges Bataille, *Erotism: Death and Sensuality,* trans. Mary Dalwood, 1957 (San Francisco: City Lights, 1986), 96.

15. Sale, "Call and Response as Critical Method," 97.

16. Susan Meisenhelder, "'The Whole Picture' in Gloria Naylor's *Mama Day,*" African-American Review 27 (1993): 413.

17. Spillers, "Moving on Down the Line," 89.

18. Lindsey Tucker, "Recovering the Conjure Woman: Texts and Contexts in Gloria Naylor's *Mama Day,*" *African-American Review* 28 (1994): 186.

19. Tucker, "Recovering the Conjure Woman," 181.

20. Sale, "Call and Response as Critical Method," 44.

WORKS CITED

Bataille, Georges. *Erotism: Death & Sensuality.* 1957. Translated by Mary Dalwood. San Francisco: City Lights, 1986.

Derrida, Jacques. *Given Time: I. Counterfeit Money.* Translated by Peggy Kamuf. Chicago and London: University of Chicago Press, 1992.

Fliegelman, Jay. *Prodigals and Pilgrims: The American Revolution Against Patriarchal Authority, 1750–1800.* Cambridge: Cambridge University Press, 1982.

Mauss, Marcel. *The Gift: The Form and Reason for Exchange in Archaic Societies.* Trans. W.D. Halls. New York: Norton, 1990.

Meisenhelder, Susan. "'The Whole Picture' in Gloria Naylor's *Mama Day.*" *African-American Review* 27.3 (1993): 405–19.

Naylor, Gloria. *Mama Day.* New York: Vintage, 1988.

Peterson, Dale E. "Response and Call: The African American Dialogue with Bakhtin." *American Literature* 65.4 (1993): 761–75.

Sale, Maggie. "Call and Response as Critical Method: African-American Oral Traditions and *Beloved.*" *African-American Review* 26.1 (1992): 41–50.

Spillers, Hortense. "Moving on Down the Line." *American Quarterly* 40.1 (1988): 83–109.

Tucker, Irene. "Writing Home: *Evelina,* the Epistolary Novel and the Paradox of Property." *ELH* 60.2 (1993): 419–439.

Tucker, Lindsey. "Recovering the Conjure Woman: Texts and Contexts in Gloria Naylor's *Mama Day." African-American Review* 28.2 (1994): 173–88.

Toward a Literacy of Empathy:
Inhabiting Gloria Naylor's *Bailey's Cafe*

CAROL BENDER AND ROSEANNE HOEFEL

My old man used to say, Always finish what you start. It's a sound principle, but it can't work in this cafe. If life is truly a song, then what we've got here is just snatches of a few melodies. All these folks are in transition; they come midway in their stories and go on. If this was like that sappy violin music on Make-Believe Ballroom, we could wrap it all up with a lot of happy endings to leave you feeling real good that you took the time to listen. But I don't believe that life is supposed to make you feel good, or to make you feel miserable either. *Life is just supposed to make you feel.* (Naylor, *Bailey's Cafe,* p. 219)

Although this founding principle of Gloria Naylor's *Bailey's Cafe* begins its final chapter, it could well serve as a musical score for the entire novel. As Henry Giroux and Peter McLaren in *Critical Pedagogy and Predatory Culture* have argued in their wake-up call to a radical cultural politics which foregrounds a conscientious critique of school culture's tacit ideology, "knowledge must be made meaningful to [readers] before it can be made critical."[1] This integral goal, we argue, can be achieved by opening cultural spaces which invite the fostering of what we call an ethic of empathy. Gloria Naylor's novels seem especially conducive to such emancipatory strategies that challenge the "master narratives of liberal, post-industrial democracy and the humanist, individual, and patriarchal discourses that underwrite it" (55), as Paulo Friere's disciples deem a critically conceived, historically situated language of hope should do. As with her novel, *The Women of Brewster Place,* for example, this novel is collective, communal and collaborative, rather than "individual," the discourse, defiantly matriarchal, rather than predictably patriarchal. *Bailey's Cafe* offers "zones of possibility [that] not only destabilize alliances among passivity, helplessness, dependency, and despair, but also invite [readers] to form partnerships dedicated to reconstructing subjectivity and redirecting the paths of human

182

desire" (54). Importantly, the particular brand of empathy Naylor fosters does not allow readers to diminish the anguish, anger or oppression of her characters. Instead it clarifies the power differentials that accrue to privilege and accentuates the need to resist such destructive dynamics.

The question arises: How do readers genuinely engage with this moving novel without being debilitated by its pervasive pain? Naylor orchestrates a framework whereby the misery does not disable but rather mobilizes readers by leading them to feel outraged at the injustice and compelled to envision alternatives. Naylor provides a narrative structure that creates a powerful consistent zone such as those advocated by Giroux and McLaren. According to these theorists, the radical pedagogy of cultural politics transforms "classrooms into social laboratories" that dismantle the nexus of "passivity, helplessness, dependency, and despair."[2] Naylor achieves this "zone of possibility" through the unobtrusive and, significantly, nameless narrator: a black male, a victim of oppression, both as a working class black man in America and as a veteran of war and pawn of government. He relinquishes his voice to the storytellers, many of whom are female and/or more disenfranchised than he. Though sympathetic, he poses no threat to their authority and seems in awe of their resiliency; he thereby serves as a model for empathy and reduces reader resistance through his own respectful demeanor and intermittent consciousness-raising. This collective, leaderless sharing of variant oppressive experiences necessitates the reader's trust and openness in its similarity to the black church's tradition of testifying.[3] Bailey's Cafe constitutes a congregation of beleaguered souls whose heart-wrenching testimonies and stories envelop readers emotionally. The characters' captivated replies to these narratives thus elicit similar reactions from readers, evoking a call-and-response pattern beyond the novel which replicates the intrinsic one.

Naylor's ingenious blend of voices suggests itself in the title of the opening chapter, "Maestro, If You Please," in which readers meet the conductor, a most amiable narrator. Though this Maestro lacks formal education, he is wise to the fact that real learning takes place elsewhere:

I went to kindergarten on the muddy streets in Brooklyn, finished up grade school when I married Nadine, took my first diploma from the Pacific; and this cafe, well now, this cafe is earning me a Ph.D. You might say I'm majoring in Life, standing in front of this grill and watching that door open and close, open and close, as they step in here from all over the United States and some parts of the world. (3)

These figurative goalposts equate the setting, Bailey's Cafe, with higher learning. The educational process seems invitingly easy, seductive in fact. The narrator entices readers to "stick around and listen to the music" (4).

Indeed, Naylor's own hand skillfully involves the reader who unwittingly requests that the narrator set the tempo: "Maestro, If You Please . . ." Clearly, he does aim to please, primarily through the humor he offers throughout, such that readers can deem this at once the funniest and most sobering book they have ever experienced. Paradoxically, the narrator's unassuming manner immediately endears readers as we learn of his disadvantaged socio-economic background, and yet we respect his class consciousness which began in his childhood when his parents worked for wealthy blacks. We learn early on that, growing up, he was surrounded by wealthy colored families: "And my eyes certainly didn't deceive me: liveried coachmen, sable wraps, and brownstone mansions meant rich, while getting up at five in the morning to stoke the furnace, start breakfast, and lay out the morning suits for people like that meant you weren't. And that's what my parents did as butler and cook for the Van Morrisons. . . ." (4).

As the narrator humorously renders his parents' dichotomous responses to an array of situations which significantly foreshadow the novel, we realize that his exemplary listening and observation skills began as a youngster. Consider, for example, the following illustrative passage: "My father would have cut his own throat for Mr. Van Morrison. My mother hated Mrs. Van Morrison with a quiet passion that's peculiar to women: it burns low, slow, and long" (5). Here, he develops the skill of reading the subtext of women's responses. He continues: "a woman can drag the whole thing out—over years—and pick, pick, pick to death . . . she relished hating that woman" (5). With the playful objectivity that time and distance allow, the narrator amuses the reader with snatches of his parents' conversation which he overheard. Regarding, for instance, "Mrs. Van Morrison's former stage career—

—Opera: my father
—Burlesque: my mother." (6)

Throughout his youth he internalized their voices and now keeps their stories, their differing and sometimes gendered perspectives alive.

This rare gift makes him a reliable narrator. Naylor conveys his uncanny ability to see the larger picture in the amusing and thought-provoking anecdote about his love for baseball. As a child, it seemed clear to him that baseball was segregated because black athletes were better. Racist envy and the repercussions for being a good player made for an exhausting non-stop season. Barnstorming in the Deep South began in February with a game a day and three on Sunday, interspersed with discriminatory/travel and lodging conditions as the players moved their way North into the Negro World Series in September, followed by winter ball in Florida or Cuba since the pay had been so poor throughout the year. This pattern of institutionalized racism's rejection of black excellence foreshadows Stanley's/Miss Maple's relentless and futile job search, much as the narrator's parents' divergent perceptions set the stage for the controversy surrounding Eve's place, for example when his parents sparred about Mrs. Van Morrison's "brief association with a London bordello—

—As interior decorator: my father
—Interiors, period: my mother." (6)

In addition, the narrator's stories anticipate his open mindedness, not only about the cafe customers, but about Eve's residents, whom he perceives as necessarily inhabiting a league of their own. Similarly, his keen ability to see through the hypocrisy of the Van Morrisons is both comic and incisive. He contends that until racism and classism dissipate, or in his words "real power get[s] shared at the top," nothing but "a game of smoke and mirrors is going on at the bottom" (12).

Remarkably, this sentiment is also prophetic in terms of the narrative structure, for our favorite grill cook shares the power of storytelling with disenfranchised and marginalized voices. Meeting Nadine, the narrator's wife, the woman who cofounded the cafe, humbles him and tempers his own egocentric tendency to monopolize conversation. Early in their courtship he was quite content with monologues: "the sound of my own voice was so pleasing to me I only needed one or two sentences from her to let me catch my breath before I started off again" (16). Nadine's refusal to laugh outwardly at his self-deprecating jokes gradually erodes his cockiness and demands that he *listen,* and not only to verbal cues. Only when she calls his bluff and the joke is on him does he realize she's been laughing all along. This epiphany informs the novel: "Sure, she taught me a lesson, and a whole different way of looking at her—and women—which doesn't negate the fact that my wife is still a little strange. While most of what happens in life is below the surface, other people do come up for air and translate their feelings for the general population now and then" (19).

So humbled is he by this deference to the women that he remains a nameless translator. He tacitly acknowledges the importance of retrieving valuable narratives. Graciously, he proffers the story of his own pain during his horrifying and futile World War II march into Tokyo. This bewildering and endless experience with the unstoppable Japanese solidifies his reckoning with the devastation incurred by an abuse of power.

> God, I am so sick of killing the living dead. What kind of people are these? . . . I could still feel it on my skin. The divine wind. Kamikaze. I took my trembling hands and plastered my body with mud. It wasn't enough. I rolled in the mud, howling up into the hills of Okinawa. Begging for any god to take it all away . . . And you gotta understand how blue it was. How beautiful, soul-wrenching blue. And you gotta understand we were winning the war. There'd be no judgement passed on me for what was to happen in Tokyo. I wasn't a coward. I could go in and do my duty. It became just too unbearable to know I'd be doomed to come out alive. Take. This. Cross. From. Me. And yes, I offered any god who would answer even the rights to my unborn children. And the only god to answer claimed them. (24–25)

Simultaneously it cultivates his empathy for those who suffer such violations and fosters his awe at their stamina. Significantly, this italicized portion of the chapter is the narrator's own unmediated story, which lands him, like all the other characters, at Bailey's Cafe.

To be sure, "Bailey" has become such a good listener that he teaches the reader how to detect nuances. In the second chapter, entitled "The Vamp"— a term which indicates, among other things, an improvised accompaniment—he reminds us that "Every one-liner's got a life underneath it. Every point's got a counterpoint" (34). Life exists in a series of keys with major and minor voices, in this case the judgmental, fundamentalist Sister Carrie and the self-absorbed pimp, Sugar Man. Bailey illustrates that, though they fancy themselves worlds apart, they have more in common than they are willing to admit. "If you don't listen below the surface," the narrator interjects, "they're both one-note players. Flat and predictable" (33–34). The narrator implies that both perceive themselves as protectors of their charges/ "(A)ngels." Sugar Man subscribes to a paternalistic worldview whereby his prostitutes need pretty things and a man to safeguard, "guide" and "spank" these "angels" when necessary. Similarly, Sister Carrie deems herself the gatekeeper of Angel's budding, or bursting, sexuality. Sister Carrie's "Lord Jesus" and Sugar Man's "Five-alive" are mere variations on the call-and-response. Thus the narrator alerts us to the importance of subtext if we are going to "listen while [they] play it all out" (35) in the Jam which follows.

If readers take his lead, we too can reconcile how it is that Sadie in "Mood: Indigo" is at once a wino, a 25-cent whore, *and* a lady. The agonizing story of her life demonstrates the inadequacy and cruelty of dismissive dualities. This, the longest of the women's narratives, shows us the complexity which is erased if we don't tune in to the entire ballad. The note of her laughter rises above the cacophony of her life-long abuse and misery: "but none of us, especially Jones, would ever be the same again. He sat there staring at Sadie, and since she only knew to read silence as disapproval, she ducked her head and mumbled into her tea, I'm sorry, I just thought it was a funny story" (73). From the time her mother called her the "one the coat hanger missed" to the time when the five stars (wine) eased the ache of a loveless life, her survival fantasies sustain her grace amid the serial grief she has endured. Naylor creates an unforgettable character whose hellish existence is bearable in large part because of her vivid and elaborate imagination which transports her to a less dreadful space. To ensure that we don't miss this fundamental point, our subtle narrator intervenes to impress upon readers the prominence of dreams:

My father used to tell me that a star dies in heaven every time you snatch away someone's dream. Dreams had been dying around Sadie all of her life. And the last star for her was dimming quickly inside. The last thing holding her back from falling to her destruction, an endless plunge through the endless space of the black hole waiting to open in her heart. (64)

Likewise, Bailey's comic intervention at the outset of "Eve's Song" provides the respite we need between these oppressive sagas. Naylor resists the standard impulse of readers to secure a central voice by having Bailey humorously put Eve in her place, that is, *behind* "the Indians closing in on the pennant" and "the first new line of Chevys since the war" (79). Ironically, Eve has lost her sense of humor in her 1000-year trek through delta dust, the latter a gauge by which she ranks the hierarchy of pain her potential residents confide. Like Bailey, she recognizes the centrality of narrating one's life; she acknowledges that "they always need to finish their stories" (82). But unlike Bailey, Eve never laughs, nor does she ever conjure laughter in her imagination (as Sadie does) both because her abusive Godfather's sinister laugh was "like shards of glass on her ears" (84) and because her premature disillusionment has wizened her to how little there is to laugh about. Rather than dreams, she cultivates year-round gardens, maintaining her childhood eroto-emotional link with the earth for which she was originally cast out of her church and home. This biblical allusion, along with that of the dust to which she returns and her significant name, contextualizes the redemptive transition, or at least the potential for redeeming the

gratuitous pain and violence which has invaded their lives, that her way station proffers for other damaged cast outs. Like the biblical mother of us all,
Eve variously mothers to wholeness those who arrive broken, with tatterd
spirits and desecrated souls.

One of the most severely damaged of these women, "Sweet Esther"—
coerced into sadomasochism by her brother from the age of 12—contains
so much rage that her Medusa-like arrival nearly cripples Bailey's sense
of humor: she "scared [him] out of a year's growth" (94). Her justifiable
hatred of men simultaneously frightens him and enables his immediate
understanding of, respect for, and deference to her unsparing anger: "that
corner of the room was turned into a block of ice" (94). His stunned silence
is unbroken throughout Esther's shocking first-person account to the reader
regarding her preference for invisibility, self-annihilation, and erasure
during and due to her "unspeakable" captivity to a man her brother claimed
was her husband. As a survival mechanism, Esther has cast this twelve-year
bondage as indentured servitude yet the conclusion of her narrative belies
that reconstruction. The residue of her mortifying past has left its indelible,
incestuous scar. She says of the male callers she allows to visit her only in
the dark: "And they must call me *little sister.* Or I no longer come" (99).

After the narrator's vocal absence we welcome the amusing interlude his
infatuated encounter with Mary/Peaches brings in "Mary (Take One)." Her
narrative is perhaps the most compelling in its shifts from first-to-third person, literally and figuratively reflecting her internalized objectification by
the desirous male gaze she has negotiated since her childhood. Her excru-
ciating revenge against the scores of men—father, husband, lovers—who
tried to contain her sexuality and possess her extraordinary beauty is laced
with a nightmarish black humor. The ultimate horror of her ingested mi-
sogyny surfaces in the epitome of her self-loathing, significantly placed
dead center of the novel. Her self-mutilation results from the schizophrenic
adoption of the Madonna-whore binary which her father's religion and other
forces have inflicted. Sardonically, after smiling into mirrors for so many
years, she traces the laugh lines as the blueprint for freedom in her self-
imposed scarification ritual.

Bailey's humor, his specifically male dimension and his honesty about
being magnetically attracted to this goddess-type body lend him even more
credibility. He doesn't pretend, like the minister who molested Mary at the
altar or the father who tried to wall in or beat out her sensuality. Further, he
defends Mary to the reader when Sugar Man exaggerates to the distraught
Daddy Jim that she has hundreds of callers. Sugar Man wants to be one of
her callers and to profit, as her pimp, from the "mileage left below her neck"

(113). Bailey counters with a more sensitive and accurate picture of Mary's status and acknowledges her value: "And it will take a special man . . . special enough to understand what the woman upstairs is truly worth" (114). Likewise, his commentary reiterates Eve's refrain, the repeated promise of restoration, making the hope of wholeness a mantra in this otherwise dissonant piece.

In fact, Bailey goes so far as to defend Peaches and Esther as "special case[s]" (117) in his first conversation involving mutual laughter: "Jesse can get you laughing" (116), he muses, and even more inspiring: "her laughter is good-natured and comes from deep down" (117). Of all the stories, Jesse Bell's rendering is closest to that of Bailey in its liberal dose of humor. After an extensive delineation of the invincible female stock from which she hails, comes this witty and insightful passage:

> Weren't nothing secret about my marriage. I got him the same way I kept him—with the best poon tang east of the Mississippi. And just cause it was 1924, don't let people tell you that nice girls *didn't*. They did then, they do now—and I'll bet my grandma's drawers they always will. But it's the smart girls—nice or not—who understand that men have a short memory in that department. So you gotta find ways of reminding 'em of how good it was while promising them it's gonna get better still. And the hardest part is to remind them without saying a word. If you spoke about such things out loud, you would be indecent. You see, the real secret is that men don't give a second thought about marrying girls that *do* as long as they stay ladies. (122)

Not surprisingly, this is a woman who loves fun—including intimate sweet potato pie parties for two—in spite of her arrogant Uncle Eli's disdain. Fortunately, his insistence on pronouncing her name Jezebel doesn't destroy her spirit, though his erosion of her nineteen-year marriage and fruitful relationship with her son leads to a heroin habit and abysmal incarceration. After rescuing Jesse through an unrelenting and painful rehabilitation, Eve defends her from further self-righteous allegations. Eve's biblical savvy in sparring with the judgmental Sister Carrie strikes a resounding cautionary note which precludes readers castigating Jesse.

> Without turning around, Eve will raise her own voice and talk straight across the counter to the lard cans up on the shelf: Somebody in here likes Ezekiel. Somebody even likes the *sixteenth chapter* of Ezekiel.
> Carrie's mouth drops open. She looks at the page and looks at Eve's back. Then she looks back at the page again, hoping some miracle will change it. But since loud is righteous in her book, she gets louder still:

—How weak is thine heart, saith the Lord God, seeing thou doest all these things the work of an imperious whorish woman!
Eve keeps holding her conversation with the lard: Somebody even likes the *thirtieth* verse of the sixteenth chapter of Ezekiel. And maybe somebody should try the *fifty-second* verse on for size. And before Carrie can lick that thumb and flip over the page, Eve is quoting it by heart:
—Thou also, which hast judged thy sisters, bear thine own shame for thy sins that thou hast committed more abominable than they: they are more righteous than thou hast justified thy sisters. (135)

Bailey's intermittent presence is a model for the reader's empathic imagination: for example, with the incredible analogies to the painstaking process of detoxification:

Jesse once tried to describe to me what it means to go cold turkey. Imagine, she said, that you're speeding along at, say like, seventy miles an hour. No car, no nothing, just your body, seventy miles an hour. And suddenly your whole body slams right into this big brick wall. But you don't go unconscious, so you can feel crushed pieces of your skull stabbing back into your brain, your lungs collapsing in, each bone snapping and crumbling, your insides busting open as your guts rip apart. That's how much it hurts. Now, imagine, she said, that your body gets slammed into that same wall again and again. Red-hot bricks one time. Blocks of ice the next. Imagine it going on for four straight days. And imagine, when it was over, that bitch put me through it all again. (139)

Here and elsewhere Naylor stages a particular reaction through our trusted conduit who displays how readers, too, can give Jesse their undivided attention: "Jesse has never tried to describe for me what it was like that second time around. She says there are no words for the experience. I can only tell you this, Bailey, I sincerely prayed to die" (141).

And in the chapter which follows, "Mary (Take Two)" there are "no words" which can be uttered by a man for Mariam's experience. In fact our "maestro" gives the floor to Nadine who, in turn, yields to Eve the telling of this pregnant fourteen-year-old Jewish girl's incredulous story. Along with Nadine, we, too, have to catch our breath when Eve confirms that, though it is 1948, the people of Ethiopia hills still practice clitoridectomy and other murderous rituals; in fact, Mariam's mother sacrificed herself in defense of her daughter, thereby enabling her daughter's escape. Readers also share Nadine's anger at what seems, from our Western perspective, an atrocity against women. But Eve, through the first tears anyone has witnessed her shed, covertly cautions both Nadine and, by extension, outraged and uninformed readers regarding the shortcomings of ethnocentric bias:

> You do understand, Eve said, how much she loved her daughter. And she couldn't deny in her heart that the girl was always going to be slow-witted. Finding her a decent husband would be difficult with so many other virgins to choose from, and that is why she had the midwives close her up that tightly. It raises a woman's value. (152)

Eve's non-judgmental effort to respect the cultural derivation of customs we are too ready to condemn helps us to understand the sociohistorical context. Nadine's fear that Eve would start laughing and not be able to regain her composure doesn't come to fruition. What Eve offers instead of the laughter her Godfather taught her to associate with cynicism and hatred is the poignant and disturbing metaphor of the ripe, juicy plum upon which she inscribes the Law of the Blue Nile. This nauseating incision links the two Mary chapters which, in retrospect, we recognize are indeed two "takes" on the same universal reductive equation of a woman's worth with her intact virginity or beauty. Eve and Nadine are anxious about the fruit of Mariam's impending virgin birth occurring in what they both deem a way station, not conducive to *beginning* a life so much as repairing one.

Fortunately, Bailey re-inserts humor and reinvokes the music motif, as does Naylor's title "Miss Maple's Blues," when he refers to their preceding conversation as a "duet" (161). Comically, he defends his earlier absence: "I want you to know right off that Nadine lied on me . . . I only used fixing the coffee grinder as an excuse to cover up the fact that I was sneaking out to buy her a Christmas present" (161). He immediately interweaves his sympathy for Mariam's predicament and exile, "And underneath it all, I hoped that [Nadine] would know I was saying that Mariam's story hurt me too" (161). Interestingly, Bailey comments more profusely in this, the lengthiest of narratives—not coincidentally the only one told by a male, Stanley, who, after an arduous but futile search for the professional employment he deserves, assumes the female persona with which Eve names him, "Miss Maple." Here, it is heartening to witness Stanley's own infusion of humor, given that he was ready to commit suicide when he arrived at the cafe two years earlier.

In his long-winded story, we learn that Stanley, like many women in this novel, has been exploited by society and raped by men—the latter, during his penitentiary incarceration for conscientious objecting. Also like many women, he has been chastised for his principles, denied jobs for which he is more than qualified, damned in *any* case—though his gender privilege makes his tale of woe much less horrific than any of the women's—no matter how he dresses. To be sure, his attire is a thread of comic relief throughout the chapter, from the hilarious scene where he and his father in drag defend themselves against racist thugs, to his preferences for cotton dresses during his housekeeping duties at Eve's. The most rewarding joke is his duping of the system by creating advertising jingles to placate white minds and making fifty thousand dollars in the process.

Readers can't help but agree with Bailey's follow-up praise: of Stanley's intelligence, his courage, his integrity and his freedom. Bailey's example tempers possible reader responses that would echo Sugar Man's homophobia or Jesse's dismissal of him as unmanly. Jesse won't even allow him to clean her linens, for it's antithetical to the conduct of rough men where she grew up who embodied masculinity: "you know what it means to be a longshoreman in the wintertime? It means my uncles and brothers having the skin between their fingers split open from the cold" (118–19). She poses questions surrounding hypothetical multi-sensory scenarios which increase our empathy with such laborers even while this chapter of her life helps to explain her disapproval of Stanley's difference.

> And the winter is the best time. Cause in the summer with everything else you gotta put up with the stink. Press your nose to a rubber tire, or take a whiff of gasoline sometimes. Now, how about a mountain of crude rubber or an ocean's worth of raw gasoline? How about doing it ten hours a day? So your sweat stinks like oil? And your bologna sandwiches taste like oil? And you welcome the breeze from the dock tides cause it's bringing only rotting seaweed and dead fish. (119)

While we can understand Jesse's experiential misgivings about Stanley/ Miss Maple, Bailey exemplifies the disdain readers should feel for those whose intolerance is unfounded. We revel in Bailey's retaliation against the ignorance Sister Carrie and Sugar Man self-righteously personify when they judgmentally claim: "I'm not messing with those people" (227). Bailey plots:

> I wanted to tell the both of them to get the hell out of my place—and don't come back. Except it's not really mine. No, I'm just the fool who's forced to stay in here and serve people like that. But I'll fix their butts. By the time they get through eating their next meal in here, they'll be in the bathroom yelling for anybody's god who'll listen. (223)

We can't help but wonder what "just desserts" Bailey has in store for them.

Indeed, such integral notions of justice embedded in this novel call to mind the ways in which readers have been inspired and empowered by Paulo Freire's seminal work on liberatory methodology, *The Pedagogy of the Oppressed*. In the last decade many feminist and postmodernist scholars have tried to expand his vision whereby teachers co-suffer with the oppressed in a praxis of solidarity intended to overcome and transform the circumstances of domination. Our ongoing task in cultivating a critical pedagogy entails a recognition of a politics of ethics, difference, and emancipation not only of our concrete lives, but of our minds, hearts, and spirits as well, from race, class, gender and other divisive constructions. Certainly, the burden of the earlier stories is somewhat alleviated if readers, like those at the cafe, dwell in the final chapter. On the cusp of a new year, one might be able to share the eager anticipation to which Nadine had alluded earlier: "But maybe it's meant for this baby to bring in a whole new era. Maybe when it gets here, it'll be like an explosion of new hope or something, and we'll just fade away" (160).

> Mariam's baby's birth is a transformative moment of awakening: Nadine hugged me so tight she almost lifted me onto my toes. Then Gabe grabbed me, whirled me around, and we started to dance. He could kick pretty high for an old goat. Miss Maple took his other hand and the three of us were out in the middle of the floor, hands raised and feet stomping. People were up on tables and cheering. Someone was banging on the counter with my spatula. Someone tore open a sack of rice and was throwing it into the air. I didn't give a damn. Jesse had her skirt raised in the throes of a mean flamenco. And, wonder of wonders, Esther smiled. But I think it was Peaches who started to sing. I know she has the best voice, and the spiritual started off high and sweet. You could hear it even above the mayhem. As everyone could still hear the lone cry of new life. (225)

The musical motif which frames the novel reaches its highest note when all sing for a rare hour of rejoicing. Those present model the benefits of inhabiting another's culture when they assume a collective Jewish identity and participate in the naming ceremony and circumcision, both cast as survival rituals. As Bailey points out, "that's what I like the most about Gabe's faith: nothing important can happen unless they're all in it together as a community" (227). Readers, too, rejoice in the medley of voices, though "a bit ragged and off-key," (226) welcoming this infant to a now-transformed community.

It is precisely this communal catharsis that makes this novel conducive to Augusto Boal's theatre of the oppressed. Crucially, Naylor's novel prioritizes the diversity of the dominant culture's destructive manifestations and, as such, posits what Kathleen Weiler seeks in theorizing a liberatory pedagogy,[4] the cost of which can be risky and painful for readers as they recognize, variously, their own privilege, their possible complicity in oppressions, or their own victimization. This richness in the novel enables an examination of one's own positionality and opens a pathway to coalition-building toward transformation. This transformation is incomplete without an acceptance of the affective realm (what Audre Lorde refers to as "feeling" or the power of the erotic) as a guide to active knowing and change agency made plausible by our genuine engagement in others' struggles, a variation on what McLaren refers to as "inhabit[ing]" the narratives we read, even as they read us.[5] Readers, in their momentary but potentially momentous alliance and shared resistance, have become co-inquirers interrogating the oppressive status quo through a genuine empathy that is neither spurious nor trivializing of the suffering they've encountered.

We contend that an Augusto Boal *Theatre of the Oppressed* approach to absorbing, processing, and enacting *Bailey's Cafe* will better facilitate not only a vicarious but also a visceral understanding which can become the wellspring of revolutionary action that Naylor's novel engenders. Ideally, this pedagogical and reading strategy will move one beyond feeling overwhelmed by the anguish to which Naylor and Bailey bear witness. Having been urged beyond passivity or inertia by the book's sheer power, readers will more than likely welcome a constructive release. Such a methodology engages critical thinking as well as now more productively and counter-hegemonically empathic imaginations.

One would be hard-pressed to find a novel which more completely attains Jeanne Brady's impulse toward functional, cultural, and critical literacy:

> literacy needs to be viewed within an ethical and emancipatory discourse providing a language of hope and transformation that is able to analyze, challenge, and transform the ideological referent for understanding how people negotiate and translate their relationship with everyday life.[6]

Along with Bailey, readers will realize that, despite innumerable "damned-if-you-do-and-damned-if you-don't" predicaments, "life will go on."[7] But he will have conducted readers to the place where we can recognize and own that empathy is the route to resolving the questions that outnumber the answers.[8]

NOTES

1. Peter McLaren, *Critical Pedagogy and Predatory Culture: Oppositional Politics in a Postmodern Era* (New York: Routledge, 1995), 43.

2. Peter McLaren with Henry Giroux, "Radical Pedagogy as Cultural Politics," in *Critical Pedagogy and Predatory Culture,* eds. P. McLaren and C. Lankshear (New York: Routlege, 1995), 54.

3. Michelle Russell, "Black Eyed Blues Connection," in *Learning Our Way,* ed. C. Bunch and S. Pollack (Trumansburg, New York: The Crossing Press, 1983).

4. Kathleen Weiler, "Friere and a Feminist Pedagogy of Difference" in *Politics of Liberation: Paths from Freire,* ed. Peter McLaren and C. Lankshear (New York: Routledge, 1994), 35.

5. McLaren, 89, 98.

6. Jeanne Brady, "Critical Literacy, Feminism, and a Politics of Representation," in *Politics of Liberation,* eds. P. McLaren and C. Lankshear (New York: Routledge, 1994), 142.

7. Naylor, 229.

8. Ibid., 229.

WORKS CITED

Brady, Jeanne. "Critical Literacy, Feminism, and a Politics of Representation." In *Politics of Liberation: Paths from Freire,* ed. P. McLaren and C. Lankshear. 142–53. New York: Routledge, 1994.

Freire, Paulo. *Pedagogy of the Oppressed.* 27th ed. trans. Jorge Mellado. Mexico: Siglo XXI, 1981.

McLaren, Peter. *Critical Pedagogy and Predatory Culture: Oppositional Politics in a Postmodern Era.* New York: Routledge, 1995.

————— and Colin Lankshear. *Politics of Liberation: Paths from Freire.* New York: Routledge, 1994.

————— with Henry Giroux. "Radical Pedagogy as Cultural Politics: Beyond the Discourse of Critique and Anti-Utopianism." In *Critical Pedagogy and Predatory Culture,* eds. P. McLaren and C. Lankshear, 29–57. New York: Routledge, 1995.

Naylor, Gloria. *Bailey's Cafe.* New York: Random House Vintage Books, 1992.

Russell, Michelle. "Black Eyed Blues Connection." In *Learning Our Way,* ed. C. Bunch and S. Pollack. Trumansburg, New York: The Crossing Press, 1983.

Weiler, Kathleen, "Freire and a Feminist Pedagogy of Difference." In *Politics of Liberation: Paths from Freire,* eds. P. McLaren and C. Lankshear. 12–40. New York: Routledge, 1994.

Contributors

Carol Bender is Associate Professor and Chair of the English Department at Alma College where she teaches rhetoric and modern American literature, with special interests in women's and African American literature. Her articles have appeared in *Beyond Bindings and Boundaries, The Language Arts Journal of Michigan, Language and Style, Masterpieces of Women's Literature,* and *Concerns.*

Mark Hall is currently pursuing a Ph.D. in Rhetoric and Composition at the University of Louisville, where he serves as both an Assistant Director of the Composition Program and an Assistant Coordinator of the Writing-Across-the-Curriculum Program. He also teaches in the Composition Program. He holds an M.A. degree in English Literature from the University of Alabama.

Roseanne Hoefel, Associate Provost and Associate Professor of English at Alma College, teaches American literatures, poetry, Caribbean literature, and composition. She taught African American literature while on a Fulbright at the University of the West Indies in Jamaica. Her work has appeared in various journals, including *Studies in American Indian Literature, Studies in Short Fiction, The Emily Dickenson Journal, Transformations, Studies in American Indian Literature, CEA Critic,* and *Feminisms.*

Carol Howard teaches English and theater at Warren Wilson College in Asheville, North Carolina. She has co-edited two books in *Scribner's British Writers* and has published articles on Restoration and eighteenth-century literature and contemporary African-American literature.

Johnny Lorenz is pursuing his doctorate in English at the University of Texas at Austin. His research interests concern American literatures that address histories of genocide and displacement, construct multiple temporalities, and complicate teleological narratives of "progress" and chronological "history." His dissertation, entitled "Haunted Cartographies," addresses

196

contemporary epics of the Americas; the presence of ghostly figures as a challenge to coerced absences, invisibility, and disappearances; and the construction of history as a haunting.

KERRY REGAN received her M.A. degree in English Literature from Indiana University. She is currently pursuing a J.D. degree at Harvard Law School, and plans to focus her future scholarship on intersections between legal discourse and narrative literature.

MARK SIMPSON-VOS (University of North Carolina at Chapel Hill) is currently investigating the intersections of literature, ethnicity, and national identity in early America. His research interests include multiethnic American literatures, print culture, and postcolonial theory.

SHIRLEY STAVE, a member of the faculty of the Louisiana Scholars' College at Northwestern State University, received her Ph.D. from the University of Minnesota in 1986, where her area of concentration was the Victorian and early modern British novel. Since that time, she has developed an interest in the contemporary woman's novel and cultural criticism as well. Her other works include *The Decline of the Goddess: Nature, Culture and Women in Thomas Hardy's Fiction* and a co-authored work, *Living Witchcraft: A Contemporary American Coven.* She has also published articles on Willkie Collins and Toni Morrison and is currently working on articles on Jayne Anne Phillips and Elizabeth Gaskell.

JULIE THARP is an Associate Professor of English at the University of Wisconsin—Marshfileld, where she teaches women's literature, multicultural literature, film studies, and creative writing. She is co-editor of *Creating Safe Space: Violence and Women's Writing* and the author of the forthcoming *This Giving Birth: Pregnancy and Childbirth in Women's Writing.*

ANISSA J. WARDI is Assistant Professor of English and Coordinator of Cultural Studies at Chatham College, where she teaches courses in African American literature. She has published articles on Jean Toomer, Gloria Naylor, and Toni Morrison.

INDEX